Communication as Culture

An Introduction to the Communication Process

D1518532

John W. Gareis, PhD
Ellen R. Cohn, PhD
University of Pittsburgh

KENDALL/HUNT PUBLISHING COMPANY
4050 Westmark Drive   Dubuque, Iowa 52002

Cover image © Jed Share and Kaoru/Corbis

Copyright © 2008 by Kendall/Hunt Publishing Company

ISBN 978-0-7575-4804-8

Printed in the United States of America
10 9 8 7 6 5 4 3

Contents

Chapter 4   Perception and Reality   45

Chapter 5   Verbal Communication   69

Chapter 6   Non-Verbal Communication   81

Preface and Acknowledgments

When we began this project last September (2006), I thought that it would be fairly easy: you transcribe some lectures, you plug in some exercises, and you have a book. Ellen, the seasoned veteran of such projects, was more aware and realistic. So here I am nearly one year later, a little more tired, a little smarter (yes, even teachers can learn new things through research and writing), and, much more respectful of those who write textbooks for a living. The great thing about a project like this is that we not only got to think about (and rethink) everything we've thought and taught about communication over the years, but we came to realize and appreciate that we owe so much to so many supportive people.

Thanks, first, to Dr. Ellen Cohn, who is not just a co-author but a good friend. Not only did she enter the project with some great text in hand, but she kept me grounded, on task, and optimistic.

Thanks also to Marc Sawyer, Carrie Maro, and all the folks at Kendall Hunt. Their ability to manage the project with both flexibility and professionalism was greatly appreciated by a first-time author.

Thanks to my teaching assistants over the years who were so willing to lead and evaluate many of the exercises that made it into this book. While there are too many to mention individually, I must point out Autumn Boyer who created the forms for some of the exercises here.

Finally, and most importantly, thanks to my wife and best friend, Lori, who endured, listened, supported, and continued to love; and thanks to my daughters, Evanne and Kaitlin, the joy of my life. It is my hope that you and your generation gain much from this or any effort to understand and improve human communication.

John W. Gareis, PhD

I am first and foremost grateful to co-author and a longtime great friend and colleague Dr. Jack Gareis and his warm and supportive family; my daughters Jamie and Abby, my parents, brothers, and friends, and the undergraduate communication majors I so enjoy teaching!

Much of my contributions to this text were directly excerpted, with permission, from several editions of study guides written for the University of Pittsburgh External Studies Program [copyrighted, Ellen R. Cohn and University of Pittsburgh Center for Instructional Development and Distance Education (CIDDE)]. I am indebted to Diane Davis, PhD, CIDDE Director, and Joanne Nicoll, PhD, CIDDE Associate Director, for their instructional design expertise and generous assistance.

Many thanks to Dr. Janet Skupien who, along with the late Ms. Carol Houston and Ms. Sheila McBride, conceived new directions for the teaching of the communication process.

Ellen Cohn, PhD

About the Authors

John W. Gareis, PhD

John W. Gareis has been the Director of Undergraduate Advising and a Senior Lecturer in the Communication Department at the University of Pittsburgh for nearly 20 years. He received a B.A. in Speech Communication and Theatre from Clarion State College (now Clarion University of Pennsylvania) in 1976, and a Masters of Divinity from Lancaster Theological Seminary in 1980. After some time away from academia, he completed his PhD in Rhetoric and Communication at the University of Pittsburgh in 1991. His dissertation, *Characteristics of Empathic Exchanges in Human Interactions*, provided much of the information presented in Chapter 7 of this text.

In addition to the introductory Communication Process course, he has taught Public Speaking, Small Group Communication, Organizational Communication, Theories of Interpersonal Communication, History of Mass Media, and Rhetoric and Culture. He was nominated for a Chancellor's Distinguished Teaching Award and received the University of Pittsburgh's Bellet Award for Excellence in Undergraduate Teaching.

Beyond the classroom, Dr. Gareis has served as a communication consultant for several professional and university related organizations and has presented and published (along with Ellen Cohn) articles on computer-mediated communication in small groups and cultural diversity in the classroom.

John, a native western Pennsylvanian, still lives in the area with his wife, Lori, and their two daughters, Evanne and Kaitlin.

Ellen R. Cohn, PhD

Ellen Cohn is Associate Dean for Instructional Development at University of Pittsburgh's School of Health and Rehabilitation Sciences and Associate Professor in the Department of Communication Science and Disorders. She has a secondary faculty appointment in the School of Pharmacy and is a Member Faculty of the McGowan Institute for Regenerative Medicine. Previously, she was a speech-language pathologist and research associate at the University of Pittsburgh Cleft-Palate Craniofacial Center and was director of the University of Pittsburgh

Speech and Hearing Clinic. Cohn earned a BA at Douglass College of Rutgers University, an MA at Vanderbilt University, and a PhD at the University of Pittsburgh.

Cohn's academic activities span multiple disciplines. She teaches in the areas of cleft palate and craniofacial disorders; pharmacy and therapeutics; orthodontics; and rhetoric and communication, where she has been teaching introductory and applied communication courses for the past 25+ years. She is a co-investigator on a Rehabilitation Engineering Research Center on Telerehabilitation at the University of Pittsburgh, funded by the U.S. Department of Education, National Institute on Disability Research and Rehabilitation (NIDRR). She recently co-authored *Diversity Across the Curriculum: A Guide for Faculty in Higher Education*, (Anker Publishing Co., 2007, with J. Branche and J. Mullinex), and has served as a communications consultant.

CHAPTER 1

Introduction to Communication as Culture

Learning Objectives

After reading this chapter, you should be able to:

- Describe this textbook's "inverted triangle" approach to communication.
- Discuss the relationship of communication to culture.
- Define culture.
- Provide examples that illustrate each of the following statements:
  - Culture is learned.
  - Culture is created.
  - Culture is rule governed.
  - Culture is composed of symbol systems.
  - Culture changes.
  - Culture is distinctive.
  - Culture is constraining.
- Describe the purpose of ethnography.
- Explain how a "participant observer" conducts ethnographic research.
- Describe Garfinkel's concept of ethnomethodology.

Introduction

This introduction is being written in the waning days of November 2006. It is five years and two months after the terrorist attacks on 9/11, and a few days after a historic midterm election in which the Democrats regained control of both the House of Representatives and the Senate, a position they have not enjoyed since 1994; and it appears that Nancy Pelosi (D-California), a grandmother of five, will be elected as the first female Speaker of the U.S. House of Representatives when it reconvenes in January 2007.

The United States is still involved in a controversial war in Iraq (and Afghanistan), which, along with concerns over immigration and illegal aliens, may have contributed greatly to the Republican defeat. The U.S. Supreme Court is debating a "partial birth abortion" case, New Jersey's Supreme Court offered a ruling last month that clears the way for New Jersey to become the second state to legalize same sex marriages (45 states have either banned or are considering a ban), and 28 states now have declared English as the official language.

Secretary of State, Condoleezza Rice, named champion figure skater, Michelle Kwan, to serve as the first Public Diplomacy Envoy. The mission of the nine-time national champion and five-time world champion is to improve the image of the United States abroad. Also in Washington, D.C., ground was broken for the Dr. Martin Luther King Jr. Memorial on the National Mall near the Jefferson and Lincoln memorials.

By way of entertainment, Tom Cruise and Katie Holmes recently announced their long anticipated wedding plans, Brittany Spears is divorcing husband number two, and the new James Bond flick will be released in a few days. We in Western Pennsylvania are anguishing over the Steelers' worst post-Super Bowl record ever, and Emmett Smith, a three-time Super Bowl champion, won the *Dancing with the Stars* competition.

We get much of our news from blogs, music and video clips from YouTube.com, and we stay connected with family and friends via instant messaging. The use of cell phones in the United States has increased from about 200,000 in 1985 to more than 197 million today (Cato, 2005).

Purpose of the Text

We are offering this snapshot of U.S. culture, not because this is a book about history, politics, or popular entertainment per se, or to "date" the text, as one of our colleagues feared. Instead we include this overview to emphasize that communication always, always, always occurs in the context of a cultured world. The historic events we just described all contribute to the way you and I view and talk about war, politics, politicians, abortion, and marriage. These events also influence how we talk to women, people of Middle Eastern descent, Jews, teenagers, and men who dance.

As a result of the political events, some people who had voices of power on the Monday before the 2006 election are suddenly outsiders, and voices that have been disenfranchised for years, now have national, if not international, exposure. Likewise, issues that were considered settled or defined may now be wide open for debate. In fact, Lynn Cullen, a Pittsburgh talk show host on WPTT 1360, suggested the relevance of politics to everyday communication when she said, "We're going to have to learn a new way to talk about the issues. We have to change the vocabulary we've been used to." (11/16/06).

If, as we argue, communication is culture-based, then you as a reader must understand the present culture to understand why we used specific words, examples, and disciplinary concepts. If we somehow enjoy the good fortune of someone picking this book up 60 years from now and wondering *why* we wrote such a thing or *if* we didn't know better—the answer is no, we didn't know better. We didn't know any better because we are for better or worse, a product of our culture. Even writing about a timeless phenomenon such as communication is constrained by the boundaries of the current culture. The point of all of this is that we are always representatives of a culture, and communication provides us with the means to exist within culture.

This point, however, is not an easy one to get across. Jack (one of the authors) says: "I remember well spending the two class periods following the 2000 presidential election making this very point. I discussed insiders and outsiders, and how something like an election impacts us and our everyday experiences communicating with others. At the end of the term, while reading my student evaluations, I came across one that said, 'He spent two class periods talking about politics and the election instead of giving us the information about communication that we really needed.'"

Now instead of criticizing, let us say something in this student's defense. It would appear that he or she has actually learned well the lesson perpetuated by many of those in education. That lesson is that subjects (like math, science, English, and communication) are distinct and separate. They are departmentalized and compartmentalized and each deals with specific, isolated subject matter. This student was (and is) a product of the culture of education that trains us to see the world as parsed and static rather that as whole and dynamic. Gregory Bateson (1978) described this segmented worldview when he wrote:

> "We have been trained to think of patterns, with the exception of music, as fixed affairs. It's easier and lazier that way, but, of course all nonsense. The truth is that the right way to begin thinking about the pattern which connects is to think of it as primarily (whatever that means) a dance of interacting parts, and only secondarily pegged down by various sorts of physical limits and by the limits which organisms impose."

Even textbooks in the discipline are guilty of perpetuating the piecemeal approach to the study of communication. A quick perusal of many current communication texts suggest, by their very organization, that communication can somehow be separated from culture or that, at best, culture is one context in which communication occurs. This difference can best be explained in terms of triangles (or pyramids if you prefer). Most communication textbooks are arranged as an upright triangle.

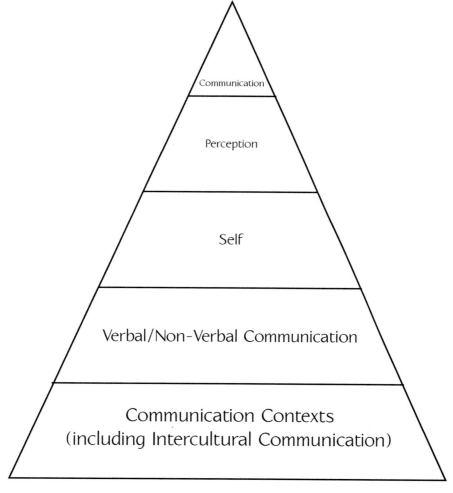

After discussing why we study communication and offering a definition, these texts move on to consider perception and the self. The implication of this standard triangle arrangement of topics is that the *self* is the starting point for communication and all communicative experiences, be they interpersonal, group, public, mass, or intercultural.

Contrast that approach to what we offer as the *inverted triangle approach*. It is illustrated as follows:

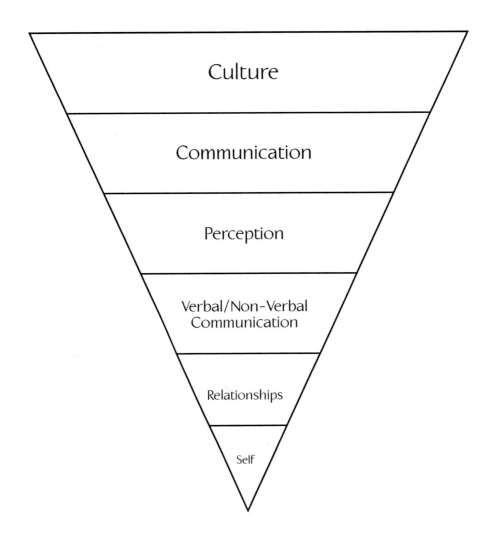

Patterned after the works of George Herbert Meade, Clifford Geertz, and others, this arrangement begins with the broader topic of culture and then uses it as the foundation for all other points of discussion. This means that, rather than being the source, the self is the product and manifestation of all things cultural. The purpose of this textbook, then, is to offer an alternative approach to the study of human communication.

Another major difference between this text and others is that this text does not suggest that culture only becomes a factor when communication occurs between representatives of two different cultural groups. It posits instead that culture is very much in play any time and every time two people speak. Consider these examples.

A recent drug awareness ad begins with *tween* to teenage children listing every slang word they know that is used as a reference to drugs. After an extensive list, the voiceover says something to the effect that "talking with kids about drugs is a lot tougher than it used to be." Why is that true?

Why does it seem like we are speaking a foreign language when we talk to members of the opposite sex?

Why do Jack's eyes glaze over when his 13-year-old or 17-year-old daughter tries to tell him how to transfer an emailed picture to his computer as a background or a screen saver?

Why does their grandmother not even know what a screen saver is? ("Oh Gram, get with it!")

The answer to each of these questions is differences in culture. Men and women, relational partners, parents and children, business associates, republicans and democrats are all totally immersed in similar but vastly different cultures. Moreover, notice that we have not even yet mentioned differences in race, nationality, or language.

Culture Defined

According to Clifford Geertz (1973), culture is "an historically transmitted pattern of meanings embodied in symbols, a system of inherited conceptions expressed in symbolic form by means of which (humans) communicate, perpetuate, and develop their knowledge about and attitudes towards life" (p. 89). Beginning with this definition, then, we can describe seven characteristics of culture.

Culture Is Learned

We are not born with a culture; we are born into a culture. Everything we think, do or say is acquired through imitation, trial and error, and positive reinforcement. Beginning at birth, the child learns the linguistic system of its culture. Humans are born with centers in our brains for formulating grammar and manufacturing metaphors. We become specialized for this uniquely human function early in childhood, perhaps losing the major capabilities of this language learning mechanism as we mature, and our brains become less plastic.

Learning simultaneously occurs in several systems of language:

Phonologic—The child acquires the phonological system, learning to perceive and produce phonemes, the minimal sound units of meaning. For example, the English-speaking child learns that the phoneme /g/, combined with the vowel /o/ in the word "go" creates a different meaning than the phoneme /n/ combined with the vowel /o/ in the word "no."

Semantic—The child acquires the minimal units of meaning, morphemes. An example of a morpheme would be the word "chair." The word "chairs" actually contains two phonemes: "chair," and the plural marker "s." Semantic competency refers to the ability to perceive and use the vocabulary of the language, and increases with the child's development.

Syntactic—The child must acquire a mastery of the grammar of the language, learning how to string series of morphemes together in meaningful and grammatically acceptable combinations. Mastery occurs in developmental stages.

Morphophonemic—Morphophonemic capabilities enable the child to master spelling, as well as to understand rules for the combination of certain morphemes and phonemes, and how these might affect meaning. For example, the final /k/ sound in the word electric (where the /k/ sound is represented by the letter /c/) changes to a /s/ sound when "ity" is added to create the word "electricity."

Pragmatic—Pragmatic language skills refer to the ability to use language to achieve various functions of communication. This would include knowledge of how to ask a question, negotiate, make a demand, and inform. The acquisition of pragmatic skills proceeds in a developmental fashion, and we master new pragmatic skills throughout our lives.

Children's success in learning the complex communicative system is integrally related to their cognitive development. Children who are delayed or impaired in their intellectual development will typically display delays and/or dysfunction in each of the aforementioned systems of language.

Cognition and language development are also linked in the development of the cognitively intact child. Consider, for example, the work of the Swiss psychologist Jean Piaget (1962). Piaget concluded that before the age of seven or eight years, the child uses both egocentric and socialized speech. When using egocentric speech, the child does not adapt his speech to the receiver, and is virtually unconcerned if the message is received. Socialized speech, on the other hand has a social purpose and takes the receiver's viewpoint into account. Before the age of seven or eight, it is estimated that at least half of children's speech is egocentric in nature.

However, others argue that the developing child is actually sociocentric, not egocentric, in that from birth on, the child's activity is focused on social interaction. Evidence for this is seen in the child's ability to engage the attention and efforts of adults. Even infants exchange glances, vocalizations and grimaces with their mothers or caretakers, and learn how to manipulate adult behavior via crying, smiles and coos to gain food, attention and physical comfort (Tubbs and Moss, 1994).

The human child, by virtue of its social communicative abilities is uniquely able to engage human adults to fulfill its needs for physical survival, affection, and socialization during an extended period of dependence on the society.

The Hidden Curriculum

George Gerbner (1974) originated the term *hidden curriculum* to describe much of what humans must learn about their culture. He says that while some of the learning occurs through direct teaching (e.g., say "please" and "thank you"), the vast majority of learning occurs incidentally, or indirectly, making it "hidden." Since the curriculum is largely unwritten, it must be acquired by simply living in the culture.

Included in this learning are the complex patterns of non-verbal and verbal communication that remain unrecognized and/or undiscussed unless the behavior is shown to be inappropriate for the culture. Consider, for example, the act of "taking-leave," of a simple conversation with a friend. The communicative norms of our culture require that we perform an untaught and rather complicated verbal and non-verbal pattern of communication to signal that the leave-taking is about to occur. We non-verbally show increased attention and reinforcement of our communicative partner by sustaining eye contact, shaking our head in agreement, and perhaps gently touching their arm. Our non-verbal behavior simultaneously signals disengagement. We might position our hips and legs toward the door, and assume a "catapult" position with our hands, so as to signal our intent to physically leave. We also verbally indicate that we are disengaging from the encounter, but that we are not doing so because we are rejecting the individual. If our friend disrupts our leave-taking, (e.g., "Hold-up, there is something I forgot to tell you."), we may momentarily relax our bodies and cease the "leave-taking," only to reinitiate the leave-taking ritual later. Constant or inappropriate violations of the rituals can be extremely annoying, as when professors say they have "one last point" to cover in a lecture, but then proceed to introduce a topic they forgot to include, or, when public speakers insert lengthy new content in their "concluding remarks."

Sometimes the culture requires that we learn unstated rules in the context of formal rule learning, such as when it is culturally acceptable to break the stated rules. A colleague sent her daughter off to her first day of kindergarten. As is customary the first day of school, the teacher proceeded to teach the children some of the expected rules of conduct: "hang your coats on the hanger;" "stop talking if I flash the lights on and off;" "no fighting or bad language;" "close your eyes during nap time;" etc. This very bright and meticulous young girl also learned to "raise your hand to get my permission if you need to go to the bathroom." After sitting quietly and learning *all* of these new rules, the child felt the need to use the bathroom. As taught, she raised her hand, but was unrecognized by the distracted teacher. The student subsequently lost bladder control, and was totally humiliated and confused. Why had the teacher failed to let her go to the bathroom when she had followed the "bathroom rule?" What occurred in this situation was that the child did not know that there are certain times when it is appropriate to violate a stated rule in the culture. That evening, her mother taught her a new rule, "if you need to go to the bathroom and your teacher doesn't see you raise your hand, it is okay to call out, 'I need to go to the bathroom,' or to just get up and use the toilet."

The work of Frederick Ford (1983) addresses when and how it is acceptable to break a rule. Ford describes his *"family of rules"* applied below to the rule: "be nice."

> *The rule:* "Be nice"
>
> *The counter-rule:* "Be bad"
>
> *Rule about qualification and exceptions:* ". . . except to people who are unkind to you"
>
> *Consequence of breaking a rule:* "We punish people who go around making trouble"
>
> *The rule that tells how the rule is to be implemented:* "Speak softly"

The learning of the "hidden curriculum" is a lifelong process, for even after we are exposed to the majority of information in the curriculum, each rule (and *its family of rules*) must be applied in a variety of potentially numerous and unique contexts.

Culture Is Created

Again it is Geertz who writes: "The concept of culture I espouse . . . is essentially a semiotic one. Believing, with Max Weber, that man is an animal suspended in webs of significance he himself has spun, I take culture to be those webs" (p. 5). What he means is that even though our culture precedes any one of us, that culture is still a product of human design. There is no given or ultimate culture.

Of course, in any culture there are those persons or groups who assert cultural superiority. They believe that their worldview, their way of doing things, their rules, and their language, set the standard by which all others are to be judged.

Culture Is Rule Governed

Picture yourself stepping onto an elevator with one person already on board. Where do you stand? Where do you look? When, if ever, do you speak? The answers to these questions show our familiarity with the rules that govern behavior in certain social situations in a particular culture. Cultural rules regulate everything in social situations from how loudly we laugh at a joke to which fork we use to eat dessert.

Based on Susan Shimanoff's (1980) work, a *rule* is defined as a followable prescription that indicates what behavior is obligated, preferred, or prohibited in certain contexts (p. 39). With this definition in mind, let us discuss Shimanoff's four characteristics of rules.

First, says Shimanoff, rules are followable. To say that a rule is followable is to say that it is well within the realm of human ability to accomplish the prescribed action. But followability is more. It also implies that if the rule can be followed, it can also be ignored or violated. In other words, one has a choice as to whether to perform the action or not. For example, the rule: *Upon entering the classroom, you will turn off all cell phones and beepers,* is certainly one that can be followed. Whether it *will* be followed, however, is another matter.

Second, rules are prescriptive. By relating prescription to "preferences as well as obligations and prohibitions" (p. 44), Shimanoff suggests that failure to follow a prescribed rule may have specific consequences. Consequences may be clearly described ($500.00 fine for littering), or more subtly enacted (If I cut line then I receive stern looks from others). Either way I know what behaviors are preferred, obligated, or prohibited.

Before leaving the concept of prescription, we must note that rules governing human behavior are not always explicit. In fact, many rules that function in interaction are not written. Shimanoff says, "*Explicit rules* are inscriptions of utterances that prescribe behavior. *Implicit rules* are unstated prescriptions for behavior. Explicit rules have a physical reality of their own; implicit rules must be inferred from behavior" (p. 54, italics added). Recall the aforementioned elevator rule governing where you stand if you enter an elevator occupied by one other person. I have yet to see a book or pamphlet that describes elevator etiquette. These are rules we learn by observing others perform appropriate and/or inappropriate behavior. This, then, suggests one further thing about implicit rules. Typically, they operate unnoticed until they are broken. Again, no one thinks much about where to stand in the elevator, until someone stands too close to the other person. When that happens, it becomes very clear that something is amiss.

The third characteristic of rules is that they are behavior specific. In other words, rules only govern behaviors, never thoughts, feelings, or attitudes. Imagine, for example, that you are standing behind me in a super market checkout line. I take a step backward and bring the bottom of my foot down sharply onto the top of yours. At that moment we find ourselves in a social situation with a prescribed course of action. I am expected to say, "I'm sorry." Notice, however, that the rule says nothing about my feeling sorry or actually being sorry. I may in fact not be sorry at all but hoping that you got the message to not stand so close to me in line. The rule simply says that in this situation I am socially obligated to enact a behavior indicative of contrition.

Characteristic number four says that rules are contextual. This means that while rules prescribe behavior and those rules operate in similar situations, they do not function in all situations. For example, if I am a student and I want to speak in class, I am obligated to raise my hand and be recognized. And unless directed otherwise, I assume that this rule functions in all classroom situations. If, however, I am on a date and raise my hand to speak, well . . . you get the picture. The hand raising rule functions in a particular situation and it functions in similar situations. The hand raising rule, however, does not function in all situations.

Culture Is Comprised of Symbol Systems

For our purposes, symbols are the verbal and non-verbal codes—the words, actions, and artifacts used by a culture. *Symbol systems,* according to Geertz, are the organized and particular ways symbols are arranged to make sense in a culture. For example, a flag is a symbol when it is used to represent a nation or a group. That same flag flying at the top of a pole means something different than it does flying at half mast, flying upside down, draping a coffin, or displayed in a triangular glass case. The symbol in different contexts, interacting with other symbols, conveys very different meanings. Likewise, the systematic nature of symbols is drilled into elementary students across the United States when they are told repeatedly that sentences must have a subject (noun or naming symbol) and a verb (action symbol) or that adjectives describe nouns and adverbs describe action words.

All of this implies that when it comes to learning a language, whether it is your native tongue or not, it is not enough to simply learn the words. In order to communicate in that culture, we must learn the symbols and the systematic rules governing those symbols.

Culture Changes

What is the role of women in this culture? How do you define *family*? How much education does someone need to get a "good job"? What is a "good job"? My guess is that if you, your parents, and your grandparents sat down and discussed these topics, you would hear at least three different points of view. Why? Because you and they would be responding according to the prevailing understandings of your respective cultures. "But," you say, "I'm a fifth generation American. My culture is the same as my grandparents.'" To a degree, that is true. However, when you consider that in their day a "good job" for someone in the Pittsburgh area was in a coal mine or a steel mill and you are hoping for something in computers or pharmaceutical sales, you can see how culture has changed.

Culture Is Distinctive

Have someone from Western Pennsylvania, Eastern Pennsylvania, and another state answer the following questions:

What do you call the carbonated beverage you get from vending machines? (pop, soda, or Coke)

What do you do to your car when it gets dirty? (worsch or wash)

What is the plural of *you?* (you, yous, younz, or ya all)

Who answered these questions correctly? The point of this exercise is that, in addition to changing over time, culture at any particular time varies from place to place. Culture is distinctive. And, while it might constitute the topic of a lively discussion in this case, overlooking this fact of cultural distinction can lead to devastating results. Consider, for example, Brian Handwerk's assessment of post-Hussein Iraq in his 2003 *National Geographic News* article.

> "Now that Iraq's regime has been toppled, the old cultural divisions are again surfacing. . . . Sunnis, Shiites, and Kurds. Each calls Iraq home, but each is unsure of what its role will be in the new Iraq. If the country's territorial integrity is to be respected, they must somehow work together."

Culture Is Constraining

W. Barnett Pearce (1994) offers an excellent description of the constraining nature of culture in *Interpersonal Communication: Making Social Worlds*. He writes:

> "You are already familiar with Wittgenstein's (1922) statement that "the limits of my language make the limits of my world." But what kind of limits are these? Pearce and Kang (1988) distinguish between "horizons" and "boundaries." Horizons are the natural limits of sight; they mark the end of what can be seen but with no sense of confinement or impediment. That is, they are not *visible* as limits. Boundaries are imposed restrictions; the bars on a cage that mark off distinctions within the array of what we know between where we can go and where we cannot.

The natural state of human beings is to be limited within cultural horizons. We can feel fully free if we move unimpeded within these horizons because, to put it simplistically, we do not know what we do not know. Horizons are the limits of our social *umwelt* (the part of the physical world available as a creature's living space). However, human beings have the ability to expand their social *umwelt* by peeking over those horizons. When we do, we find ourselves thrust into social world for which we are unprepared or aware of social worlds into which we cannot gain admittance. Thus, horizons become boundaries.

Wittgenstein's project was to convert horizons into boundaries, thus freeing us from limits built into our language of which we were unaware. Thus freed, we can avoid repeating old mistakes and develop new ways of acting." (Pearce, p. 302)

Here Pearce is saying that while our culture restricts our ability to see beyond our individual, social world, we live as though we have no such constraints. Humans tend to believe that they are open and non-discriminating toward others; it is just that others have not yet discovered or been civilized to know the right way (our way) to live. Pearce counters this by pointing out that, not only do we not know that these ethnocentric limits exist in our culture, we don't even know that we don't know. He hopes to help us see the limits as limits, so we can then be open to differences beyond those limits.

The Study of Culture

Now that we have discussed the meaning and intent of *Communication as Culture*, we can examine one of the primary ways of studying culture. That approach, forwarded by Geertz and others is Ethnography. *Ethnography* is defined as: "A qualitative methodology that uncovers and interprets artifacts, stories, rituals, and practices in order to reveal meaning in a culture" (West and Turner, 2000, p. 233).

In order to conduct ethnographic research, the ethnographer must spend time living among and observing the everyday life of the group or culture in question. In other words, she or he must become a *participant observer*. An ethnographer becomes part of the community, but always maintains a distance so that she or he can watch the action unfold. Ethnographers must, in essence, make phenomenon or action *anthropologically strange*. It must be seen as if for the first time.

The purpose of ethnography is not to provide universal truths or to suggest similarity between us and them. The purpose is to provide a detailed description of a culture or group, sometimes like, sometimes very different from our own. As Geertz says about the job of the ethnographer: "The claim to attention of an ethnographic account does not rest on it's author's ability to capture primitive facts in faraway places and carry them home like a mask or a carving, but on the degree to which he is able to clarify what goes on in such places, to reduce the puzzlement—what manner of men are these?—to which unfamiliar acts emerging out of unknown backgrounds naturally give rise" (1973, p. 16).

Ethnomethodology

It was in the spirit of ethnography that sociologist, Harold Garfinkel (1994), introduced his unique type of inquiry known as Ethnomethodology. *Ethnomethodology* is the "study of a particular subject matter: common-sense knowledge and the range of procedures by which ordinary members of society make sense of, find their ways about in, and act on circumstances in which they find themselves" (Heritage, 1984, p. 4).

Garfinkel and his students would spend their time examining such everyday occurrences as elevator rituals, conversation structures, and as we shall see later, the social construction of gender identity. By engaging in his now famous "breaching experiments," Garfinkel would have his students identify a social norm that seemed to operate in a specific situation (e.g., When you enter an elevator occupied by one other person you take your place in the opposite corner), then break the norm to test reactions (e.g., I enter the elevator and stand as close to the other person as I can). From these experiments, Garfinkel was then able to determine the value of the rule that had been identified and the level of expectation we hold for "what others should know" regarding actions in various situations.

Summary

In this introductory chapter we have argued that, far from being a context in which communication occurs, culture is the very basis of communication. Whether you are talking with a family member or someone from another country, you are never anything more or less than an enculturated person. You abide by the limits of your language and your values and ideals. You talk about certain things and view others in certain ways. Everything you do and say reinforces or shows your opposition to your culture. The discussion of Communication as Culture was followed by a look at ethnography as a means of studying culture and an overview of Garfinkel's Ethnomethodology. In the next chapter we will offer a definition of communication.

CHAPTER 2

Definition of Communication

Learning Objectives

After reading this chapter, you should be able to:

- Provide two reasons why it is difficult to define communication.
- Explain what is meant by "the transactional nature of communication."
- Provide an example that illustrates that communication is a process.
- Explain why communication is both "irreversible" and "unrepeatable."
- Explain how communication "creates and sustains social order."
- Provide an example that illustrates: "meanings not inherent in words or actions."
- Define what is meant by "communication is symbolic."
- Define "metacommunication" and provide an example.
- Describe the symbol as a distinct feature of human life.
- Explain how communication is both "context shaped" and "context shaping."
- Define "theory."
- Explain the functions and forms of theory.
- Distinguish between inductive and deductive theory building.
- Describe the scientific method.
- Describe metatheory.
- Define "ontology," "epistemology," and "axiology."
- Define hypothesis.
- Explain the terms: independent variable, dependent variable, and intervening variable.

Blind Men and the Elephant

(by John Godfrey Saxe)

It was six men of Indostan
To learning much inclined,
Who went to see the Elephant
(Though all of them were blind),
That each by observation
Might satisfy his mind

The First approached the Elephant,
And happening to fall
Against his broad and sturdy side,
At once began to bawl:
"God bless me! but the Elephant
Is very like a wall!"

The Second, feeling of the tusk,
Cried, "Ho! what have we here
So very round and smooth and sharp?
To me 'tis mighty clear
This wonder of an Elephant
Is very like a spear!"

The Third approached the animal,
And happening to take
The squirming trunk within his hands,
Thus boldly up and spake:
"I see," quoth he, "the Elephant
Is very like a snake!"

The Fourth reached out an eager hand,
And felt about the knee.
"What most this wondrous beast is like
Is mighty plain," quoth he;
"'Tis clear enough the Elephant
Is very like a tree!"

The Fifth, who chanced to touch the ear,
Said: "E'en the blindest man
Can tell what this resembles most;
Deny the fact who can
This marvel of an Elephant
Is very like a fan!"

The Sixth no sooner had begun
About the beast to grope,
Than, seizing on the swinging tail
That fell within his scope,
"I see," quoth he, "the Elephant
Is very like a rope!"

And so these men of Indostan
Disputed loud and long,
Each in his own opinion
Exceeding stiff and strong,
Though each was partly in the right,
And all were in the wrong!

(Linton, 1878)

Introduction

In this chapter we are embarking on a nearly impossible but absolutely necessary task: we must define communication. I began this chapter with the parable of the *Blind Men and the Elephant* to illustrate the difficulty one encounters when attempting to define anything, especially a phenomenon like communication. Frank Dance suggested as much when in 1970 he surveyed the literature in an effort to discover the definitive definition of communication. What he discovered was 126 different but equally valid definitions. Why the differences? Pessimists might say it is because of a lack of focus and discipline in communication studies. Optimists, on the other hand, have a different explanation.

One of the reasons for such diversity is the breadth of this field of study. Talk to 50 different communication scholars about their research and you will get 50 different responses. Some study interpersonal communication, some public address, some media, some new technologies; but each is legitimately involved in the study of communication.

A second reason for the diversity is the nature of definitions themselves. It is important that there is no such thing as an all inclusive definition of anything. The problem that arises when we think that we have discovered *the* definition is highlighted in the poem with which this chapter began. While each of the blind men had encountered an aspect of the elephant, no one of them had experienced its totality. That is an important insight for any seasoned or beginning scholar to realize.

So, with the vastness of scholarship and the limits of definitions clearly in mind, I (optimistically) am offering the following definition as a starting point for our discussion of communication.

Communication Defined

Communication is *the transactional process of creating and sustaining social order through symbolic action.* Based on this definition, then, we can discuss some of the generally acknowledged characteristics of communication.

1. Communication is **transactional.** Of all of the words in this definition, "transactional" is probably the most unfamiliar, especially in relation to communication. Its use arises from the need to correct two historic misconceptions of communication: communication is something I do to you (action), or, communication is a series of messages and responses that occur reciprocally between us (interaction) like a game of ping-pong.

To say that communication is a transactional experience is to suggest that it is not only something that we engage in (or create) together, but that it is an experience that affects us. As a result of our having communicated, in any situation or with anyone, we are changed. Either we have new insight, our relationship with the other has improved or deteriorated, we have successfully obtained the cup of coffee we so desperately needed, or we have reconnected at the end of a day apart. In any case we are not the same people we were prior to the encounter.

Likewise, the transactional nature of communication says something about the roles that we as communicators play. Unlike the *action view*, which sees one communicator as the sender and the other as the receiver, or the *interaction view*, which sees each communicator as constantly switching roles between sender and receiver, the *transactional view* suggests that each communicator is simultaneously both a sender and receiver.

To illustrate this, imagine being at a party where you are about to meet someone for the first time. You make and maintain eye contact with the person you hope to meet. While you are sending this message you are also processing messages (receiving) from the other. Does s/he seem interested? Is s/he alone? Is this person someone I might like to get to know? And while you are sending and receiving your messages, the other person is doing exactly the same thing. There are multiple messages being sent and received through multiple channels before you even move toward the person or open your mouth to speak.

2. Communication is a **process.** A process is defined as a series of recognizable steps that produce some end. This suggests that *a process is something you do* rather than something that is. The problem with much of our thinking about human phenomena in general, communication specifically, is that we tend to see them as objects rather than as activities. We talk about being in love, in a relationship, or a part of a family as though these were states or containers (Lakoff and Johnson, 1980) that somehow surround us. Notice how these same phenomena take on a different sense when we view them as verbs. Now we say that we are loving, relationshiping, or familying.

Two other qualities associated with the process nature of communication are that it is *irreversible* and *unrepeatable*. Communication is irreversible in that we can never "take back" something we said, nor can a jury ever really "disregard the witness's comments." Once something is said or done we can explain, refute, reframe, or apologize, but we can never reverse.

Communication is unrepeatable to the extent that, while we can have similar experiences, we can never have the same experience twice. You might indeed have a series of first dates with different people, but you will only ever have one first date. If I were to enter class two days in a row and attempt to give the same lecture, students would remind me all too quickly that I had already said that before. We expect non-repeatable experiences when it comes to communication.

3. Communication **creates and sustains social order.**

The next time you are in a mall or department store with an escalator, watch people getting on or off. Which of them are couples or social groups? Who is alone? How do you know who is with whom? My guess is that those whom you are observing will enact behaviors that you associate with connecting or maintaining distance.

The next time you approach a counter at a fast food restaurant notice your behaviors. How do you know when to speak? What do you say? What does the person taking the order say? Does your behavior mirror or differ from others placing orders around you?

A friend tells you that he or she was on a first date last night. Before getting the details, imagine the situation: Where did they go? What did they talk about? My guess is that your imagined scenario is relatively close to their experience; and if it is not, you will undoubtedly be surprised.

These simple exercises suggest that there are culturally recognized behaviors that do indeed signal relationships, transactions, or social situations. In fact, we can function well in our everyday lives precisely because we have mastered the means to maintain social order via our behaviors. We know, for example, how to *act* in class, when meeting strangers for the first time, and at home with family and friends.

When we communicate, we do it generally to be understood, to be normal, and to maintain social order. You might recall that it did not take long for the singer Prince, after changing his name to the symbol, to change it back. For better or worse, social order demands commonly known labels for participants, objects, and experiences.

4. Communication involves **meaning.**

Contrary to popular perception, meanings are not inherent in words or actions. Meanings are assigned, not given. Even a dictionary does not record the "true meaning" of a word. As S. I. Hayakawa (1964) says, "The writing of a dictionary, therefore, is not a task of setting up authoritative statements about the "true meanings" of words, but a task of *recording,* to the best of one's ability, what various words *have meant* to authors in the distant or immediate past. *The writer of a dictionary is a historian, not a lawgiver*" (pp. 55–56, italics in original).

If we could in fact transfer or send meanings to each other, there would never be miscommunication. We would always say what we mean and mean what we say, and no one would ever misunderstand our message or intent. Unfortunately that is not the case, and departments of communication are there to study the results.

5. Communication is **symbolic.**

Kenneth Burke defines human being as "the symbol-using (symbol-making, symbol-misusing) animal" (Burke, 1968, p. 16). Regardless of how intelligent you may believe your pet to be, the chances are slim of her or him being able to sit down and converse with other animals about a past experience.

Think, for a moment, about where most of your knowledge comes from. What do you know about Sacagawea? How do you know it? My guess is that even if she happens to be a distant relative, you still know about her life and adventures through the words of others.

Likewise, symbols not only allow humans to communicate, but to communicate about communication. This experience is called **metacommunication** and occurs as you read this book, take a public speaking class, or talk with your friends about relationships. Symbols enable humans to think, reflect, and engage in critical analysis.

Thinking again of your pet, even if s/he can in some unknown way discuss the immediate past, your pet will never be conducting or attending seminars by which others can learn from his/her experiences. As far as we know, only human beings can use and create symbols as a means of communicating about things not immediately present, even about the communication process itself.

6. Communication is both **context shaped and context shaping.**

When someone says, "Is the Pope Catholic?" what does s/he mean? Before you answer, consider the following conversation.

1Freda:	What religious group holds the Pope in high esteem?
2Fred:	Is the Pope Catholic?
3Freda:	Yes.
4Fred:	The Catholics.

Does Fred's utterance (2Fred) mean what you thought? Probably not. Why? Because the context has a direct influence on the meaning of the utterance. "Is the Pope Catholic?" only means what we think it means because we envision a context. The utterance is so much a part of our culture that we simply cannot imagine it occurring and consequently meaning anything else. Anyone who has ever had a statement taken "out of context," however, is very aware of the fact that communication is shaped by the context in which it occurs.

Communication is also context shaping. This means that each utterance of an ongoing conversation or each communication experience contributes to our understanding of what each subsequent utterance or experience means. For example, receiving an unexpected sign of affection (like a kiss or a pat on the hand) from someone we really like, certainly helps contextualize anything that comes next. Likewise, a good or bad day at work might easily contextualize anything that happens with the first person who speaks to us when we get home.

A Side Note on Theory

"There is nothing so practical as a good theory."

—Kurt Lewin

Your roommate walks into the kitchen as you are eating your breakfast and announces that this is the big night.

"What big night?" you ask.

"The night I declare my love for Pat!"

"Wait a minute!" you say. "Are you sure that's the best thing to do? After all, this will only be your third date."

"Yeah, so?" says your roommate. "What are you saying?"

What exactly are you saying? What led you to say it? Why do you have reservations about your roommate's actions? Without even thinking of it, you have just engaged in theorizing.

Too often students in disciplines like Communication see theory as something that belongs to the sciences or, if applied to communication, something you have to wade through to get to the good (practical) stuff. Nothing, however, could be further from the experiences of life. In fact, most times we ask questions like, "Why did . . .?" or "What if . . .?" we are theorizing.

Theory Defined

The *American Heritage Dictionary* defines *theory* as "a set of statements or principles devised to explain a group of facts or phenomena, especially one that has been repeatedly tested or is widely accepted and can be used to make predictions about natural phenomena." From this definition then we glean two basic functions of theories: to explain and to predict.

Theories *explain* when they purport to tell us why something occurred. Looking back at the third date example with which this section began, we see an explanatory theory in the making when you try to tell your naïve roommate why third dates and the words, "I love you" don't mix.

If this approach fails, you might try the *predictive* approach. "Here is what will happen if you go through with this plan," you say. And even though you don't know for sure what will happen, you have enough past experience to make an educated guess.

Approaches to Theory Construction

Typically the scientific method of inquiry is conducted in two ways. *Inductive reasoning* is utilized when the researcher begins with a number of particular cases then moves upward to a more generalized theory to account for them. If, for example, you observed three separate cases of relationships ending after one of the actors said, "I love you," you might begin to make a probable connection between the pronouncement of love and relationship longevity.

On the other hand, you would engage in *deductive reasoning* if you assumed that there was a definite connection between the timing of certain statements and the probable termination of the relationship. In this case you might encourage your roommates to say, "I love you" at different times in their relationships to test your theory. Either way you are engaged in scientific inquiry.

Metatheories

Regardless of your approach to theory construction, all theories and theorists are guided by three metatheoretical positions. A *metatheory* is a theory of theories that describe "what aspects of the social world we can and should theorize about, how theorizing should proceed, what should count as knowledge about the social world, and how theory should be used to guide social action" (Miller 2002). The three metatheories are: ontology, epistemology, and axiology.

Ontology

Does love exist apart from those who experience it? Is love something we can "fall into" or "fall out of?" What is the nature of power or charisma? What is happiness? These are all questions of ontology.

Ontology is the study of the reality or nature of things. It addresses the nature of being. We established our ontological position regarding communication above when we proclaimed it to be a transactional rather than an actional or interactional experience. This means that we believe that communication is not something I do to you or something we take turns doing (like a ping-pong game). Instead the very nature, essence, or reality of communication is that it is a co-created, transforming experience. Every theory, in every discipline is driven by an understanding of what is real.

Epistemology

Epistemology is the study or science of knowledge. It asks the general question: How do we know what we know? When it comes to conducting researching the communication process, what is the best approach? This is a question of epistemology. And the two most common approaches to research are quantitative methods and qualitative methods.

Quantitative research methods rely upon empirical data generated through counting or statistical analysis (Smith 1988). It is most often associated with the scientific method of inquiry. The *scientific method* is a four-fold approach in which we:

1. Formulate a Hypothesis. A *hypothesis* is declarative sentence "predicting that a particular kind of relationship exists between specified classes of phenomena" (Smith, 1988). A hypothesis works best if presented in the if/then format. For example: *If you say 'I love you' too soon in a relationship, then the other will respond by ending the relationship* might be a working hypothesis in your roommate's situation.

Notice at this point, we know nothing about the actual outcome. Instead we are hypothesizing an outcome that will be proven or disproven later.

2. Identify and Operationalize the Variables. Each hypothesis usually contains three variables. The *independent variable* causes or contributes to the outcome. The *dependent variable* is the outcome or resulting action/condition. The *intervening variable* affects the relationship between the other two (Smith, 1988). In our example, saying "I love you" is the independent variable; ending the relationship is the dependent variable; and timing is the intervening variable. This is because saying "I love you" is not only acceptable but expected at a later point in the relationship.

When we *operationalize* our variables we are suggesting a means of measuring them. In our example it is easy to determine if one says "I love you" and if the relationship ends. In other cases, however, we may be dealing with less apparent variables like charisma, persuasiveness, or self esteem. In these cases we must prescribe a test or other means of measuring the variable so others can follow or replicate our study exactly for the purposes of verification.

3. Describe Methodology. At this point we must explain in detail how we will conduct our research. Again this is necessary so that others can see exactly where we are going and how we propose to get there. This necessitates our describing the characteristics and size of the sample and the data gathering process or instrument we are using. As per our ongoing example, we might ask 100 people of various ages in ongoing relationships and 100 people who have experienced a breakup when they said, "I love you" to the other person. In this case we would be using a *self-report measurement* to collect data.

4. Code and Analyze Data. In this final stage we report our findings. Keep in mind here that, while it may be satisfying to confirm our original hypothesis, an equally valid outcome is to disprove your theory. The current television show, *Mythbusters*, has gained a great deal of popularity doing just that.

The second epistemological approach to acquiring knowledge is through *Qualitative Research Methods*. Unlike their quantitative counterparts, qualitative researchers tend to prefer narrative and textual data over numbers (Smith, 1988, p. 180). A good qualitative study will be more interpretive or critical than predictive, will explore individual or culture-specific behavior rather than attempt to make broad generalizations, and will often take years to complete. The potential longevity of the study is significant since many qualitative researchers choose to become entirely immersed in the culture of those being studied. They will also rely most often on speeches, diaries, artifacts, narrative accounts, and transcribed conversations as rich sources of data. One of the more popular qualitative approaches to the study of communication is Ethnography as discussed in Chapter 1.

Axiology

The third metatheory, *Axiology*, deals with questions of objectivity and bias in research. Imagine that I want to conduct research on the dating habits of U.S. adults. As my sample population I chose the undergraduate students from my introductory communication process class. What, if any, potential biases might flaw this study?

Is there bias in research? Can research be completely bias-free? What is the impact of any form of bias on any given research project? On one hand there are those who still believe that even the most rigorous scientific research can be absolutely objective. On the other hand, there are those who believe that bias not only permeates research, but is a necessary component in some instances (West and Turner, 2000). Consider, for example, those who argue that Al Gore's *An Inconvenient Truth* is biased, but that the ends justify the means; an argument that many Iraq war supporters make in reference to intelligence reports about Iraqi weapons of mass destruction and involvement in the 9/11 attacks.

Beyond these extreme positions, then, there are those few who intentionally manipulate research to ensure success every time. When it comes to issues of axiology it seems most logical to affirm that there are inherent biases in all research, even without the intentional breeches. Given that fact, it is incumbent upon the research community to police its ranks and do the best they can to keep research bias in check.

Summary

In our effort to define communication we encountered the problem that plagues anyone who attempts to define anything: the temptation to see their definition as *the* definition. Recognizing fully this temptation, we offered this definition as a starting point for discussion: *communication is the transactional process of creating and sustaining social order through symbolic action.*

After describing the general characteristics of the communication process, we described the functions of and approaches to theory building that are most often associated with communication studies. Far from being a process associated strictly with the natural or human sciences, theorizing is actually a function of everyday life. This revelation was followed by a discussion of two basic methods for conducting research and an overview of the three metatheoretical positions that govern every act of theorizing.

As a supplement to this chapter we will read an excerpt from *Pragmatics of Human Communication* (1967). In it, Paul Watzlawick, Janet Beavin, and Don Jackson apply the basic tenants of Systems Theory to communication. These authors rejected the long-standing ontological position that communication was something one person does to another and posited the view that communication and relationships are interactive, co-created phenomena. Because of the influence of their text on the field of communication studies, we thought it important for you to read a portion of their work. As you read this selection, note their definition of communication and the *axioms* (assumed truths) they attribute to it.

The Organization of Human Interaction

Paul Watzlawick, Janet Beavin Bavelas, and Donald D. Jackson

4.1 Introduction

The relatively isolated examples presented in the previous chapters served to present, specifically and immediately, certain basic properties and pathologies of human communication. These are the elements out of which the complexity of communication is built. In turning now to the organization of interaction (as this unit of communication was defined in s. 2.22), we will consider the patterning of recurring, ongoing communications, that is, the *structure* of communication processes.

This level of analysis was implicit in earlier discussions, such as of cumulatively symmetrical or complementary interaction (s. 2.6 and 3.6). Similarly, the "self-fulfilling prophecy" (s. 2.44) encompasses more than the particular punctuation of a unique communicational sequence: repetition of this pattern of punctuation over time and over a variety of situations is a vital element. Thus the concept of pattern in communication can be seen as representing repetition or redundancy[1] of events. As there are certainly patterns of patterns and probably even higher levels of organization this hierarchy cannot be shown to be limited. However, for the moment, the unit of study will be the next higher level than that of our previous discussion: the organization of sequential messages, first in general and then with specific consideration of ongoing interactional systems. This chapter is primarily theoretical, with the complex problem of illustrating such macroscopic phenomena left mostly for Chapter 5. Thus, these two chapters have essentially the same relation (first theory and then illustration) as in Chapters 2 and 3.

4.2   Interaction as a System

Interaction can be considered as a system, and the general theory of systems gives insight into the nature of interactional systems. General System Theory is not only a theory of biological, economic, or engineering systems. Despite their widely varying subject matter, these theories of particular systems have so many common conceptions that a more general theory has evolved which structures the similarities into formal isomorphies.[2] One of the pioneers in this field, Ludwig von Bertalanffy, describes the theory as "the formulation and derivation of those principles which are valid for 'systems' in general" (25, p. 131). Von Bertalanffy has also anticipated the concern of those who will shrink at our eagerness to treat human relationships with a theory better known— which is not to say better suited—or application to distinctly nonhuman, notably computer, systems and has pointed out its faulty logic:

> The isomorphy we have mentioned is a consequence of the fact that in certain aspects, corresponding abstractions and conceptual models can be applied to different phenomena. It is only in view of these aspects that system laws will apply. This does not mean that physical systems. organisms and societies are all the same. In principle, it is the same situation as when the law of gravitation applies to Newton's apple, the planetary system, and the phenomenon of tide. This means that in view of some rather limited aspects a certain theoretical system, that of mechanics, holds true; it does not mean that there is a particular resemblance between apples, planets, and oceans in a great number of other aspects. (26, p. 75)

4.21

Before any of the special properties of systems are defined, we should point out the obvious and very important variable of time (with its companion, order) must be an integral part of our unit of study. Communication sequences are not, to use Frank's words, "anonymous units in a frequency distribution" (45, p. 510) but the inseparable stuff of an ongoing process whose order and interrelations occurring over a period of time, shall be our interest here. As Lennard and Bernstein have put it:

> Implicit to a system is a span of time. By its very nature a system consists of an inter-action, and this means that a sequential process of action and reaction has to take

place before we are able to describe any state of the system or any change of state. (*94*, pp. 13–14)

4.22—Definition of a System

Initially, we can follow Hall and Fagen in defining a system as "a set of objects together with relationships between the objects and between their attributes" (*62*, p. 18), in which *objects* are the components or parts of the system, *attributes* are the properties of the objects, and *relationships* "tie the system together." These authors further point out that any object is ultimately specified by its attributes. Thus, while the "objects" may be individual humans, the attributes by which they are identified herein are their communicative behaviors (as opposed to, say, intrapsychic attributes). The objects of interactional systems are best described not as individuals but as persons-communicating-with-other-persons. By pinning down the term "relationship" the present vagueness and generality of the above definition can be considerably reduced. Conceding that there is always some kind of relationship, however spurious, between any objects whatever, Hall and Fagen are of the opinion

> that the relationships to be considered in the context of a given set of objects depend on the problem at hand, important or interesting relationships being included, trivial or unessential relationships excluded. The decision as to which relationships are important and which trivial is up to the person dealing with the problem, i.e., the question of triviality turns out to be relative to one's interest. (*62*, p. 18)

What is important here is not the content of communication per se but exactly the relationship (command) aspect of human communication, as defined in s. 2.3. Interactional systems, then, shall be *two or more communicants in the process of, or at the level of, defining the nature of their relationship.*[3]

4.23—Environment and Subsystems

Another important aspect of the definition of a system is the definition of its environment; again, according to Hall and Fagen: "For a given system, the environment is the set of all objects a change in whose attributes affect the system and also those objects whose attributes are changed by the behavior of the system" (*62*, p. 20). By the authors' own admission,

> the statement above invites the natural question of when an object belongs to a system and when it belongs to the environment; for if an object reacts with a system in the way described above should it not be considered a part of the system? The answer is by no means definite. In a sense, a system together with its environment makes up the universe of all things of interest in a given context. Subdivision of this universe into two sets, system and environment, can be done in many ways which are in fact quite arbitrary. . . .
>
> It is clear from the definition of system and environment that any given system can be further subdivided into subsystems. Objects belonging to one subsystem may well be considered as part of the environment of another subsystem. (*62*, p. 20)

The very elusiveness and flexibility of this system-environment or system-subsystem concept in no small way accounts for the power of systems theory in the study of living (organic) systems, be they biological, psychological, or interactional as here. For

> . . . organic systems are *open*, meaning they exchange materials, energies, or information with their environments. A system is *closed* if there is no import or export of energies in any of its forms such as information, heat, physical materials, etc., and therefore no change of components, an example being a chemical reaction taking place in a sealed insulated container. (62, p. 23)

This distinction between closed and open systems can be said to have freed the sciences concerned with life-phenomena from the shackles of a theoretical model based essentially on classical physics and chemistry: a model of exclusively *closed* systems. Because living systems have crucial dealings with their environments, the theory and methods of analysis appropriate to things which can be reasonably put in "a sealed insulated container" were significantly obstructive and misleading.[4]

With the development of the theory of hierarchically arranged open subsystems, the system and its environment need no longer be artificially isolated from one another; they fit meaningfully together within the same theoretical framework. Koestler describes the situation as follows:

> A living organism or social body is not an aggregation of elementary parts or elementary processes; it is an integrated hierarchy of semiautonomous sub-wholes, consisting of sub-sub-wholes, and so on. Thus the functional units on every level of the hierarchy are double-faced as it were: they act as whole when facing downwards, as parts when facing upwards. (87, p. 287)

With this conceptual model we can easily place a dyadic interactional system into larger family, extended family, community, and cultural systems. Also, such subsystems may (with theoretical impunity) overlap other subsystems, since each member of the dyad is involved in dyadic subsystems with other persons and even with life itself (see Epilogue). In short, communicating individuals are seen in both *horizontal* and *vertical* relations with other persons and other systems.

4.3   The Properties of Open Systems

Thus we have shifted our discussion from the most universal definition of general systems to focus on one of two basic kinds of systems, the open system. Now some of the macroscopic formal properties of open systems can be defined as they apply to interaction.

4.31—Wholeness

Every part of a system is so related to its fellow parts that a change in one part will cause a change in all of them and in the total system. That is, a system behaves not as a simple composite of independent elements, but coherently and as an inseparable whole. This characteristic is perhaps best understood in contrast with its polar opposite, summativity: if variations in one part do not affect the other parts or the whole, then these parts are independent of each other and constitute a "heap" (to use a term from systems literature) that is no more complex than the sum of its elements. This quality of summativity can be put on the other end of a hypothetical continuum from wholeness, and it can be said that *systems are always characterized by some degree of wholeness.*

While they were not at the time formalized into a metatheory, the mechanical theories of the nineteenth century can now be seen to have been primarily analytical and summative, "The mechanistic world-view found its ideal in the Laplacean spirit, i.e., in the conception that all phenomena are ultimately aggregates of fortuitous actions of elementary physical units" (25, p. 165). Thus it will be that historical contrasts will provide the best examples. As Ashby has noted:

> Science stands today on something of a divide. For two centuries it has been exploring systems that are either intrinsically simple or that are capable of being analyzed into simple components. The fact that such a dogma as "vary the factors one at a time" could be accepted for a century, shows that scientists were largely concerned in investigating such systems as allowed this method; for this method is often fundamentally impossible in the complex systems. Not until Sir Ronald Fisher's work in the '20's, with experiments conducted on agricultural soils, did it become clearly recognised that there are complex systems that just do not allow the varying of only one factor at a time—they are so dynamic and interconnected that the alteration of one factor immediately acts as cause to evoke alterations in others, perhaps in a great many others. Until recently, science tended to evade the study of such systems, focusing its attention on those that were simple and, especially, reducible.
>
> In the study of some systems, however, the complexity could not be wholly evaded. The cerebral cortex of the free-living organism, the ant-hill as a functioning society, and the human economic system were outstanding both in their practical importance and in their intractability by the other methods. So today we see psychoses untreated, societies declining, and economic systems faltering, the scientists being able to do little more than to appreciate the full complexity of the subject he is studying. But science today is also taking the first steps towards studying "complexity" as a subject in its own right. (5, p. 5)

4.311

Nonsummativity, then, as a corollary of the notion of wholeness provides a negative guideline for the definition of a system. A system cannot be taken for the sum of its parts; indeed, formal analysis of artificially isolated segments would destroy the very object of interest. It is necessary to neglect the parts for the gestalt and attend to the core of its complexity, its organization. The psychological concept of gestalt is only one way of expressing the principle of nonsummativity; in other fields there is great interest in the *emergent quality* that arises out of the interrelation of two or more elements. The most obvious example is supplied by chemistry, where relatively few of the known elements produce an immense variety of complex new substances. Another example would be the so-called "Moiré patterns"—optical manifestations of the super-position of two or more lattices (114). In both cases, the result is of a complexity for which the elements, considered separately, could never account. Furthermore, it is very interesting that the slightest change in the relationship between the constituent parts is often magnified in the emergent quality—a different substance in the case of chemistry, a very different configuration in the Moiré pattern. In physiology, Virchowian cellular pathology contrasts in this regard with modern approaches such as Weiss's (162), and in psychology, classical association contrasts with Gestalt theory; so in the study of human interaction, we propose to contrast essentially individual-oriented approaches with communication theory. When interaction is considered a derivative of individual "properties" such as roles, values, expectations, and motivations, the composite—two or more interacting individuals—is a summative heap that can be broken into more basic (individual) units. In contrast, from the first axiom of communication—that all behavior is communication, and one cannot not communicate—it follows that communication sequences would be reciprocally inseparable; in short, that interaction is nonsummative.

4.312

Another theory of interaction that is contradicted by the principle of wholeness is that of *unilateral* relations between elements, i.e., that A may affect B but not vice versa. Recalling the example of the nagging wife and the withdrawing husband (s. 2.42), it was seen that although an interactional sequence may be *punctuated* (by the participants or the observer) into a pattern of one-way causality, such a sequence is in fact circular, and the apparent "response" must also be a stimulus for the next event in this interdependent chain. Thus, to assert that person A's behavior causes B's behavior is to ignore the effect of B's behavior on A's subsequent reaction; it is, in fact, to distort the chronology of events by punctuating certain relations in bold relief while obscuring others. Especially when the relationship is complementary, as in leader-follower, strong-weak, or parent-child relationships, it is easy to lose the wholeness of the interaction and break it up into independent, linearly causal units. This fallacy has already been warned against in s. 2.62 and 2.63 and needs only to be made explicit in terms of long-term interaction here.

4.32—Feedback

If the parts of a system are not summatively or unilaterally related, then in what manner are they united? Having rejected these two classical conceptual models, we would seem to be left with what in the nineteenth and early twentieth centuries were their disreputable alternatives—vague, vitalistic, and metaphysical notions which, since they did not fit the doctrine of determinism, were branded teleological. However, as already shown in s. 1.3, the conceptual shift from energy (and matter) to information has finally led us away from the sterile choice between deterministic and teleological causal schemes. Since the advent of cybernetics and the "discovery" of feedback, it has been seen that circular and highly complex relatedness is a markedly different but no less scientific phenomenon than simpler and more orthodox causal notions. Feedback and circularity, as described in detail in Chapter 1 and as illustrated repeatedly in Chapters 2 and 3, are the appropriate causal model for a theory of interactional systems. The specific nature of a feedback process is of much greater interest than origin and, frequently, outcome.

4.33—Equifinality

In a circular and self-modifying system, "results" (in the sense of alteration in state after a period of time) are not determined so much by initial conditions as by the nature of the process, or the system parameters. Simply stated, this principle of equifinality means that the same results may spring from different origins, because it is the nature of the organization which is determinate. Von Bertalanffy has elaborated on this principle:

> The steady state of open systems is characterized by the principle of equifinality; that is, in contrast to equilibrium states in closed systems which are determined by initial conditions, the open system may attain a time-independent state independent of initial conditions and determined only by the system parameters. (*27*, p. 7)

If the equifinal behavior of open systems is based on their independence of initial conditions, then not only may different initial conditions yield the same final result, but different results may be produced by the same "causes." Again, this corollary rests on the premise that system parameters will predominate over initial conditions. So in the analysis of how people affect each other in their interaction, we will not consider the specifics of genesis or product to be nearly so important as the ongoing organization of interaction.[5]

This issue is illustrated by the changing conceptions of the (psychogenic) etiology of schizophrenia. Theories of a unique trauma in childhood gave way to the postulation of a repetitive though unilateral and statically conceived relationship trauma inflicted by the schizophrenia-producing mother. As Jackson has pointed out, this is only the first phase in a larger revolution:

> Historically the place of psychogenic trauma in etiology appears to be shifting from Freud's original ideas of a single traumatic event to the concept of repetitive trauma. *The next step would be not who does what to whom, but how who does what.* Perhaps the next phase will include a study of schizophrenia (or schizophrenias) as a family-borne disease involving a complicated host-vector-recipient cycle that includes much more than can be connoted by the term "schizophrenogenic mother." (68, p. 184; italics ours)[6]

What has just been said about origins (etiology) can also be applied to the resultant clinical picture (nosology). To take schizophrenia as an example again, there are two ways to understand this term; as the label for a fixed disease entity or for a mode of interaction. It has already been proposed (s. 1.65 and 1.66) that the behavior traditionally classified as "schizophrenic" no longer be so reified but rather be studied only in the interpersonal context in which it occurs—the family, the institution—where such behavior is neither simply result nor cause of these usually bizarre environmental conditions but a complexly integrated part of an ongoing pathological system.

Finally, one of the most significant characteristics of open systems is found in equifinal behavior, especially in contrast to the closed-system model. The final state of the closed system is completely determined by initial circumstances that can therefore be said to be the best "explanation" of that system; in the case of the open system, however, organizational characteristics of the system can operate to achieve even the extreme case of total independence of initial conditions: *the system is then its own best explanation,* and the study of its present organization the appropriate methodology.[7]

Endnotes

1. The relevance of redundancy and constraint to our concept of pattern has been discussed in detail in s. 1.4; it is only necessary here to emphasize that a pattern is information conveyed by the occurrence of certain events and the *nonoccurrence* of other events. If all possible events of a given class occur randomly, there is no pattern and no information.
2. As will be noted, our focus herein is limited to certain aspects of ongoing interactional systems, especially families. For a recent, comprehensive application of this frame of reference to living systems in general, see Miller's series (*105*), which signals the potentially fruitful integrative aspect of such an approach.
3. While primary emphasis will be on human communicants, there is no theoretical reason to exclude the interaction of other mammals (9) or of groups, such as nations, which may interact much as two or more individuals do (*125*).
4. An interesting and relevant example of the indirect effect on diverse disciplines of the metatheory most articulated by classical physics can be found in psychiatry: Pathologies of interaction were virtually

unknown in the early days of psychiatry with one exception, the *folie à deux* and related symbioses (s. 3.62). These dramatic relationships were from the first considered interactional, not individual, problems and, as such, were little more than nosological freaks. Still, the fact that they were even admitted while many other relationship problems were ignored is intriguing, especially since we can now see that only the *folie à deux* fitted precisely the closed system model of the day.

5. Cf. Langer, who has put the choice another way:

> There is a widespread and familiar fallacy, known as the "genetic fallacy," which arises from the historical method in philosophy and criticism: the error of confusing the *origin* of a thing with its *import*, of tracing the thing to its most primitive form and then calling it "merely" this archaic phenomenon . . . e.g. words were probably ritualistic sounds before they were communicative devices; that does not mean that language is now not "really" a means of communication, but is "really" a mere residue of tribal excitement. (91, p. 248) (Italics and quotation marks in original).

6. There is evidence to support such an equifinal view of psychopathology; Kant (82) and Renaud and Estess (124) have found, respectively, no precipitating traumatic factors in fifty-six consecutive cases of schizophrenia, and overwhelming reports of traumatic experiences in the life histories of men who were considered psychiatrically normal. Noting that their normal group was indistinguishable from clinical samples on this basis, Renaud and Estess go on to say:

> Such a conclusion is not incompatible with basic assumptions underlying twentieth century behavioral science (e.g., that in substantial degree human behavior is a product of life experience); neither is it in conflict with the basic proposition that the early years of human life are crucial for later development. This view does question, however, elementalistic conceptions of simple, direct causal relations insistently presumed to exist between certain kinds of events and later development of mental illness. (124, p. 801)

7. The same point has been made by writers as scientific as Wieser (167, p. 33) and as facetious yet realistic as C. Northcote Parkinson (115).

CHAPTER 3

A Short History of the Study of Communication

Learning Objectives

After reading this chapter, you should be able to:

■ Recognize that human communication has been studied from several different perspectives.

■ Describe the origins of communication studies in ancient Greece.

■ Define concepts advanced by Aristotle: ethos, pathos, and logos.

■ Explain Aristotle's view of the role of the audience.

■ Discuss the new technologies and societal conditions that influenced the study of communication in the 1920s and 1940s.

■ Explain how scholars in the Chicago School conceptualized communication vis-à-vis symbolic interactionism, mass communication, film effects on children, and female communication scholars.

■ Name and describe the communication model proposed by Shannon and Weaver.

■ Provide an example of each of the following sources of noise: physical noise, psychological noise, semantic noise, and intra-listener discomfort.

■ Explain the nature of the shift in communication studies that occurred in the 1950s through the 1970s.

■ Discuss the nature of communication models, and how they relate to reality.

■ Explain how one's personal orientation may affect communication.

■ Describe what is meant by the communication context.

■ Explain why no piece of behavior has meaning in and of itself.

■ Explain why a communicative act must be interpreted in light of the context in which it occurs.

■ Explain how one's personal orientation may affect communication.

■ Identify the major types of psychological defense mechanisms and their impact on communication.

■ Describe why relationships develop.

■ Outline the stages of relationship development and the stages of relationship deterioration.

■ Give examples of strategies to end relationships.

■ Describe the small group communication context and identify the five commonly found types of small groups.

■ Describe the symptoms of groupthink and risky-shift phenomenon.

■ Describe four stages of group development and the types of group roles.

■ Analyze the accuracy of the grapevine.

■ Explain the phrase "culture is invisible."

■ Define and provide examples of the assembly effect bonus and the dynamogenic effect.

■ Provide examples of types of organizations.

■ Discuss the following characteristics of organizations: division of labor, span of control, chain of command, and downward, upward, and horizontal communication

"If you would understand anything, observe its beginning and its development."

—Aristotle

Introduction

While the practice of communication has been a part of human societies since their inception, the study of communication has not. In fact, concerted efforts to discover the hows and whys of human communication are relatively recent phenomena. In this chapter, we will explore the history of the discipline known as Communication.

As we move quickly through this 2500 year history, it is important to note that, as with the study of any phenomenon, the study of communication does not occur in isolation. Instead it is a pragmatic discipline that responds directly to the sociopolitical events of the day.

450 B.C.E. to the 1900s

The earliest known efforts to explain and teach communication skills occurred in ancient Greece about 450 B.C.E. The newly formed democracy required any citizen who wished to reclaim family land that had been taken by the tyrannical government to argue their case before a panel of judges and a citizen jury of some 500 peers (Poulakos, 1995), since the one seeking restitution could not solicit the aid of a lawyer to present the case, one had to rely upon one's own ability to persuade. To aid citizens in their quest for justice, teachers of rhetoric became staples in Greek culture. Corax and Tisias and Sophists like Gorgias, Protagoras, and Isocrates, established competing schools of rhetoric, each promising to outdo the other in teaching students to handle themselves well in a public forum.

One of the more prolific authors of the time was Plato. While Plato is probably best known for his relentless attacks on the aforementioned Sophists for practicing the art of deception, he, too, made a living tutoring wealthy students in the art of public speaking.

Although bits and pieces of the Sophists' "handbooks" on public speaking remain, and Plato's *Dialogues* continue to fascinate and educate philosophers and teachers of rhetoric, the most influential figure in the study and practice of rhetoric was Aristotle. Aristotle, a student of Plato, went well beyond the purview of his teacher in exploring the pragmatics of public address.

In one of his surviving texts, *On Rhetoric,* Aristotle describes the "available means of persuasion" that any rhetor can and should use. These means fall into three distinct categories: *ethos,* the character of the speaker; *pathos,* the emotion a speaker is able to generate in an audience; and *logos,* the logic of the arguments or words themselves.

There are two important things to note in relation to Aristotle's approach to communication: 1) the major emphasis in the communication process is on the speaker; and 2) the communication process is unidirectional (i.e., one-way). This means that communication was viewed by Aristotle (and subsequently much of the western world) as something a speaker does to an audience, making the audience little more than passive recipients of information.

So profound was Aristotle's work that it continued to influence the understanding of communication until the early 1900s. Even today we see examples of Aristotle's understanding of communication being exhibited through such things as the "sponge model" of education.

The 1920s to the 1940s

The next significant era in the study of communication as an emerging discipline occurred between the 1920 and 1940s. Many communication scholars maintain that, because of the advances taking place in the new technologies like radio, telephone and television, and because of the ensuing world wars, communication was receiving a new-found attention from researchers and disciplines outside of traditional communication studies. These researchers, like Harold Lasswell, Paul Lazarsfel, Kurt Lewin, and Carl Hovland were most interested in exploring the effects of propaganda on mass audiences. And while this represents an important advancement in mass communication, there was an arguably more influential group working simultaneously (Rogers, 1994).

Unlike those who studied communication as a means of manipulating and propagandizing the masses, the *Chicago School* was more interested in communication as a means of human connection (Rogers, 1994). Under the influence of scholars like W. I. Thomas, John Dewey, George Herbert Mead, and Robert Parks, there was, according to Rogers, a fivefold contribution to the study of communication:

1. It conceptualized symbolic interactionism, a theoretical viewpoint that put communication at the center of how human personality is formed and changed.
2. It thought of mass communication as a possible means for American democratic society to survive in the face of urban social problems.
3. It conducted the Payne Fund studies of film effects on children in the late 1920s, which provided an early prototype for the many later studies of communication effects.
4. It shunted female scholars like Jane Addams and her sociological colleagues connected with Hull House into social work as a separate and applied field.
5. Its methodological approach led to a contemporary set of communication scholars called the interpretive school (Rogers, 1994).

The 1940s to the 1950s

Given the post war boom in technology and the growing fascination with all things scientific, it was only a matter of time before communication established itself as a legitimate member of the

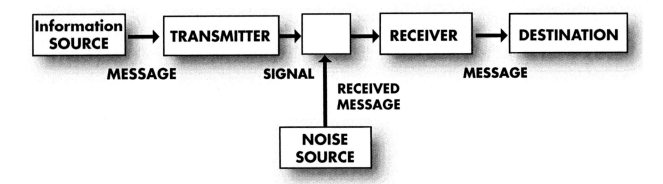

Figure 1: Shannon and Weaver Model.
Source: The Mathematical Theory of Communication, Claude E. Shannon and Warren Weaver. Copyright © 1949 by the University of Illinois. Renewed 1977.

human or social science community. This was accomplished during this period by introducing the more predictive and corrective approaches to the communication process like Psycholinguistics (Psychology of Language), Speech-Language Pathology and Audiology, and Voice and Diction. There was, however, a second, influential event that spurred the Study of Communication to becoming more scientific. It was the introduction of Shannon and Weaver's Mathematical Model of Communication.

While working for Bell Telephone laboratories, *Claude Shannon and Warren Weaver* created an engineering-based model of communication.

According to Shannon and Weaver, the information source sends a message (e.g., written or spoken words, music, dance, etc.) to the transmitter. The transmitter changes the message into a signal (e.g., speech), which is sent over the communication channel, and processed by the receiver into a message that can be understood by the destination. Shannon and Weaver's model was the first to include a noise source, as well as a correction channel to compensate for the noise. There can be many sources of noise, which is defined as anything which interferes with the transmission of the message. Examples of noise sources include:

Physical noise: loud machinery; traffic sounds; papers rustling; talking, cell phones ringing

Psychological noise: anxiety; depression; boredom; anger

Semantic noise: the perceived meaning of a word is upsetting distracting or unclear; bias against the speaker.

Intra-listener discomfort: lack of sleep; stomachache; headache; hunger; room temperature too hot or too cold; hard chairs

A Side Note on Models of Communication

Since Shannon and Weaver, communication theorists have developed models to represent their conceptions of the communication process. It should be stressed that these models are representations of reality, not identical replicas of the process. For as Miller (1972), points out, models of speech communication are always symbolic, employing numbers, pictures or words, but never physical representations. This is because "communication is best viewed as a psychological phenomenon, rather than as a physical entity." Miller (1972) describes a model of speech communication as being "a kind of classificatory system that enables one to abstract and to categorize potentially relevant parts of the process." He further points out that it is useful to think of "models" as "arbitrary constructs as judgments made by the person who creates the model."

The 1950s to the 1970s

Without a doubt these decades were among the most revolutionary in United States, if not world history. The same thing might be said of the study of communication.

Because of growing civil and equal rights movements, ongoing dissatisfaction with the Vietnam conflict, and a growing distrust of national and international political leaders, it is no surprise that there was a radical change in the discipline. For the first time since its start in ancient Greece, public or platform speaking was beginning to falter as the primary focus of communication studies. The discipline was beginning to emphasize interpersonal communication.

Also, because public platforms were open mostly to those in positions of power, there was a growing sense of communication as a critical study.

The 1970s to the Present

The current state of communication studies is very eclectic to be sure. All one needs to do is look at the research divisions called contexts of communication offered by most textbooks in the discipline. The following is a sample of the areas of study and some specific types of research relative to each. Remember two things as you read this section: 1) Because communication is both context shaped and context shaping, we do not want to give the impression that these are independent, real contexts in which communication occurs. Instead we want to emphasize that a context like an organization or a small group exists because the members agree to enact certain communication behaviors specific to the expectations of such a context. 2) The order of contexts listed below, while representing the traditional divisions within the discipline, have been reordered to align with our ontological position represented through the text.

Organizational/Institutional Communication

Definitions

We spend a large part of our lives as members of organizations and institutions. An organization is:

> "A collection or system of individuals, who commonly through a hierarchy of ranks
> and division of labor, seek to achieve a predetermined goal" (Rogers and Rogers,
> 1975).

Institutions may be defined as collectives containing considerable numbers of people, but can also refer to the formalization of interaction between two people, such as "the institution of marriage." However, for the purposes of this Unit, we will concentrate primarily on communication within organizations.

Types of Organizations

For many people the term "organizational communication" conjures up an image of a corporate giant such as IBM or United States Steel Corporation. However, it is important to bear in mind that these groups represent just one type of organization. The following list illustrates a number of different types of organizations:

1. *Business organizations*: Owners receive the greatest benefits or profits. Examples: banks, hotels, retail stores.
2. *Service organizations*: Clients, rather than the organization, receive the most benefits. Examples: hospitals, civil rights groups, schools, and social work agencies.
3. *Mutual benefit organizations*: Members derive the most rewards out of participation. Examples: professional organizations, private country clubs, religious or fraternal organizations, and political parties.
4. *Commercial or commonwealth organizations*: These organizations serve the public interest. Examples: public transportation systems, post offices, armed forces, and public radio or television stations.
5. *Coercive organizations*: Coercive organizations exert force over individuals to assert power and control. Examples: prisons and government dictatorships.
6. *Utilitarian organizations*: Utilitarian organizations control members via the dispensing of rewards for employees' work. Rewards might take the form of wages, tenure, and advancement. Examples: industries and workers' cooperatives.
7. *Normative organizations*: These organizations control the actions of their members by invoking societal norms. Examples: religious, voluntary, and political organizations.

It is important to note that an organization may have more than one goal or function and that this might fit the definition of more than one of the above categories (Barker, 1987).

Characteristics of Organizations

If one is to communicate effectively within an organization, it is important to understand typical organizational structure and function.

At the time of the Industrial Revolution, it was determined that an organization, or collection of people, could produce more than individuals working alone by allowing individuals to specialize. Thus, instead of one artisan producing a single product, tasks were divided among various job specialists. This resulted in division of labor. Previously, a factory produced 20 pins per day when each worker was solely responsible for the completion of an entire pin. However, when the labor was divided into 18 separate operations, 4,800 pins were produced per person, each day.

The concept of span of control also evolved. This refers to the limit of the authority of a single supervisor. Span of control is determined by the number of people who can be effectively managed by one supervisor.

As the Industrial Revolution progressed and more supervisors were employed, it became evident that the supervisors needed supervision. More and more levels were added to the organization, and a hierarchy or pyramid of control was established. This resulted in a chain of command, the formal communication pathway. Thus, an employee admonished to "follow channels" is not being advised to watch more television. Instead, he or she is being told never to "jump the chain of command" by seeking a higher authority other than their immediate supervisor.

Communication Pathways

Organizational communication can proceed through formal or informal channels.

Formal Channels

Formal communication channels proceed in three directions: downward, upward, and horizontal.

Downward Communication. Downward communication is initiated by the organizations' upper management, then filters downward through the "chain of command." Typical methods of downward communication are as follows: department meetings, company newsletter, letters sent home, a speech to all employees, and even videotape recordings. Downward communication consists of messages such as job instructions, job rationale, policy and procedures, employee performance appraisal, and motivational appeals (Hamilton and Parker, 1990).

With downward communication, there is a loss of information as information proceeds from level to level. For instance, it has been estimated that the amount of a message formulated by a company's board of directors will be received as follows: 63 percent by the vice-president; 56 percent by the general supervisor; 40 percent by the plant manager; 30 percent by the general foreman, and only 20 percent by the worker. Reasons for this information loss includes loss of detail and shortening of the message. The effective communicator must realize that information loss is likely, and prepare for this problem.

Upward Communication. *Upward Communication* has multiple functions. Subordinates tell their supervisors about the highlights of their work and unsolved work problems. This generally occurs via written reports, supervisor-subordinate meetings, staff meetings, and even the company "suggestion box."

Effective upward communication occurs in an organizational environment of trust. The subordinates must not feel they will be penalized if they are the "bearers of bad news."

In *Horizontal Communication*, messages flow laterally between persons of the same rank or department. This is important in coordinating work tasks, solving problems, resolving conflict, and building alliances in the workplace.

Informal Channels

Informal channels of communication flourish when formal channels fail to develop or are not accepted by the people for whom the messages are intended. The most typical informal channel is the *grapevine*, which has been estimated to be 75 percent to 95 percent accurate (Hamilton and Parker, 1990).

Organizational/Institutional Realities

The world of an organization or institution is experienced as an objective reality:

- the organization/institution has a permanent history of events and communication;
- the institution has an effect on the individual, and the individual has an effect on the institution, in that individuals in the institution establish patterns and standards of human conduct;
- there is institutional segmentation, in that there are socially segregated subunits of meaning, such as departments at the University of Pittsburgh.

Knowledge is transmitted within the institution as follows:

- by language, written and spoken, as in memos, the Annual Report, meetings, and interpersonal conversations;
- symbolic objects, such as religious or military emblems;
- symbolic activities such as religious or military rituals, graduation ceremonies, retirement dinners, and "parents'-day" at summer day camp.

For example, let us consider some of the organizational/institutional realities at institutions of higher learning. Language is used to define your role, in that you are given the label "student," (though you may also be an "employee" of the institution). As a student, language further expresses your relationship to the institution. You may be categorized as full-time or part-time, in-state or out-of-state, a communication or other major, a member of an anticipated graduating class. Similarly, others are characterized as faculty, staff, members of a department, or administrative personnel. As students you talk of grades, papers and credit hours. Faculty refer to their Faculty Activity Reports and their teaching loads. There is even a peculiar form of "institutional time" associated with universities, colleges, and community colleges, such as midterm and finals weeks, semesters, semester breaks, and class times. These times, created by communication, assume objective reality, even dictating when faculty may take vacations and when students must study.

Small Group Communication

Consider, for a moment, how important small groups are in your life. Families, sports teams, and long-standing "lunch-table" companions are all examples of groups which fulfill our need for belongedness. Indeed, the world would be a lonely place without one or more groups to belong to.

Definition

For the purpose of definition, we will consider a small group to be "a collection of individuals, from three to fifteen in number, who meet in face-to-face interaction over a period of time, generally with an assigned leader, who possess at least one common characteristic, and who meet with a purpose in mind" (Barker et al., 1991).

Three's a Crowd?

Why devote a section in this book specifically to communication in the small group? Because "extensive studies by social scientists indicate that the small group is an identifiable social entity. The introduction of a third person into a social field changes the nature of communication" (Bormann, 1990). The addition of the third person into the group allows for coalitions to form. The tendency for groups of three individuals to become "two against one" can significantly change the nature of communication from that found in the two-person dyad. And when the group size exceeds three members, there is the possibility for counter-coalitions to form.

The Importance of Small Groups

Small groups can be exceedingly powerful entities in our society, and the decisions made by these groups have great impact upon our lives. Influential small groups include: The U.S. Supreme Court, a board of citizens that assigns ratings to movies, the editorial staff of the local newspaper, juries, the presidential cabinet, and college admissions committees.

There are many, sometimes overlapping purposes of small groups. Groups may exist to solve problems, accomplish tasks, gather information, satisfy social needs, increase psychological well-being, engage in recreation, or share religious, avocational or vocational pursuits.

One setting in which the small group is important is the health care setting. The sphere of the small group's influence begins with the recruitment, selection, and training of health care professionals. It is a small group of faculty members that typically determines who will be admitted to a health care training program. Another, perhaps overlapping, faculty group establishes the curriculum and standards for graduation. As students proceed through their training, much support is gained from the friendships established in small groups of students.

Small groups are also significant within the larger health care organization. Groups of practicing physicians, medical standards committees, and groups within administrative and staff departments formulate policy and operational guidelines. The governing body of any major health care organization also has standing committees that dictate policy. For example, a hospital's Board of Trustees typically contains several small groups such as the Executive Management Committee, Finance Committee, Investment Committee, Buildings and Grounds Committee, Conflict of Interest Committee, Long Range Planning Committee, and Personnel and Compensation Committee. While the precise numbers and missions of the committees vary from institution to institution, these small groups provide a mechanism for trustees, professional staff, and management staff to address important areas of institutional function. Whether we work in a hospital or visit as a patient, our lives will no doubt be affected by the decisions made by these small groups.

Types of Small Groups

Small groups can be classified as follows:

1. *The Primary Group* is the most basic group, consisting of family or good friends. The primary group is typically a long-lasting entity.
2. *The Social Group* gets together to exchange friendship and conversation. This might include a group of neighbors or a group of high school students who eat lunch together in the cafeteria each day.
3. *The Educational Group* meets to learn a new skill or body of knowledge. A study group, small aerobics class, or a photography club are all forms of educational groups.
4. *The Therapy or Support Group* attempts to offer mutual support and psychological growth under the leadership of a trained therapist, and
5. *The Problem Solving or Task Group* works together to determine a solution to a particular problem.

Characteristics of Small Groups

The following are characteristics of small groups which render each small group unique. The first two characteristics provide reasons why the small group is more effective than one or two people working alone:

1. *Assembly Effect Bonus:* Productivity increases when there is a) division of labor, b) specialization of tasks, and c) reduction of physical and psychological tension that occurs when working within a group.
2. *Dynamogenic Effect:* The dynamogenic effect holds that the presence of others releases latent energy that the individual is unable to release on his own" (Burgoon and Ruffner, 1978). This phenomenon was first identified by Triplett (1897), who investigated the effects of

competition on individual performance by examining bicycle race data from the records of the Racing Board of the League of American Wheelman. He found that race times were fastest for the races where several riders competed, next fastest for "paced races" (i.e., another rider set the pace), and slowest for unpaced events.

In more recent competitions, professional tennis players have noted that their performance improves as the size and enthusiasm of the crowd increases.

The next group of characteristics allows observers to describe a particular group:

3. *Group Personality:* Each group takes on a unique personality or identity. Surprisingly, a group's orientation is not necessarily a conglomeration or "average" of the personalities of individual group members. Such incongruity is possible because the presence of others can calm even the most enthusiastic group members or stimulate passive individuals into action. Thus, a group of "rigid" individuals can exhibit a "flexible" group personality, while a collection of "flexible" individuals can be part of a highly traditional and "rigidly" functioning group (Burgoon and Ruffner, 1978).

4. *Group Norms:* Group norms are in essence a "shared acceptance of rules," which express what is considered to be the normative behavior and values of most members of the group. Group norms function to ensure a group's survival. These may be reflected in the group's values, traditions, by-laws, and rituals. The longer an individual is exposed to a group's norms, the greater the tendency for that person to adopt the group's norms as his or her own.

5. *Group Cohesiveness:* Group cohesiveness refers to the degree to which group members are attracted to each other and to the group, and to the desire to remain within the group.

6. *Commitment to Task:* Groups exist for a designated purpose, usually to accomplish an identified and agreed-upon goal. This recognized purpose may relate to information sharing, group maintenance, problem solving, or task completion. In order to achieve the goal, it is important that group members subordinate their own needs and desires to those of the larger group. Group members seek to 1) avoid group failure, and 2) achieve group success (Burgoon and Ruffner, 1978).

7. *Group Size:* A small group has been characterized as a collection of at least three individuals. Some have arbitrarily placed the upper limit for the small group at 20 individuals. It is important that the group be small enough to permit face-to-face communication. Group size should allow members to "recall personal characteristics of other members accurately" (Burgoon and Ruffner, 1978; Tompkins, 1982).

Finally, due to the nature of the small group, two major problems can occur during the decision-making process:

8. *Groupthink:* Janis (1982) examined a group of government decisions of foreign policies and found that well-established and long-standing groups tended to make decisions in characteristic ways. A possible danger of such cohesive groups is that the pressure for group conformity causes individuals within the group to censor any deviations they might have with group policy. In addition, the group as a whole may 1) share an illusion of invulnerability so that they are willing to take extreme risks; 2) engage in collective rationalization of their shortcomings or failures; 3) ignore the ethical or moral implications of their decisions because they believe that the group's morality is unquestionably acceptable; 4) pressure a dissident group member to conform; 5) mistakenly believe that all group members unanimously support a decision when such is not the case; 6) stereotype other "enemy" group leaders as too evil or unworthy of negotiation attempts, and 7) contain self-appointed "mindguards" who shield other group members

from information that runs counter to the expressed group position (Janis, 1982; Burgoon and Ruffner, 1978).

9. *Risky Shift Phenomenon:* This refers to the finding that the decisions made by small groups are consistently "riskier" than those made by individual members of the group. It has been postulated that group decision-making increases the likelihood of a "risky" decision because the group diffuses the responsibility, and thus the anxiety, generated by a risky decision.

Development of Small Groups

Much like the evolution of interpersonal relationships, the communication within small groups engaged in decision-making moves through predictable stages of development (Barker et al., 1991).

> *Stage One: Orientation.* During the Orientation Stage, group members function as if in a "honeymoon period." They become acquainted with one another, try to avoid conflict, and begin to "test the waters" by tentatively expressing their viewpoints.
>
> *Stage Two: Conflict.* Groups enter the Conflict Stage when group members feel secure enough to express disagreement. It is in this stage that attempts are made to persuade and coalitions are formed.
>
> *Stage Three: Emergence.* Groups in the Emergence Stage begin to resolve their conflict and tentatively reach agreement. Coalitions weaken, and the areas of agreement are identified. Group members begin to compromise, cooperate, and make positive statements.
>
> *Stage Four: Reinforcement.* The Reinforcement Stage is characterized by the reaching of consensus. The group develops a unified approach and strengthens its commitment to the decision.

While many regard the Conflict Stage as an uncomfortable and undesirable state of group function, it is during this stage that the group begins to engage in critical thinking and problem solving. A failure to do so may cause the group to suffer from Groupthink or Risky Shift Phenomenon described above.

Roles in Small Groups

People play different roles within small groups. Benne and Sheats (1948) divided these roles into three broad categories: *group task roles; group building and maintenance roles;* and *self-centered roles.* The following section will define and give examples of these categories (Barker et al., 1991). Perhaps you will be able to identify what roles you and others assume in the small groups you have participated in. You might also widen your communicative repertoire by experimenting with new group roles.

Group Task Roles

The group member who focuses energies on group task roles is primarily concerned with completing the group's task or achievement goal. Specific task roles are as follows:

> *Coordinator:* Shows how statements made by different group members relate to one another. ("Don's statistics support the observations made by Mary.")

Elaborator: Explains and elaborates on another group member's idea. ("Perhaps Joan is suggesting that we need to consider alternatives to this problem.")

Evaluator-critic: Evaluates the group's work in light of higher standards. ("This is a start in the right direction, but I don't think that the evidence we've gathered is sufficient to convince a Congressional committee of our position.")

Energizer: Stimulates group members to take action. ("Who is going to help me analyze the data?")

Information-giver: Provides useful information to group members. ("The library closes at 11:00 p.m.")

Information-seeker: Asks group for information or clarification. ("Can anyone explain why we can't get this to work today?")

Procedural technician: Takes responsibility for completing routine tasks. ("I scheduled the audio-visual equipment for our presentation.")

Recorder: Keeps minutes of the meetings or otherwise records the group's progress. ("We've dispensed with only two items of the agenda in the last hour.")

Group Building and Maintenance Roles

Group building and maintenance activities enable the group to function harmoniously so that conflicts are resolved, disruptive behavior is eliminated, and interpersonal relationships are positive. Quite simply, the social-emotional leader attempts to make the group experience pleasant and desirable for all group members.

Compromiser: Attempts to arrive at a solution that will be acceptable to everyone. ("You both have good ideas. Perhaps we can combine them to formulate a workable solution.")

Encourager: Provides positive feedback to another group member. ("Keep trying, Jim; you're on the right track.")

Follower: Accepts the ideas of others in the group. ("I'll go along with that—sounds good to me.")

Gatekeeper: Facilitates equal participation from everyone in the group. ("Let's hear from the people who have not had a chance to speak yet.")

Group Observer: Provides an evaluation of the group's progress ("I think we've reached an impasse here.")

Harmonizer: Reduces interpersonal conflict and tension, often by use of humor. ("One thing we can surely agree upon tonight is that we need to break for pizza.")

Self-Centered Roles

While group task behaviors and group building and maintenance behaviors serve to promote the mission and solidarity of the group, self-centered behaviors either prevent the group from achieving its goals, or waste the group's time with conversation that is unrelated to the group's goals. Barker and colleagues (1991) delineates seven types of self-centered roles. These are:

Aggressor: Is antagonistic toward other group members and their ideas. ("I think that's the dumbest thing I've ever heard.")

Blocker: Does not accept any ideas and refuses to cooperate. ("I'll never accept that. We're going nowhere fast.")

Dominator: Dominates the group speaking time.

Help-seeker: Behaves in a helpless, dependent way so as to avoid work. ("I've never been very good at dissection—I think someone should do that for me.")

Social-loafer: Avoids work by engaging in non-relevant discussion or activities. ("Let's go swimming instead.")

Self-confessor: Discusses topics related to self rather than to the group task. ("I finally figured out why I don't like computers. It's all because of . . .")

Special-interest pleader: Presents his/her own viewpoint and needs, sometimes introducing irrelevant information. ("Let's wait to start that project until next Friday; it falls on a full moon and is good luck.")

Group Leadership

While there is often a designated group leader, group leadership can also be assumed by a non-designated member. In fact, when forming a group, it is effective to designate a task leader and to include a member likely to be a social-emotional leader. Any member of the group has the potential to learn and display leadership qualities, though not all may choose to do so.

Interpersonal Communication

Interpersonal communication refers to the communication that occurs between two people, in the context of a relationship.

The Nature of Relationships

No two relationships are alike. The type of relationship may vary according to the focus of the relationship, whether this is emotional, intellectual, and/or physical. For example, the relationship that one achieves with a professional mentor will differ in its primary focus from a relationship with one's closest friend. The former will be primarily professional in nature and the latter social. Relationships also assume different levels of intensity, according to the frequency of contact, duration of the relationship, and the depth of the intimacy that is achieved.

Reasons Relationships Develop

Relationships develop for a variety of reasons. According to DeVito (1985), relationships help us to feel less lonely, to obtain intellectual, emotional, and physical stimulation, and to learn more about ourselves. Relationships also enable us to share the "good times" and the "bad times" with others.

When we develop relationships, we generally do so with individuals to whom we feel attracted. This attraction may be physical and/or relate to the individual's personality or behavior.

Relationships also tend to develop on the basis of proximity. Studies of students living in student housing show that friendships tend to develop between those who live close by. Also, an overwhelming majority of marriages occur between people who have lived near each other.

Another reason relationships seem to thrive is based upon reinforcement. We tend to like people who like us and to dislike people whom we sense dislike us.

Similarity is also another strong reason for the development of relationships. There is a tendency for people of like attitudes and who demonstrate a similar level of physical attractiveness, intelligence, and ability to be attracted to one another.

While individuals who are similar seem to seek one another, *complementarity*, resulting in attraction to dissimilar individuals, also operates in the development of relationships, though to a lesser extent. This principle explains why "opposites attract."

Stages of Relationship Development

Relationships typically progress through a series of predictable stages, though it is possible for a stage to be skipped or for development to cease at a particular stage.

Contact Stage: In the first stage, contact is made, and the two people decide whether they wish for the relationship to progress. Conversation relates to the exchange of basic information, such as name, place of residence, and so on. At this stage, physical attraction is very important, and basic assumptions are made about the person's warmth, friendliness, and character.

Involvement Stage: In the second stage, involvement occurs, and there is a mutual disclosure of interests and attitudes.

Intimacy Stage: The third stage establishes intimacy such that the other person becomes one's closest friend, companion, and/or lover.

Certain types of intimate relationships may at some point be institutionalized in the form of "going steady," or marriage. DeVito (1991) writes that this stage is reserved for the closest of friends and/or family members. With the exception of close family members, it is rare to have more than four intimates.

Dissolution Stage: Relationships can also experience a weakening of the bonds of intimacy. The beginnings of this weakening occur in the deterioration stage and are formalized in the dissolution stage.

So Many Ways to End a Relationship!

There are so many ways to end your relationships, whether they are business, social, or professional in nature. The strategies you use will depend upon the duration and intensity of the relationship and the reasons for the termination of the relationship.

One or more of five major strategies are typically used to end relationships. These include:

Behavioral De-escalation: Simply avoid all future contact, phone calls, letters, etc.

Negative Management Identity: Try to convince the individual that it would be best to end the relationship, as both parties need to enter a more positive relationship.

Justification: Justify your actions by explaining the positive consequences of disengaging (i.e., the relationship should benefit both parties, and it doesn't) or negative consequences of non-disengaging (i.e., continuing the relationship will be damaging to both parties).

De-escalation: decrease the intensity of the relationship for the present time, with the possibility that the relationship might resume in the future.

Positive Tone: try to end the relationship on a positive note.

Intrapersonal Communication

Intrapersonal communication is defined by Ruben (1988) as "the processing of messages of which we, ourselves, are the source" is one of the most fascinating, though difficult to study forms of communication. Intrapersonal communication performs a "self-monitoring" function, in which we engage in self-reflection, examining our own communicative behavior and its effects upon others. As such, intrapersonal communication allows us to reflect upon our internal use of cognitive strategies and development, as students often do when they consider whether they have studied "the right way" for a particular test.

Intrapersonal communication is also used to plan our cognitive strategies. For example, when students ask an instructor whether an examination will be multiple-choice, true-false, or essay, they are gathering information with which to formulate a cognitive strategy for study. This type of internal communication is also important as we attempt to engage in self-development, self-expression, decision-making, and stress management.

Intrapersonal Variables That Affect Communication

What accounts for two people watching the same presidential debate, yet arriving at different conclusions as to the victor? Or two businessmen entering a partnership to find that they have very different perceptions of their roles and responsibilities? These variations in perceptions are largely due to the effects of the intrapersonal variables of communication. Individual differences in experience, perception and psychological make-up greatly affect our interpretation of internal and external communicative stimuli. The following psychological variables are known to affect our perceptions:

Personal Orientation

Values: Moral or ethical principles we consider to be important (e.g., honesty).

Attitudes: "A learned tendency to react positively or negatively to an object or situation" (Barker, 1987).

Beliefs: Anything that is accepted as true.

Prejudices/Stereotypes: Pre-established judgments about a person, thing, or group.

Personality Traits

Locus of Control: The degree to which we believe that we are responsible for our own successes and failures (*internal locus of control*), or that positive or negative outcomes are the result of factors beyond our efforts and control (*external locus of control*) (Barker, 1987).

Manipulation: The degree to which we are willing to engage in manipulation to achieve our goals. Individuals who are willing to dominate and manipulate others are said to be high in their Machiavellian tendencies, i.e., "high Mach" personalities. At the other end of the "manipulation scale" is the "low Mach" person who will infrequently, if ever, engage in manipulation for his or her own gain (Baron, 1986).

Dogmatism: The ability to consider new ideas or opinions (Barker, 1987).

Tolerance of Ambiguous Information: How well we are able to deal with conflicting or unclear information.

Self-esteem: Our sense of our own self-value and worth.

Maturity: This encompasses aspects of our psychological, emotional, and intellectual development, as well as intangible qualities such as "wisdom."

Defense Mechanisms:

Our psychological defense mechanisms enable us to deal with the anxiety and emotional pain that stem from intrapersonal conflicts. These conflicts often arise because of incongruity between our psychological needs and the realities of our external environment.

It is important to recognize that appropriate and moderate use of these psychological defense mechanisms can be healthy and adaptive. However, their overuse can result in an unhealthy distortion of reality. The following are examples of a few common defense mechanisms.

Repression: A way of dealing with unpleasant or unacceptable feelings by relegating them to our unconscious minds and not consciously thinking about them.

Rationalization: Attempts to justify our failures or inadequacies by stating that an undesirable outcome is due to some external source, or that the outcome was really unimportant to us anyway.

Projection: The attribution of our qualities, attitudes, or behaviors to someone else. For example, a wife remarks to her husband: "you're angry" when, in actuality, she is the one who is upset.

Identification: When an individual seeks security by psychologically identifying with one or more qualities of another individual (e.g., a "helpful" little girl with a new sibling identifying with her mother as the baby's caretaker) (Barker, 1987).

Denial: Refusing to recognize the reality of something that is negative.

A Side Note on the National Communication Association

One way to track the focus and state of research in any academic discipline is to look closely at its professional organizations. The Communication discipline is no different. In fact, the movement and development of the discipline's growth, internal power and politics, and current research interests can be seen in the various name changes that have occurred throughout the organization's history. The following is a list of those name changes that have occurred since the organization was founded in 1914:

- National Association of Academic Teachers of Public Speaking, 1914–1922
- National Association of Teachers of Speech, 1923–1945
- Speech Association of America, 1946–1969
- Speech Communication Association, 1970–1996
- National Communication Association, 1997–Present

Summary

In this chapter we offered an overview of the history of communication studies from their roots in ancient Greece to the present day. Along with a brief discussion of the nature of models, we examined the ways in which communication forms and functions within the contexts of organizations/institutions, small groups, interpersonal relationships, and intrapersonal experiences. The chapter ended with a look at the history of the discipline as it is reflected through the name of the National Communication Association.

CHAPTER 4

Perception and Reality

Learning Objectives

After reading this chapter, you should be able to:

- Define perception.
- Explain the statement, "reality is created, rather than given."
- Understand Gorgias' threefold summary of reality.
- Describe Watzlawick's view of the connection between communication and reality.
- Provide an example of how an automobile driver might experience multiple, internal realities.
- Name the parts of the threefold process whereby humans create reality.
- Explain in what ways our social interaction is highly patterned.
- Provide reasons why human beings seek to perceive patterns.
- Explain the following statement: "patterns are interpreted in context."
- Distinguish between first order reality and second order reality.

http://eluzions.com/Illusions/Ambiguous/

Introduction

Look at the picture above. What do you see? Some undoubtedly see a woman's face while others see a man playing a saxophone. This picture is referred to as an *ambiguous* or *optical illusion* because it allows different people to see very different things. Unfortunately we are so accustomed to seeing pictures like this in psychology textbooks that we forget that the same principle operating here operates in our everyday lives. That principle is **perception.**

Consider the following:

- Three people witness the same traffic accident at the same intersection. Upon questioning them, however, investigators hear three different accounts of what happened.
- You and a friend are introduced to the same person. Sometime later, when asked to describe the person, your friend says she was tall while you contend that she was medium height.
- Within ten seconds of meeting a person for the first time, you know whether you want to see this person again.
- You and a friend watch the latest installment in the *Fantastic Four* series. At the movie's end, you think that it was a waste of time and money while your friend thinks that it was an amazing action film.

The question one might ask in each of these instances is: How can different people possible have different views or accounts when experiencing the same stimuli? The answer again, is perception.

Perception Defined

Perception refers to the unique way we order and interpret stimuli to create reality. You might notice immediately that this definition begins with a specific notion of reality: that reality is created rather than given. While this might seem like a radical understanding of reality, it is actually as old as rhetoric itself. In fact, it can be traced to the works of Gorgias (ca. 487–376 B.C.E.), a Greek philosopher and rhetorician who became known as the "father of sophistry." Gorgias' three-fold summary of reality was:

1. Nothing exists.
2. Even if something exists, nothing can be known about it; and
3. Even if something can be known about it, knowledge about it can't be communicated to others.

What this suggests, then, is that all I can do is offer you descriptions of my personal experiences of reality. This is accomplished via communication.

Communication and Reality

Paul Watzlawick (1977) much more recently explained the connection between communication and reality when he wrote: "reality is what is, and communication is merely a way of expressing or explaining it." He goes on to say: "Our everyday, traditional ideas of reality are delusions which we spend substantial parts of our daily lives shoring up, even at the considerable risk of trying to force facts to fit our definition of reality instead of vice versa. And the most dangerous delusion of all is that there is only one reality. What there are, in fact, are many different versions of reality, some of which are contradictory, but all of which are the results of communication and not reflections of eternal, objective truths."

Multiple Realities

The world consists of different internal realities. For example, while sitting in class, you may experience different spheres of reality. As I write on the board, you listen and take notes. You may also be daydreaming about where you are going Saturday night or what you will do if you win this evening's lottery drawing.

As you move from one reality to another, you will experience some degree of shock. Imagine, for example, that I ask you to answer a question in the middle of your "lottery winning fantasy." The most dramatic shift would occur if, when calling upon you, I were to awaken you from a deep sleep.

Think of all of the realities that people experience when they drive a car. Here are some of my simultaneously experienced auto realities:

- listen to the radio
- think about a problem at work
- talk to a friend in the front seat
- attend to the car's noises
- watch the traffic
- steer the car and navigate home
- be certain my children are not fighting in the back seat

I would continue to move effortlessly through these multiple internal realities, unless some urgent situation demanded otherwise (e.g., emergency vehicle approaches with its sirens on). This is all possible because our consciousness can move through different spheres of reality.

The Perceptual Process

Now that we have discussed the nature of perception and reality and their connection to communication, we must turn our attention to the perceptual process. How exactly do humans create reality?

Most will say that it is the result of a three-fold process. This process includes: *selection, organization, and interpretation.*

Selection is choosing to attend to some stimuli and ignore others. It occurs because, given the vast amount of stimuli that bombards us in the course of a day, we must necessarily make choices as to which stimuli we will attend. No one can watch every news channel or read every article. No one will be equally excited about every topic we discuss in this text. Most typically we attend to the stimuli that interest us the most. Which of the following can you do?

Name the two U.S. senators from your state.

Name the winner of last season's *American Idol* competition?

My guess is that your attention is piqued by one or the other. This is not a test of right or wrong or a measure of intelligence. It is instead an example of different selections of important data which will impact a sense of reality and communication.

But selection not only occurs on the basis of interest. Often *physiology* can be a factor. For example, you might notice a person's height more readily if that person is much taller or shorter than you. If, however, you are used to others being taller or shorter, then you might be more aware of someone who is as tall as you. Other physiology factors that affect selection would be whether you wear glasses, contacts, or have 20/20 vision; whether you hear well out of both ears; or whether you are color-blind or not. Each of these has a direct bearing on our ability to select stimuli.

Organization is an attempt to make sense of or to order the selected stimuli. Look again at the picture at the start of this chapter. For some, the essence of the picture lies in the lighter stimuli while for others the picture is formed by the darker images. This organizational process is known as **figure/ground** and is used whenever we draw certain stimuli to the foreground as the most important and push the other aside as background.

A second organizational process is called **patterning.** Patterning occurs when we attribute patterns to stimuli. Webster defines pattern as: "A combination of qualities, acts, tendencies, forming a consistent or characteristic arrangement." Consider the following sequence:

If you were called upon to remember these figures, you might perform some specific cognitive functions:

Sorting: ○ ○ ○ ○ ■ ■
Categorizing: ○   or a   ■
Labeling: circle   or   square
                  figure that is empty   or   figure with shading

The recognition and formation of patterns are equally important in our social interactions as seen in the example that follows concerning the proper time to kiss in a dating relationship in the United States versus England during World War II.

Human beings are inherent pattern seekers (Birdwhistell, 1970). Here are four possible reasons why we seek patterns to help us to organize our world:

1. Patterns help us to live in a world of constant and potentially overwhelming sensation. Were it not for our ability to create patterns, human beings might experience an overwhelming degree of "sensory overload."
2. Patterns help us to process "the new," by seeking similarities with the patterns we already know in "the old."
3. Patterns help us to deal with the unknown. Even though you might not know how a particular instructor conducts a class, you know from your prior academic experience that it would be unlikely for the final examination to be given the first day of class, and for the syllabus to be first introduced the week of final exams.
4. Patterns help us to deal with the potentially dangerous, or to seek healthy mates. Patterns have survival value, in predicting the course of an illness, the path of a hurricane, or the aftershocks of an earthquake. Some of this perception may be unconscious, such as humans' tendency to seek others with symmetrical (i.e., "beautiful") faces and bodies. This may be because physical symmetry can often be equated with underlying health. We notice the unilaterally drooping lip, a limp, and eyes that do not match in color.

Interpretation is the meaning we attach to the organized stimuli. In order to understand the interpretative process, it is helpful to examine Watzlawick's idea of first order reality and second order reality. **First order reality** is that "which is purely physical, objectively discernible properties of things and is intimately linked with correct sensory perception, with questions of so-called common sense or with objective, repeatable, scientific verification." **Second order reality** is "the attribution of meaning and value to these things and is based on communication."

Watzlawick offers an example of the red traffic light, which may appear as virtually the same physical entity to both the child and the adult. The physical properties of the red light create its first order reality. However, the second order reality of the traffic light may differ for the adult and the child, as the child is not aware that one should not cross at the light. In fact, the second order reality of the red traffic light may even vary for two adults, one of whom is in a car, (i.e., "stop the car at the light, or risk getting a ticket or having the car damaged"), versus the adult who wishes to cross the street, (i.e., "don't step out into the curb or risk getting hit by a car"). Second order realities emerge as a result of our cumulative experiences, which include our prior communication with others and ourselves.

An example of culturally differing second-order realities was described by Watzlawick (1977):

> "During the last years of World War II and the early postwar years, hundreds of thousands of U.S. soldiers were stationed in or passed through Great Britain, providing a unique opportunity to study the effects of large-scale penetration of one culture by another. One interesting aspect was a comparison of courtship patterns. Both American soldiers and British girls accused one another of being sexually brash. Investigation of this curious double charge brought to light an interesting punctuation problem. In both cultures, courtship behavior from the first eye contact to the ultimate consummation went through approximately thirty steps, but the sequence of these steps was different. Kissing, for example, comes relatively early in the North American pattern (occupying, let us say, step 5) and relatively late in the English pattern (at step 25, let us assume), where it is considered highly erotic behavior. So when the U.S. soldier somehow felt the time was right for a harmless kiss, not only did the girl feel cheated out of twenty steps of what for her would have been proper behavior on his part, she also felt she had to make a quick decision: break off the relationship and run, or get ready for intercourse. If she chose the latter, the soldier was confronted with behavior that according to his culture rules could only be called shameless at this early stage of the relationship."

In this fascinating example, the second order reality of "the kiss" is obviously quite different for each culture. The man and the woman have divided up and organized their respective worlds in different ways. This is because they have learned different sequences of behavior, employing different punctuation. *Punctuation* here refers to the way in which we divide communication into chunks to best manage it (Leeds-Hurwitz, 1992). As such, each expects "the kiss" to occur in a different phase of the relationship. Thus, the meaning of the behavior of the kiss can only be interpreted if it is viewed as to where it occurs within the entire context of the relationship.

Consider the controversial policy that had been instituted on the Antioch College campus. An article in the *New York Times*, ("Combating Rape on Campus in a Class on Sexual Consent," September 25, 1993) described how, in sexual consent workshops, students were taught that they must be certain to share the same "second order reality" concerning communication about sexual consent. One Antioch College instructor advised the students that the Antioch policy required "willing and verbal consent" for each individual sexual act. Students were informed that asking "do you want to have sex?" was not sufficient communication because "sex means something different to different people."

Thus, in each of these two examples (Antioch College in the 1990s, and Great Britain during World War II) there were different definitions of what constitutes the reality of sexual consent. Communication is the key to creating mutually agreed upon definitions in these, and other matters.

Summary

In this chapter we talked about perception and the creation of reality via communication. The section ended with a discussion of selection, organization, and interpretation, the three processes associated with perception. We have not yet, however, discussed the impact that personal perception has on our everyday interactions. In the following article by Laing, Phillipson, and Lee, we see how directly our perceptions of ourselves and others create, mould, and modify our relationships. As you read, note particularly the authors' discussion of the "spiral of interpersonal perceptions."

Self and Other

R. D. Laing, H. Phillipson, and A. R. Lee

The human race is a myriad of refractive surfaces staining the white radiance of eternity. Each surface refracts the refraction of refractions of refractions. Each self refracts the refractions of others' refractions of self's refractions of others' refractions . . .

Here is glory and wonder and mystery, yet too often we simply wish to ignore or destroy those points of view that refract the light differently from our own.

Over a hundred years ago Feuerbach effected a pivotal step in philosophy. He discovered that philosophy had been exclusively orientated around "I." No one had realized that the "you" is as primary as the I. It is curious how we continue to theorize from an egoistic standpoint. In Freud's theory, for instance, one has the "I" (ego), the "over-me" (super-ego) and "it" (id), but no *you*. Some philosophers, some psychologists, and more sociologists have recognized the significance of the fact that social life is not made up of a myriad I's and me's only, but of you, he, she, we, and them, also, and that the experience of you or he or them or us may indeed be as primary and compelling (or more so) as the experience of "me."

The critical realization here is that I am not the only perceiver and agent in my world. The world is peopled by others, and these others are not simply objects in the world: they are centres of reorientation to the objective universe. Nor are these others simply other I's. The others are you, him, her, them, etc.

The presence of these others has a profound reactive effect on me. This has been expressed by a number of thinkers in different ways. Philosophically, the meaninglessness of the category "I" without its complementary category of "you," first stated by Feuerbach, was developed by Martin Buber. Scheler and Husserl have incorporated our primary experience of inter-subjectivity into their philosophical reflections. George Herbert Mead reflected on how my concept of myself is mediated by the "generalized other," and Cooley had the concept of "the looking-glass self". Talcott Parsons, in his social action theory, describes the relations between ego and *alter*," and Heider (1959) has given us some basic constructs for a genuinely interpersonal psychology.

If we obstinately continue to regard human beings as persons, then it is clear that there can no more be "simple location," in Whitehead's sense, in the human scene than anywhere else. But many languages (English included) express a further complexity, arising from the refractions a person undergoes as he is seen from different personal perspectives. Language expresses this by forcing the one person through various pronominal transformations, according to his relation to the signifier. This curious and highly significant fact is, we believe, specific to those forms of relationship we are calling personal.[1]

My field of experience is, however, filled not only by my direct view of myself (ego) and of the other (alter), but of what we shall call *meta*perspectives—*my view* of the *other's* (your, his, her, their) *view* of me. I may not actually be able to see myself as others see me, but I am constantly supposing them to be seeing me in particular ways, and I am constantly acting in the light of the actual or supposed attitudes, opinions, needs, and so on the other has in respect of me.[2]

From this we see that as my identity is refracted through the media of the different inflections of "the other"—singular and plural, male and female, you, he, she, them—so my identity undergoes myriad metamorphoses or *alter*ations, in terms of the others I become to the others.[3]

These alterations in my identity, as I become another to you, another to him, another to her, another to them, are further reinteriorized by me to become multifaceted *meta-identities,* or the multifacets of the other I take myself to be for the other—the other I am in my own eyes for the other. The concept of a meta-identity should not lead to any error that it is in some way secondary to self-identity, whether ontogenetically, cause-effect-wise, or in importance.

To summarize: we have ego (self) and alter (other). We recognize that I have my own view of myself (direct perspective) in terms of which I establish my self-identity. However, self-identity is an abstraction.

We recognize furthermore that ego exists for alter. This gives my being-for-the-other, or one's identity for the other. The existence one has for the other is not that of the "I." For the other, *I* am another. The other I am for the other is a constant concern of us all. My view of the others' view of me, my perspective on the others' perspective on me, is what we are calling a metaperspective, and the other that I take myself to be for the other, how *I* think you see *me,* is what we are calling my meta-identity. Now this scheme can be extended to encompass meta-meta and meta-meta-meta perspectives and identities, logically extendible to infinity.

Self-identity (**my** view of myself) and meta-identity (my view of your view of me) are theoretical constructs, not concrete realities. *In concreto,* rather than *in abstracto,* self-identity ("I" looking at "me") is constituted not only by our looking at ourselves, but also by our looking at others looking at us and our reconstitution and alteration of these views of the others about us. At this more complex, more concrete level, self-identity is a synthesis of my looking at me with my view of others' view of me. These views by others of me need not be passively accepted, but they cannot be ignored in my development of a sense of who I am. For even if a view by another of me is rejected it still becomes incorporated in its rejected form as part of my self-identity. My self-identity becomes my view of me which I recognize as the negation of the other person's view of me. Thus "I" become a "me" who is being misperceived by another person. This can become a vital aspect of my view of myself. (E.g., "I am a person whom no one really understands.")

Similarly my meta-identity (in which we can incorporate all my meta-identities and my meta-meta-identities) is intimately interwoven with my self-identity. The "me" that I think another sees, the "me" that I feel I perceive that another sees, can be cognitively created only in conjunction with the basic structure of the "me" that I perceive. Thus meta-identity is woven into the fabric of self-identity, as self-identity is woven into the fabric of meta-identity.

But before we go on to consider this, we shall pause to develop certain basic minimal constructs that will enable us to conceive of two persons each a self to himself each an other for the other, *together,* in relation.

At the very least, we need concepts which indicate both the interaction and interexperience of two persons, and help us to understand the relation between each person's own experiences and his own behaviour, always, of course, within the context of the relationship between them. Our concepts must also help us to understand the persons and their relations, in relation to the *system* which their relationship creates.

It is useful to consider briefly the help that existing theories can offer in this task: for instance, classical psychoanalytic theories, object relations, transactional analysis, and what we might call the idiom of games theory.

Psychoanalytic theory has no constructs for the dyad as such, nor indeed for any social system generated by more than one person at a time. Psychoanalytic theory has, therefore, no way of placing the single person in any social context. Nor, as we have stated, has it any category of "you." Indeed, in classical psychoanalysis there are only objects. Even the "ego" is itself an object, as are the superego, the id, and any other "internal objects." The ego is one part of a mental apparatus. Internal objects are other parts of this system. Another ego is part of a different system or structure. How two mental apparatuses or psychic structures, each with its own constellation of internal objects, are conceived to relate to each other, is totally unexplained. Indeed, within the concepts that are theory provides it is inconceivable. The concepts of projection and introjection, as we shall see in more detail below, do not bridge the gap *between* persons.

Attempts have been made recently to express the facts of the relational system by constructs felt to be more adequate than those of early psychoanalysis.

Object-relations theory is concerned with *internal* dynamic structure, supposed to consist of a central ego and other egos, each with correlated objects. Once more, objects not persons are involved; once more the relationship *between* persons is undeveloped theoretically. What has been said above applies equally to object-relations theory. The "objects" in object-relations theory are *internal objects* not *other persons.*

Transactional analysis conceives the person to consist of three centres (parent, adult, child) that interact with equivalent or complementary elements in the other person. Although "transaction" remains an ambiguous word, applicable equally to the relation between the endocrine and reticulo-endothelial systems as to one person and another (so that what is specific to a personal system is not made explicit, or even is lost), Berne's (1961) schema is undoubtedly a valuable contribution to the study of interpersonal systems.

The individual acts from these three separable centres of orientation. (Of course one can conceive of other centres of orientation, but these have an overall universality and significance.) It is highly significant in interpreting behaviour, and hence in experiencing another individual, which centre or centres of orientation one imposes or evokes, on one's self and on the other. Stress occurs if a particular centre of orientation is neglected or invalidated in self or in the other. The "programming" for each centre that each individual incorporates can be distinctly different from that incorporated by the other member of the dyad. When this happens, disjunction of interpretation and attribution are inevitable. The individual who refuses to acknowledge, for instance, that the other is capable of lending support or of helping or of teaching may produce intense discomfort in the other. The quality of such support, help or guidance may appear benignly paternal to the giver, but presumptuous or patronizing to the recipient, etc. These disjunctions are likely to be based on past experience and learning.

In the games theory idiom, everyone has a certain limited repertoire of games, based on particular sets or sequences of interactions that have been learned. Actual others may have games that mesh with the subject sufficiently to allow a greater or lesser variety of more or less stereotyped dramas to be enacted. The games a person plays have certain rules, some public, some secret. The games that certain people have come to play break the rules that most other people play by, and certain people play undeclared, secret and unusual games. The latter tend to be regarded as neurotic or psychotic, and to be required to undergo the ceremonials of psychiatric consultations, diagnoses, prescriptions, or treatment and cure, which consists in pointing out to them the unsatisfactory issues of the game they play (e.g., Loser wins, Poor little old me, This one will fool you) and teaching them new games. A person reacts by despair more to loss of a game than to losing his partners as real persons. Critical is maintenance of the game rather than the identity of the players, e.g., Berne (1961) and Szasz (1961).

This idiom saves those who use it from committing at least some of the most banal and unproductive errors that some psychologists have perpetuated.

The failure to see the behaviour of one person as a function of the behaviour of the other has led to some extraordinary perceptual and conceptual aberrations that are still with us. For instance, in a sequence of moves in a social interaction between person (a) and person (b), $a_1 \rightarrow b_1 \rightarrow a_2 \rightarrow b_2 \rightarrow a_3 \rightarrow b_3$, the sequence $a_1 \rightarrow a_2 \rightarrow a_3$ is *extrapolated*. Direct links are made between $a_1 \rightarrow a_2 \rightarrow a_3$, and this artificially derived sequence is taken as the entity or process under study. It is in turn "explained" as an *intra*personal sequence (process) due to intrapsychic pathology.

The games theory, has not, however, addressed itself fully to the sector of the problem we shall now consider.

Interaction and Interexperience in Dyads

In a science of persons, we state as axiomatic that:

1. behaviour is a function of experience;
2. both experience and behaviour are always in relation to some one or something other than self.

The very simplest schema for the understanding of the behaviour of one person has to include at least two persons and a common situation. And this schema must include not only the interaction of the two, but their interexperience.

Thus:

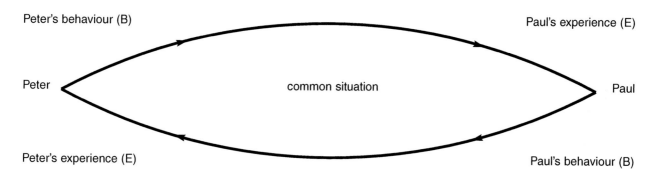

In terms of this schema, Peter's behaviour towards Paul is in part a function of Peter's experiences of Paul. Peter's experience of Paul is in part a function of Paul's behaviour towards Peter. Paul's behaviour towards Peter is in turn partly a function of his experience of Peter, which in turn is in part a function of Paul's behaviour towards him. Thus, the behaviour of Peter towards Paul, and of Paul towards Peter, cannot be subsumed under an exclusively inter*behavioural* schema (much less any *intra*personal schema) if Peter and Paul are axiomatic persons. For, if Peter and Paul are persons, the behaviour of each towards the other is mediated by the *experience* by each of the other, just as the experience of each is mediated by the behaviour of each.

The transformation of Paul's behaviour into Peter's experience entails all the constitutional and culturally-conditioned learned structures of perception that contribute to the ways Peter construes his world. Much of this learning has never been open to reflective awareness. To a much greater extent than most of us realize, and any of us wish to believe, we have been "programmed" like computing machines to handle incoming data according to prescribed instructions. Often this has been accompanied by meta-instructions against being aware that we are being thus instructed. This is an additional factor in the frequently great difficulty that many people have in opening their own "programming" to their own conscious reflection.

If each of us carries around a set of criteria by which we judge certain acts as loving and tender or hating and brutal, what may be a loving act to one person may be a hating act to another. For example, one woman may be delighted if her suitor uses a "caveman approach" with her; another woman may think of him as repugnant for just the same behaviour. The woman who sees the caveman approach as loving may in turn interpret a more subtle approach as "weak," whereas the woman who is repelled by a caveman approach may see the more subtle approach as "sensitive." Thus behaviour even of itself does not directly lead to experience. It must be perceived and interpreted according to some set of criteria. Although these intervening variables are not for the most part explicitly focused upon in this book, this does not mean that we are relegating them to a place of secondary significance in a comprehensive theory of interpersonal systems.

In order for the other's behaviour to become part of self's experience, self must perceive it. The very act of perception entails interpretation. The human being learns how to structure his perceptions, particularly within his family, as a subsystem interplaying with its own contextual subculture, related institutions and overall larger culture. Let us take, for example, a situation in which a husband begins to cry. The behaviour is crying. This behaviour must now be experienced by his wife. It cannot be experienced without being interpreted. The interpretation will vary greatly from person to person, from culture to culture. For Jill, a man crying is inevitably to be interpreted as a sign of weakness. For Jane, a man crying will be interpreted as a sign of sensitivity. Each will react to a greater or lesser extent according to a preconceived interpretive model which she may or not be aware of. At its simplest level, Jill may have been taught by her father that a man never cries, that only a sissy does. Jane may have been taught by her father that a man can show emotion and that he is a better man for having done so. Frequently such intermediary steps (regulative schemata) that contribute to the determination of the experience are lost to awareness. Jill simply experiences her husband as weak; Jane simply experiences hers as sensitive. Neither is clear why. They might even find it difficult to describe the kinds of behaviour which have led them to their conclusions. Yet we must not simply attribute these interpretations to phantasy, as this term is often employed as a form of crypto-invalidation.

Our experience of another entails a particular interpretation of his behaviour. To feel loved is to perceive and interpret, that is, to experience, the actions of the other as loving. The alteration of my experience of my behaviour to your experience of my behaviour—there's the rub.

I act in a way that is *cautious* to me, but *cowardly* to you.

You act in a way that is *courageous* to you, but *foolhardy* to me.

She sees herself as *vivacious*, but he sees her as *superficial*.

He sees himself as *friendly*, she sees him as *seductive*.

She sees herself as *reserved*, he sees her as *haughty and aloof*.

He sees himself as *gallant*, she sees him as *phoney*.

She sees herself as *feminine*, he sees her as *helpless and dependent*.

He sees himself as *masculine*, she sees him as *overbearing and dominating*.

Experience in all cases entails the perception of the act *and* the interpretation of it. Within the issue of perception is the issue of selection and reception. From the many things that we see and hear of the other we select a few to remember. Acts highly significant to us may be trivial to others. We happen not to have been paying attention at that moment; we missed what to the other was his most significant gesture or statement. But, even if the acts selected for interpretation are the same, even if each individual perceives these acts as the same act, the interpretation of the identical act may be very different. She winks at him in friendly complicity, and he sees it as seductive. The act is the same, the interpretation and hence the experience of it disjunctive. She refuses to kiss him goodnight out of "self-respect," but he sees it as rejection of him, and so on.

A child who is told by his mother to wear a sweater may resent her as coddling him, but to her it may seem to be simply a mark of natural concern.

In one society to burp after a good meal is good manners; in another it is uncouth. Thus, even though the piece of behaviour under consideration may be agreed upon, the interpretation of this behaviour may be diametrically disagreed upon.

What leads to diametrically opposed interpretations? In general, we can say interpretations are based on our past learning, particularly within our family (i.e., with our parents, siblings and relatives) but also in the larger society in which we travel.

Secondly, the act itself is interpreted according to the context in which it is found. Thus, for example, the refusal of a goodnight kiss after one date may seem to be perfectly normal for both parties, but after six months' dating a refusal would seem more significant to each of them. Also a refusal after a previous acceptance will seem more significant.

What happens when two people do not agree on the meaning to be assigned a particular act? A very complicated process ensues. If communication is optimum, they *understand* that they differ on the interpretation of the act, and also *realize that they both understand* that they differ in its interpretation. Once this is established they may get into a struggle over whether or not to change the act under consideration in the future. This struggle may take various forms:

Threat—Do this or else.

Coaxing—Please do this.

Bribery—If you do this I will do that in return.

Persuasion—I believe it is a good idea for you to do this because, etc.

However, often in human affairs where there is a disagreement there is also a *misunderstanding* and *failure of realization of misunderstanding*. This may be deliberate, i.e., a simple attempt to ignore the other person's point of view, or it may be an unwitting overlooking of the opposing viewpoint. In either case a disruption of communication occurs. It seems to us that, *for the first time,* our notation (*see* Chapter V) makes it possible to characterize and pinpoint the levels and pattern of disruption of this kind.

Thus, in the schema on page 9, E and B are categories of variables, each interposed or intervening between the direct impact of B on B and E on E. There is no naked contiguity, as it were, in interpersonal behaviour, between the behaviour of the one person and the behaviour of the other, although much of human behaviour (including the behaviour of psychologists) can be seen as a unilateral or bilateral attempt to eliminate E from the transaction. Similarly, in this schema it is presumed that there is no direct contiguity or actual conflux of one person's experience with the other. The one person's experience is presumed always to be mediated to the other through the intervening category of the *behaviour* (including verbal) of the one person, which in turn has to be perceived and interpreted in order to be experienced by the other. This means that, for the purpose of this enquiry, neither behaviour that is the direct consequence of physical behavioural impact (as when one billiard ball hits another) nor experience in the one person generated directly through the experience of another (as in possible cases of extrasensory perception) is regarded as personal.

Now, we know that to different extents in different people and circumstances Peter's view of himself is related to what Peter thinks Paul thinks of him; that is, to Peter's metaperspective and meta-identity. If what Peter thinks Paul thinks of him is not what Peter wants to have thought of him, Peter has, in principle, as a means of controlling the condition that controls him, the option of acting upon Paul to change Paul, or of acting upon his own experience of Paul to change his experience of Paul. By acting on Paul, Peter may intend to act upon Paul's experience of Peter, or he may intend merely to act on Paul's action. If, for instance, he says "Shut up," this injunction may say in effect: "I don't care what you feel about me, just keep it to yourself."

That is, any act may be primarily addressed to the other or to myself, but if perceived it must affect both. If directed to the other, the immediate goal may be to effect change in the other, or to prevent change in the other. Similarly, if directed to self, the immediate aim may be to effect change in self, or to prevent change in self. But in dyadic relationships, any action on the other has effects on me, and any action on self affects the other. I may so act as to induce the other to experience me in a particular way. A great deal of human action has as its goal the induction of particular experiences in the other of oneself. I wish to be seen by the other as generous, or tough, or fair-minded. However, I may or may not know what it is that I have to do to induce the other to interpret my action and experience me as I desire, whether generous or tough or fair-minded. His criteria for making these evaluations may be diametrically opposed to my criteria, and this I may or may not be aware of. Thus a passively resistant person (e.g., a Gandhi) may seem to one person to be tough, whereas to another he may seem to be weak.

Further, the other may wittingly or unwittingly be set to interpret every possible action of mine as indicating a preconceived hypothesis (e.g., that I am hurtful). For example, at a conjoint therapy session a wife interpreted her husband's absence as proof that "he wished to hurt her." When he showed up late she quite calmly assumed that he had finally decided to *come* "in order to hurt her." This is a particularly difficult bind if at the same time the person implies that there is a right course of action that the other just hasn't found. In such a situation the covert operative set is that no matter what he does he intends to hurt, whereas the overt implication is that if he did not intend to hurt he would be doing the right thing.

I therefore tend to select others for whom I can be the other that I wish to be, so that I may then reappropriate the sort of meta-identity I want. This requires that I find another who agrees with my criteria. But such stratagems may entail a remarkable alienation. My centre of gravity may become *the other I am to the other*. In such circumstances, in order to achieve the identity that I wish, through being the desired other for the other, the other must be malleable by me, or pervious to me. I must select carefully those others with whom I shall have to interact, acting towards them in such a way that I will be able to be to them what I want to be. I shall be in a serious dilemma, however, if I cannot make the other person regard me as that other that I wish to be for him. I may wish to be a mother to someone who is also wanting to be a mother, or to be generous to someone who insists on seeing me as mean, and so on. Alternatively, under those circumstances I may in desperation adopt the strategy of acting upon my *own* experience of the other, so that in a sense I render my meta-identity independent of the other.

Let us consider this latter strategy in more detail. We see it in one form of self's action on self, namely, Peter's action on his own experience of Paul, under the name of projection. Projection is a form of action directed at one's own experience of the other. It is called a "mental mechanism." This is a very misleading term, since it is neither mental nor mechanical. It is an action whose intentional object is one's own experience of the other. It is to the credit of psychoanalysis that it has brought to light actions of this kind.

Projection is clearly a most important stratagem and may function in different ways in an inter-personal system, but in every case it is one of a class of *actions whose primary object is not the other's experience of me, but my experience of the other*. Secondarily, of course, it must also affect the other's experience of me. For example, when the paranoid individual "projects," he may experience the other as hurting him and not helping him. This in turn forces the other to experience the para-noid as a person who sees him (o) as a hurtful person.

We said above that part of the theoretical problem constantly facing us is that we find it eas-ier to think of each person in a dyad separately, or one at a time, rather than together. This is true, for instance, in terms of the theory of projection. There are a number of different aspects and ver-sions of the concept of projection, not all rendered explicit.

We have already suggested that projection is one way of acting on the other by, paradoxically, not acting directly on him as a real person, but on one's experience of him. But if I convey to the other how I experience him I am certainly influencing him. Indeed, one of the most effective ways to affect the other's experience of me is to tell him how I experience him. Every flatterer knows that, all things being equal, one tends to like someone by whom one is liked. If I am ugly, I am not ugly only in my eyes, I see myself in the looking-glass of your eyes as ugly too. You are the witness of my ugliness. In fact, insofar as ugliness is relative, if you and everyone else saw me as beautiful, I might be ugly no more. If I cannot induce you to see me as I wish, I may act on my experience of you rather than your experience of me. I can invent your experience of me. Many projections, of course, are the apparently compulsive inventions of persons who see themselves as ugly, and wish to extrude this perception from their own self-self relation. At any rate, this is a commonly ascribed motive for projection. All projection involves a simultaneous negation of what projection replaces.

In Zarathustra, the ugliest man abolishes God because he cannot stand an eternal witness to his ugliness, and replaces him with nothing.

Projection refers to a mode of experiencing the other in which one experiences one's outer world in terms of one's inner world. Another way of putting this is that one experiences the per-ceptual world in terms of one's phantasy system, without realizing that one is doing this. One may seek to make the world actually embody one's phantasy, but this is another story, and projection can occur without so doing.

Pure projection tells us nothing about the other. Projection refers only to one area of the dyadic interaction, namely, the way you act on your own experience of me, or the way I act on my own experience of you, although it will, we know, be influenced by, and will influence, the other areas, since your way of experiencing me interrelates with the way I act towards you, and so on. The way Peter acts towards Paul will have something to do with the way Paul experiences Peter, and with the way Paul, for his part, now acts towards Peter. Unfortunately, there is no systematic theory to guide us here, and a paucity of empirical data. We have no language even to describe various things that can happen in other parts of the dyadic circuit when projection occurs in one section. For instance, how does Paul react to his realization that Peter's experience of Paul is largely projection, and to his realization that Peter's actions are not addressed to the Paul that Paul takes himself to be, but to a Paul who is largely Peter's invention? One way to ease the situation is for Paul systematically to discover the data upon which Peter is constructing him into a person he does not recognize. This is more exacting than to assume that Peter is purely inventing his view of Paul. By this tactic, it becomes Paul's job to discover the criteria by which Peter is coming to his discordant conclusions. These are inevitably there, but they may be hidden or so strange, even to Peter, let alone to Paul, that they are neglected, ignored, or considered insignificant; that is, invalidated in one way or another.

For example, a husband and wife, after eight years of marriage, described one of their first fights. This occurred on the second night of their honeymoon. They were both sitting at a bar in a hotel when the wife struck up a conversation with a couple sitting next to them. To her dismay her husband refused to join the conversation, remained aloof, gloomy and antagonistic both to her and the other couple. Perceiving his mood, she became angry at him for producing an awkward social situation and making her feel "out on a limb." Tempers rose, and they ended in a bitter fight in which each accused the other of being inconsiderate. This was the extent of their report of the incident. Eight years later, however, we were able to tease out some of the additional factors involved. When asked why she had struck up the conversation with the other couple, the wife replied: "Well, I had never had a conversation with another couple as a wife before. Previous to this I had always been a 'girl friend' or 'fiancee' or 'daughter' or 'sister'. I thought of the honeymoon as a fine time to try out my new role as a wife, to have a conversation as a wife with my husband at my side. I had never had a husband before, either." She thus carried into the situation her expectancy that the honeymoon would be an opportunity to begin to socialize as a couple with other couples. She looked forward to this eagerly and joyfully. By contrast, her husband had a completely differing view of the honeymoon. When questioned about his aloofness during the conversation he said: "Of course I was aloof. The honeymoon to me was a time to get away from everyone—a time when two people could learn to take advantage of a golden opportunity to ignore the rest of the world and simply explore each other. I wanted us to be sufficient unto ourselves. To me, everyone else in the world was a complication, a burden and an interference. When my wife struck up that conversation with the other couple I felt it as a direct insult. She was telling me in effect that I was not man enough for her, that I was insufficient to fill her demands. She made me feel inadequate and angry."

Eight years later they were able to laugh at the situation. He could say, "If I had only known how you felt it would have made a great difference." The crucial point is that each interpreted the other's action as inconsiderate and even deliberately insulting. These attributions of inconsiderateness and insult and maliciousness were based on hidden discrepant value systems and discrepant expectations based on these value systems.

Peter's concrete experience of Paul is a unity of the given and the constructed: a synthesis of his own (Peter's) interpretations of his perceptions based on his expectations and his (Peter's) phantasy (projection), and of the distal stimulus that originates from "Paul." The resultant fusion of projection-perception is the phenomenal Paul as experienced by Peter. Thus Paul-for-Peter is neither a total invention nor a pure perception of Peter's, nor a simple duplication of Paul's view of Paul. Paul as actually experienced by Peter will be compounded of perception, interpretation and phantasy. One might speak of a perception coefficient, according to the degree to which perception prevails over projection, or projection over perception. Also, one might speak of a coefficient of mismatching or disjunctive interpretive systems. Now Peter's actions towards Paul may follow from Peter's experience of Paul that is largely projective (has a high phantasy-coefficient) or from mismatched interpretive systems. Peter's experience and consequent actions are likely to be disjunctive with Paul's view of Paul, and with Paul's view of Peter's view of Paul. It is likely that if Peter's view of Paul is very disjunctive with Paul's view of Paul, whether itself highly phantasized or not, then Peter's actions will be addressed to a Paul that Paul does not recognize. Paul may register that Peter treats him with more or less deference than Paul expects, or is too familiar, or is too distant, or is too frightened of him, or not sufficiently so. Paul may find that Peter acts not towards the Paul that Paul takes himself to be, but as a mother, a father, a son, a daughter, a brother, a sister, etc.

All this suggests that Peter cannot perceive himself as Peter if he does not perceive Paul as Paul. If the coefficient of phantasy or of mismatched expectancy systems rises in Peter's experience of Paul, one expects that Peter's view of himself will become correspondingly mismatched between his self-identity, meta-identity, and Paul's view of Peter, and Paul's view of Peter's meta-identity (not as yet trying to exhaust the different disjunctions) and that this will express itself in the increasingly "strange" way, that, in Paul's eyes, Peter acts towards Paul. It is not necessary to repeat this whole state of affairs, *mutatis mutandis,* exchanging Peter for Paul and Paul for Peter.

What we have to try to understand is how Peter's mismatched interpretations and phantasization[4] of his experience of Peter and Paul effects Paul, and how Paul's experiences of Paul and Peter in turn affect Peter's tendency to experience projectively and to act accordingly.

One might suppose that the easiest part of the circuit to become phantasized by Peter might be what was going on inside Paul, for here there is the minimum of validation available to Peter, except from the testimony of Paul.

Thus, Peter says, "I think you are unhappy inside."

Paul says, "No I'm not."

Peter may, however, attempt to validate his attribution about Paul's relation to Paul by watching the actions of Paul. He may say, "If *I* acted in that way I would be unhappy," or, "When mother acted that way she was unhappy." He may have nothing that he can "put his finger on," but "senses" that Paul is unhappy. He may be correctly reconstructing Paul's experience by succeeding in synthesizing many cues from Paul's behaviour, or he may be "wrong" to construe Paul's behaviour in his own terms (Peter's) rather than Paul's, or he may put inside Paul unhappiness that he is trying not to feel inside himself. It is not easy to discover criteria of validity here, because Peter may actually make Paul unhappy by "going on" about it. Let us suppose, however, that Peter's view of Paul is disjunctive with Paul's view of Paul over the issue of Paul's relation to Paul. Is Paul unhappy? Peter, wittingly or unwittingly, may register from witting or unwitting cues from Paul's behavior that Paul is unhappy. Paul may be seeking to deny his unhappiness. On the other hand, Peter may be attributing to Paul what he is denying himself. Furthermore, Peter may seek to avoid feeling unhappy himself by *trying to make Paul unhappy.* One of his ways of doing this may be to tell Paul that he or Paul is unhappy. Let us suppose he does the latter. Paul may accuse Peter of trying to make him unhappy by telling him he is. Very likely, Peter will repudiate this attribution in favour, perhaps, of one of the order, "I am only trying to help you."

Sometimes, what appears to be projection is really a complicated mismatching of expectations, i.e., the interpretation that p gives to o's not fulfilling his expectation. Thus, if Peter becomes upset about something, Paul may hope to help him by remaining calm and detached. However, Peter may feel that this is just the wrong thing for Paul to be doing when he is upset. His feeling may be that a really friendly, helpful person would get upset with him. If Paul does not know this and Peter does not I communicate it, Peter may assume that Paul is deliberately staying aloof to hurt him.

Paul may then conclude that Peter is "projecting" angry feelings onto him. This, then, is a situation where projection is attributed by Paul to Peter, but it has not actually occurred. This commonly happens in analytical therapy when the analyst (Paul) assumes that a detached mirrorlike attitude is the most helpful stance he can adopt towards the patient (Peter). However, the patient may feel that only an open self-disclosing person could be of help, and if he goes on to interpret the analyst's stance as not only unhelpful in effect but unhelpful in intention, then the analyst may in turn counter-attribute "projection" to the patient. A vicious circle of mismatched interpretations, expectancies, experiences, attributions and counter-attributions is now in play.

It starts to whirl something like this:

Peter:

1. I am upset.

2. Paul is acting very calm and dispassionate.

3. If Paul cared about me and wanted to help he would get involved and show some emotion also.

4. Paul knows that this upsets me.

5. If Paul knows that his behaviour upsets me, he must be intending to hurt me.

6. He must be cruel, sadistic. Maybe he gets pleasure out of it, etc.

Paul:

1. Peter is upset.

2. I'll try to help him by remaining calm and just listening.

3. He is getting even more upset. I must be even more calm.

4. He is accusing me of hurting him.

5. I'm really trying to help.

6. He must be projecting.

Attributions of this kind, based on a virtually inextricable mix of mismatched expectations and phantasy and perception, are the very stuff of interhuman reality. One has, for instance, to enter into this realm in order to understand how one person's attributions about others may begin to be particularly disturbing and disjunctive to the others, and come to be repeatedly invalidated by them, so that he may begin to be subject to the global attribution of being mad (Laing, 1961, 1964, 1965).

However, even all-round conjunctions—between Peter's view of Peter and Paul's view of Peter, Peter's view of Paul and Paul's view of Paul, Peter's view of Paul's view of Paul and Paul's view of Peter's view of Paul's view of Paul, Peter's view of Paul's view of Peter and Paul's view of Peter's view of Paul—do not validate a perceptive circle. They achieve all-round "reliability" but not "validity." They "validate" equally readily a *phantasy circle*. These whirling phantasy circles, we suggest, are as destructive to relationships, individual (or international), as are hurricanes to material reality.

To summarize so far. Through my behaviour I can act upon three areas of the other: on his experience of me; on his experience of himself; and upon his behaviour. In addition, I cannot act on the other himself directly, but I can act on my own *experience* of him.

The Spiral of Reciprocal Perspectives

Human beings are constantly thinking about others and about what others are thinking about them, and what others think they are thinking about the others, and so on. One may be wondering about what is going on inside the other. One desires or fears that other people will know what is going on inside oneself.

A man may feel that his wife does not understand him. What may this mean? It could mean that he thinks she does not realize that he feels neglected. Or he may think that she does not realize that he loves her. Or it may be that he thinks that she thinks that he is mean, when he just wants to be careful; that he is cruel, when he just wants to be firm; that he is selfish when he just does not want to be used as a doormat.

His wife may feel that he thinks that she thinks he is selfish when all she wants is to get him to be a little less reserved. She may think that he thinks that she thinks he is cruel, because she feels he always takes everything she says as an accusation. She may think that he thinks he understands her, when she thinks he has not begun to see her as a real person, and so on.

One sees both that this area is the very heart of many relationships, and that we have in fact very little systematic and scientifically tested information about it. But let us first of all *think* about the problem a little further.

One or both persons in a twosome may spiral off into third, fourth, even fifth levels of what we have suggested may be called *meta*perspectives. Such a spiral develops, for instance, whenever two persons mistrust each other.

We do not know how people resolve mistrust that takes on this formal structure, but we know that such mistrust is common, and that it sometimes seems to go on endlessly. Logically, the possibilities are that it may end by unilateral or bilateral disarmament; by unilateral separation or mutual divorce; or by a parametric change occurring. Let us consider a simplified version of this spiral.

Jack and Jill are ostensibly in love, and each feels he or she loves the other, but Jack is not sure whether Jill loves Jack, and Jill is not sure whether Jack loves Jill. Jack feels he loves Jill, but does not know whether Jill really believes in his love. Jill feels she loves Jack, but is not sure whether Jack believes she loves him. How can each prove to the other that each loves the other?

Suppose that Jack is what is psychiatrically termed paranoid. This term is a rather inadequate descriptive generalization for certain regularities in Jack's experience and actions, one of which is a persistent tendency to mistrust certain significant others. He persistently refuses to infer from Jill's behaviour towards him, however loving, that she "really" loves him, but believes, despite evidence from Jill's manifest behaviour (he may sooner or later have to invent her "behaviour") that she loves Tom, Dick or Harry. A curious feature of Jack's tendency to attribute to Jill a lack of love for him and a love for Tom, Dick or Harry (for reasons we do not pursue at present) often seems to be that he tends to make this attribution in inverse proportion to Jill's testimony and actions to the contrary.

Jack may reason: "Look at all the things that Jill is doing to try to prove to me that she loves me. If she really loved me she would not have to be so obvious about it and try so hard. The fact that she is trying so hard proves she is pretending. She must be trying to cover up her feelings— she must be trying to cover up her true feelings. She probably loves Tom."

At this point Jill is in a double-bind (Bateson, 1956). If she tries to act even more loving, she further activates Jack's assumption that she is pretending. If, on the other hand, she pretends to act less loving and more aloof then she certainly will activate his view that she does not love him. He then can say: "See, I told you so, she really doesn't love me. Look at how aloof she has become."

Jack's phantasy coefficient in his experience of Jill rises as his perception of her tends to discount his phantasy of her.

Thus, the *issue* that he is preoccupied with is love. The *direction* of this issue is Jill's love for Jack. His prototypical expectation is that Jill does not love him. For Jack this issue shapes every other issue in that he coordinates his whole field of experience and his whole field of action around this issue. Now, let us suppose that Jill feels she loves Jack, but realizes that he thinks she does not.

The situation then is: Jack thinks Jill does not love him. Jill thinks she loves Jack, but Jill realizes that Jack thinks that she does not love him.

Now, Jack may decide to resolve his mistrust by various moves that one generally regards as part of the paranoid strategy. He may pretend to Jill that he does think she loves him, so that, in his view of her, she will think she has fooled him. He will then mount evidence (she has exchanged glances with a man, she smiled at a man, her walk gives her away because it is the way a prostitute walks, etc.) that seems to him to substantiate his secretly held view that she does not love him. But as his suspicion mounts, he may discover that the evidence he has accumulated suddenly looks very thin. This does not prove, however, that his attribution is incorrect; it proves that he has not taken into account how clever she is. In other words, he invents a meta-meta-perspective for her, to cap his metaperspective. Thus, he reasons: "I have not been smart enough. She realizes that I am suspicious so she is not giving anything away. I had better bluff her by pre-tending to some suspicions that I do not feel, so that she will think I'm on the wrong track." So he pretends to her that he thinks she is having an affair with Tom, when he "knows" that she is hav-ing an affair with Dick.

This type of reflection occurs empirically in almost the "pure" form outlined above. This aspect of the paranoid's strategy has still not been adequately explored, but even less is known about how Jack's behaviour and experience is really influenced by and influences Jill and others.

Another form of unilateral spiral is the spiral of concern. Here, the decisive direction of issue is Jill's view of Jack's view of Jill's acts towards Jack. (I want you to know I love you.) The persons in whom we see this in purest form are, in clinical terms, depressed and/or obsessional.

However, I may act not only on my own experience but on the other person's experience, by acting on the other so that he will experience me and himself as I wish him to do and act in the way that will enable me to experience him in the way I wish. Reciprocally, the other is experi-encing and acting in relation to me, so that I am subject to his actions as he is to mine.

We saw in Chapter I how Peter may attempt to control the situation by acting directly on Paul, so that Paul will act towards Peter in a way which Peter wishes, and that this may be either so that he, Peter, can continue to experience himself and Paul suitably, or so that he can be experienced by Paul as he wishes to be. (In a system constantly sustained by two agents and comprising noth-ing other than their behaviour and experience, action either "internally" on self or outwardly through behaviour on the other is the medium for effecting change or for negating change.) If it is a steady state that is desired, then, in this dyadic system, it is by *action* by each on self and on other that the steady state of the system is maintained.

Let us consider the way a husband's behaviour towards his wife functions in terms of the husband-and-wife conceived *as a system*.

Husband acts on wife so that wife will experience husband's actions in a particular way. But wife has to *act* in such a way before the husband can realize that she experiences his act conjunc-tively or disjunctively to his intention; thus, husband's behaviour towards wife affects her experi-ence of him, which, mediated back to him by her behaviour towards him, in turn influences his experience of her. Through this circuit he may feel that his experience is directly related to her experience. For instance, let us say he has acted in some way that he meant to be helpful, but she feels is unhelpful and even cruel. Through the circuit of B and E he then may feel that he *has* been unkind, so that his own self-experience is now implicated. In order to keep his own self-experience and self-identity as he wants it (I am a helpful person, now I feel unhelpful and even cruel), he has to initiate another dyadic circuit by actions towards *her*, by saying, for instance, "I'm sorry," and making amends, reparation, and so on.

We see that in a dyadic system, there is no isolated individual person. The one person, in order to maintain *his own* self-identity, has to *act towards the other,* and however adroit a strategist he may be, he can never rely on controlling the other. She wishes to see herself as kind, but he feels her to be cruel. He wants to be helpful; she finds him a nuisance. Each person has to act outwardly in order to achieve and maintain his or her own inner peace. At best this intimate intermeshed coexistence can be reciprocally confirmatory; at worst it is a mish-mash in which both can lose themselves.

If the other is at one and the same time a threat and necessary to self's identity, then he or she may require to be permanently disarmed and controlled.

There are a number of ways of doing this. We have mentioned to some of them. One acts towards the other to control his experience; through his experience, his behaviour; through his behaviour one's experience of his behaviour; finally, by a sort of ellipsis, through one's experience of the other's experience, one's experience of oneself. What I think you think of me reverberates back to what I think of myself, and what I think of myself in turn affects the way I act towards you. This influences in turn how you feel about yourself and the way you act towards me, and so on. One may, however, seek to eliminate this dyadic circuit, at any rate from one's own point of view. If one can act upon one's *own* experience of the other, so that one can shape to one's own desire the way one sees the other and hence the way one supposes the other sees oneself, is it worth the bother to act toward the other in order to shape *the other's* experience? Perhaps not, if it could work. Action towards the other would then be only a gesture performed before a mirror.

Let us consider one facet of an extremely simplified dyadic phantasy system, reverberating around the issue of greed and meanness.

Jack feels Jill is greedy. Jill feels Jack is mean. That is, Jack feels Jill wants too much from him whereas Jill feels Jack does not give her enough. Moreover Jack feels that Jill is mean as well as greedy. And Jill feels that Jack is greedy as well as mean. Each feels that the other has and is withholding what he or she needs. Moreover, Jack does not feel he is either greedy or mean himself, nor does Jill. Jack, however, realizes that Jill thinks he is mean, and Jill realizes that Jack thinks she is greedy. In view of the fact that Jack feels he is already overgenerous, he resents being regarded as mean. In view of the fact that Jill feels that she puts up with so little, she resents being regarded as greedy. Since Jack feels generous but realizes that Jill thinks he is mean, and since Jill feels deprived and realizes that Jack thinks she is greedy, each resents the other and retaliates. If, after all I've put up with, you feel that I'm greedy, then I'm not going to be so forbearing in the future. If, after all I've given you, you feel I'm mean, then you're not getting anything from me any more. The circle is whirling and becomes increasingly vicious. Jack becomes increasingly exhausted by Jill's greed and Jill becomes increasingly starved by Jack's meanness. Greed and meanness are now so confused in and between each and both that they appear to take on a life of their own. Like two boxers dominated by the fight that they are themselves fighting, the dyad, the system, the marriage, becomes "the problem" to each of the persons who comprise it, rather than they themselves. Jack and Jill are not divorced from each other, but they are divorced from the system that their own interaction and interexperience has generated, which now presents itself to each of them as a container, a mechanical machine in which both are being mangled. Each has now become caught and entangled in the properties of a system of a relationship that is experienced by *both* as a prison. Each may now experience the system as a third party—in phantasy terms, a container, a persecuting machine, a suffocating prison, something one is inside, in which one cannot move or breathe, in which one is entangled. Only when it is impossible to live in an impossible situation any more may the process be reversed. It is just from the experience of the *common situation,* now *shared,* that a ray of deliverance may be glimpsed.

Jack and Jill in the above example are much more in touch with each other than usually is the case. On the level of direct perspective that each has of self and other, they are in disagreement. However, each realizes how the other feels. That is, each person's metaperspective is in play, and is correct. Furthermore, each realizes that he or she is understood, in so far as one's point of view is at least recognized. That is, no disjunction is postulated between direct and meta, or between meta-meta and metalevels of experience.

Now, in the terms of the present discussion:

a) *understanding* can be defined as the conjunction between the metaperspective of one person and the direct perspective of the other;
b) *being understood* is the conjunction between the meta-meta-perspective of the one person and the metaperspective of the other;
c) the *feeling* of being understood is the conjunction of one's own direct perspective with one's own meta-metaperspective.

There is a peculiar satisfaction in feeling that one understands another person, and in feeling that one is being understood.

Patently, however, two people may neither understand each other completely nor wish to. They may understand each other while supposing that they do not understand. Understanding may be greater over some issues than in others. The relationship may be relatively symmetrical, in that each understands the other to about the same extent over the same issues, or it may be lop-sided, one person, in Jung's sense, being the container and the other the contained. The feeling of being understood entails feeling that the other person's *meta*perspective is correct; in other words, that one's own meta-metafeeling corresponds to one's own direct perspective. One is now operating between all three levels. The feeling of being understood or misunderstood may be desired or feared. Its presence may be comforting or disconcerting. Its presence may mean a sense of being together, its absence a sense of solitude.

People will vary as to whether or not they would rather be understood or understand. An important aspect of each person's *self*-concept is the extent to which he feels capable of being understood. An important aspect of one's image of the other is the extent to which one feels the other can or does understand oneself.

Whether or not it is easier to make guesses between second and first order perspectives, or between third and second order perspectives, is an interesting question, and one towards which our method can contribute an answer.

We must remember that some people feel extremely persecuted because they persist in attributing to the others a capacity to know what is going on in them far higher than the others actually do possess. This may be because they grew up with another who had such an ability (e.g., identical twin), or who in fact laid claims to such understanding. In intergroup and international as well as in interpersonal dyadic systems, the desires to be understood in some respects, the fears of being known in others, the efforts taken towards being understood, and the precautions taken against being known, together with the complementary manoeuvers to achieve knowledge of the other, legitimately and illegitimately (espionage), quite evidently play a large part.

From the point of view of the subject, the starting point is often between the second and third order level of perspective. Jill thinks that Jack thinks that she does not love him, that she neglects him, that she is destroying him, and so on, although she says she does not think that she is doing any of these things. In this position, it is open to Jill to do a number of things. She may constantly complain to Jack that Jack does not realize how much she is doing for him, and that he is always sorry for himself. He may protest that he thinks she is doing all sorts of things for him, but she does not believe him. She may express fears lest he think that she thinks that he is ungrateful to her for all she is doing, when she wants him to know that she does *not* think that he thinks she thinks he thinks that she does not do enough. Here, the *initial* situation from Jill's point of view is: Jill thinks that Jack thinks that Jill neglects him. One move that the other may make in order to break such a unilateral spiral is to break into it at one level of perspective. Thus, Jill thinks Jack does not believe that Jill loves Jack. Jack's move may be to say: "But I *do* believe you *do*." This direct contradiction, in this case intended as reassurance, is usually thought by psychiatrists, psychoanalysts, marriage counsellors, and so on to be ineffective.

A way to enter such a situation therapeutically is to get both Jack and Jill to define their criteria for generosity and to define how their parents defined generosity. One discovers that Jack's father treated his mother very differently than Jill's father treated her mother. Jack's father was too poor to have brought home enough money to make his family feel secure against the possibility of being evicted or not having enough food. Jack remembers vividly how his mother complained to his father about his inadequate income. From this Jack developed the viewpoint that if his father had simply made enough money his mother would have been eternally grateful. Since he is now successful financially, he expects Jill to be eternally grateful to him for providing her with a security that his mother never had. On the other hand, Jill has come from a wealthy family in which there was never any comparable issue of financial insecurity. In Jill's family, consideration, love and kindness were expressed through the giving of gifts, the remembering of anniversaries, etc. She had learned to take it for granted that the man will provide her with an economically secure home. What she looks for are the little niceties which she feels indicate true considerateness, kindness and love. For Jack these niceties are irrelevant; they are minor details, trivia by comparison to the other things he does for the family. However, if each can discover his or her own and the other's value system and thereby see the conjunctions and discrepancies between them, it becomes possible for each to explain himself or herself to the other. It is now, for the first time, feasible for Jack to say: "Well, if it really is that important to you that I remember your birthday, I'll do my darndest to try." It is now possible for Jill to "appreciate" Jack more as a provider in the family. If bitterness and revenge (I am going to hurt you for the hurt you have done to me) have not intensified too much, it may still be relatively simple for each to satisfy the other's expectations according to their idiosyncratic value systems. Such an incredibly simple move can sometimes produce very powerful effects, particularly, early in a relationship. Once a history has been developed of pain and misery, the matter becomes correspondingly more complex and difficult to reorient.

There are innumerable such unilateral and bilateral spirals as well as those of giving-taking, trust-mistrust, indifference and concern. There are "ascending" "manic" spirals (I'm happy that you're happy I'm happy), and "descending" "depressive" ones (I'm sad that you're sad, etc.); all are in a sense "obsessive." Such spirals can be attempts to get out of a *false or untenable position*. The danger to the persons involved is that the next *move* may be catastrophic. It may be the *last move ever*; it may be the end of the relationship, or the end of the world.

Here we are particularly concerned with how such a unilateral spiral functions in the dyad system. After the twists of the spiral have been extended to a third, even fourth, level, at some point a relatively steady state of reciprocal mistrust, precarious happiness, common misery or terror becomes established. It may be that the only hope at the precatastrophic position is to make a move to change the whole axis of orientation, to change the issue, both in content and direction, and one person has to make the change initially.

Psychoanalytic interpretations often have this form.

Thus, Jack maintains that the issue is: does Jill love Jack, or Tom, Dick or Harry? An analytic interpretation to Jack might be that the "real" or more basic issue is: does *Jack* love Jill, or Tom,

Dick or Harry? That is, the analyst (Freud in the Schreber case) registers that in Jack's view the issue is whether or not Jill is unfaithful to him, but feels that Jack should come to examine both the nature of his relation to *Jill* (rather than Jill's relation to him) and of *his* relation to Tom (rather than Jill's relation to Tom). That is, in the twosome Jack and Jill, the analyst would wish to change Jack's axis of orientation away from his attempt to infer the quality of Jill's experience of him *from* the testimony of her behavior towards him *to* the nature of his feelings about Jill and Tom. The analyst's thesis in this case might be expressed as: Jack attributes to Jill's feelings towards Tom what he is afraid to infer about his own feelings about Tom, if he were to examine his own behavior.

A family therapist would feel that it was insufficient to relate to Jack alone in such an interpersonal nexus. He would wish to observe directly how Jack, Jill, Tom, Dick or Harry all relate to one another. In the course of his close examinations of how Jill, for instance, actually behaves with Jack and with Tom, Dick or Harry, he may discover that she indeed is much more demonstrative with them than she is with Jack. And this might even fit her idea of how a wife should be. Jack, however, may feel that Jill's increased demonstrativeness to them is proof that she loves these other men more than himself. One such wife in therapy stated: "But of course I make a bigger fuss over your friends than I do over you. When I am with your friends I put on my social self. When I am with you I'm my real self." The implication being that she saw it as her duty to act in a "charming" way in social situations, but with her own husband she felt able to "be herself." Said she, "Would you want me to act with you, too"? Said he, "No I just would prefer that you would stop acting with others and be your natural self all the time."

Another form of reciprocal alienation gives rise to some very strange situations. Let us suppose again that the pivotal issue between two persons is love. Then my concern may be my love for you, or your love for me. My concern, however, may not be whether I love you or you love me, but whether you need my love. Similarly, your concern may not be whether you love me, or whether I love you, but whether I need your love.

This is a common issue in modern marriage, how common one does not know. Neither party is concerned so much about direct perspectives or direct issues, but about a second or third level. In these terms, I do not want someone to love or someone to love me, but I need someone to need me, and the other is someone who needs me to need her. This reciprocal dependence on the other's dependence is a form of reciprocity tending towards a spiral effect wherein each may become reciprocally more estranged from the act of directly giving or receiving love, and each in greater and greater alienation may even suppose that this is to grow deeper and deeper "in love."

This can be elevated to a system of rights and obligations. If each person is concerned about what the other thinks, feels, does, he may come to regard it as his *right* to expect the other to be concerned about him, and to be under an obligation to feel concern toward the other in turn. I make no move without feeling it as my right that you should be happy or sad, proud or ashamed, of what I do. And I regard you as callous if you do not concern yourself about my concern for you when you do anything.

My need has then ceased to be a matter of direct loving and being loved. My need is for the *other's* need of me. His or her need is that I need him or her. It is my need to be needed by the other. My desire is no longer to love and to be loved. My solicitude is not for another, but for another to want me. My want is a want to be wanted; my longing, a longing to be longed for. And in the same way, my emptiness is that the other does not require me to fulfill him or her. Similarly the other wants to be wanted by me, longs to be longed for by me.

The most natural thing in the world is the desire to love and to be loved. Which is the greater misfortune, to love without being loved or to be loved without loving? Very few people would admit to wanting either contingency. Yet we find people driving themselves into such situations all the time. Why? We say it is "compulsive." We are fortunately not trying to explain the why of this, but to describe the what. And one of the most hellish whirligigs of our contemporary interpersonal alienation is that of two alienated loves, two self-perpetuating solitudes, each in emptiness feeding on the other's emptiness, an inextricable and timeless confusion, tragic and comic—the ever fertile soil of endless recrimination and desolation.

Endnotes

1. The pronominal alterations (I, you, me, she, her, him, we, them) are not, of course, found in all languages, and this syntactical fact seems to reflect profound differences in the phenounenology of personal relations in different cultures. See the discussion of this issue by Dorothy Lee (1959).
2. For a particularly elegant presentation of self in relation to self's view of the other's view of self see Maucorps (1962).
3. Alteration in this sense is a Sartrean term; *see* Laing and Cooper (1964).
4. The concept of phantasy as a mode of experience in a social system is developed by Laing elsewhere (1961, 1966).

CHAPTER 5

Verbal Communication

Learning Objectives

After reading this chapter, you should be able to:

- Define "language."
- Describe the symbol as a distinct feature of human life.
- Provide an example that illustrates the Sapir-Whorf hypothesis.
- Construct a "semantic differential" that includes three major sets of judgments: evaluation, potency, and activity.
- Describe gender differences in communication.
- Identify sources of problems in translation.
- Describe how to accomplish "back-translation."
- Explain how culture and language are inextricably linked for human communication.

Introduction

During his January 28, 2003 State of the Union address, President Bush offered this now famous 16-word assessment of pre-war Iraq: "The British Government has learned that Saddam Hussein recently sought significant quantities of uranium from Africa." Since then supporters and critics alike have debated the intent and accuracy of these words (Jacoby 2004). (http://www.boston.com/ news/globe/editorial_opinion/oped/articles/2004/07/11/new_look_at_bushs_16_words/).

Was the 16-word sentence true or false? Did the President believe them or was he intentionally distorting facts to justify an attack on Iraq? Regardless of where you come down on the issue, it is impossible to deny that words have consequences. In fact, these words have changed the course of history, altered the political composition of the world, and determined future U.S. actions and relationships.

Granted, very few of us will ever utter words that will have the same level of international effect as those spoken by a sitting president of the most powerful nation in the world. That, however, does not mean that our words, whether intentionally or unintentionally spoken, will not influence our own or others' lives. Consider, for example the potential consequences of utterances like, "Pass the pepper." "Are you one of those mindless conservatives?" or "Will you marry me?"

In this chapter, we will focus on one of the two fundamental means of human communication: language. After defining and discussing some general characteristics associated with language, you will read an excerpt from S. I. Hayakawa's seminal text, *Language in Thought and Action*.

Language Defined

Language is *the means by which we define ourselves, others, and all phenomena in our world through written or spoken symbols.* As we concluded earlier, humans uniquely create symbols and combine them into concepts used in naming. The act of naming may be broadly defined to include not just the assignment of meaning of an object, but an evaluation of the object as well as a scripted response to the object.

Sapir-Whorf Hypothesis

In 1940, Benjamin Lee Whorf, a fire inspector who studied linguistics on the side, wrote *The Relation of Habitual Thought and Behavior to Language,* in which he discusses how people respond to a situation on the basis upon an assigned name or label. In the essay, Whorf described how his investigation of fires at a local company in Hartford led eventually to his hypothesis that language affects thought. He wrote:

> "My analysis was directed toward purely physical conditions, such as defective wiring, presence of lack of air spaces between metal flues and woodwork, etc., and the results were presented in these terms. . . . But in due course it became evident that not only a physical situation qua physics, but the meaning of that situation to people, was sometimes a factor, through the behavior of people, in the start of a fire. And this factor of meaning was clearest when it was a LINGUISTIC MEANING [Whorf's emphasis], residing in the name or the linguistic description commonly applied to this situation. Thus, around a storage of what are called 'gasoline drums,' behavior will tend to a certain type, that is, great care will be exercised; while around a storage of what are called 'empty gasoline drums,' it will tend to be different—careless, with little repression of smoking or of tossing cigarette stubs about. Yet the 'empty' drums are perhaps the more dangerous, since they contain explosive vapor. Physically, the situation is hazardous, but the linguistic analysis according to regular analogy must employ the word 'empty,' which inevitably suggests a lack of hazard. The word 'empty' is used in two linguistic patterns: (1) as a virtual synonym for 'null and void, negative, inert,' (2) applied in analysis of physical situations without regard to, e.g., vapor, liquid vestiges, or stray rubbish, in the container" (Whorf, quoted in Carroll, 1956, p. 135).

Later, Whorf and his mentor, Edward Sapir formulated their now famous **Sapir-Whorf Hypothesis** which suggests that one's view of reality is directly related to one's language.

The Semantic Differential

Any introductory overview of the "impact of language" would not be complete without a description of an instrument called the "Semantic Differential." Developed by Osgood and his associates (1957), it enables a researcher to select a concept or term and assess the reactions of people to the word(s).

The Semantic Differential consists of pairs of bipolar adjectives which relate to a particular concept. As can be seen in the example below, the person is asked to rate the concept by checking one of the seven intervals that lie between the bipolar adjectives.

Research by Osgood, et al. suggests that when completing a Semantic Differential scale, three major sets of judgments are made:

EVALUATION: is it good or bad?

POTENCY: is it strong or weak?

ACTIVITY: is it active or passive?

An example of the Semantic Differential is as follows:

"HIGHER EDUCATION"

Stimulating	X	—	—	—	—	—	—	Boring
Worthwhile	X	—	—	—	—	—	—	Worthless
Fair	—	X	—	—	—	—	—	Unfair
Fast	—	—	—	—	X	—	—	Slow
Good	X	—	—	—	—	—	—	Bad

The Semantic Differential can be constructed for any concept and thus, is a highly flexible research tool.

Verbal Differences

Let us now consider variations that exist in verbal communication. There are many sources of differences in the verbal message. Differences in pronunciation may result from faulty learning, neurological or structural problems of a physical nature, or dialectal differences. While some misinformed individuals consider dialectal differences to be inferior English, linguists and other experts in communication have shown that while dialects are different, they are *not* deviant.

Other differences in the verbal message occur in the language components which include vocabulary and grammar. Culture-specific differences are the most common source of these language variations. Dialectal influences may result in grammatical errors which are typical of the speaker's native language or dialect. Again, it is important to note that these dialectal variations reflect "differences," rather than "deviations."

A less frequent source of language differences are variations that occur because of psychological problems. The "private" language of schizophrenics, for example, is often idiosyncratic. Language may also differ relative to one's age, socioeconomic status, profession, religion, vocation, and work-setting.

Finally, gender difference can account for differences in verbal behavior. Eakins and Eakins (1981) have written that women and men often employ different verbal strategies. They report that while "women's speech" represents an alternative, one that is not "better" or "worse" than "men's speech," "some elements of female speech do not strengthen the position of women in our society." Examples of potentially non-empowering linguistic devices are as follows:

Tag Questions: The inclusion of a phrase that suggests a question, at the end of a sentence.

"It sure is a nice day, isn't it?"

"I believe I should get a promotion, don't you think?"

While tag questions are appropriate for cocktail party conversation (e.g., "Nice party, isn't it?"), their inclusion at the end of a sentence weakens the speaker's message. A positive aspect of the tag question is that its presence can "soften" the impact of a strong statement.

Fillers:	The use of extra words which are unnecessary and which suggest uncertainty. Examples: "well," "uhumm"
Qualifiers:	The use of qualifying words and sentences which, like fillers, also signal speaker uncertainty. Examples: "I think," "perhaps," "well," and "I see."
Disclaimers:	A specific type of qualifier is the disclaimer. According the Eakins and Eakins (1978), disclaimers come in many forms including:

Suspension of judgment: "I don't want you to be too mad at me."

Cognitive disclaimers: "Now I think this is a bit crazy, but . . ."

Sin license: "Now, I know this isn't totally 'legal,' but I am going to set aside company policy and. . . ."

Credentialing: "Now, some of my best friends are . . ." (fill in the appropriate ethnic or religious group)

Hedging: "Now, I might not have all of the details in order to make a decision, but . . ."

With regard to style, women's speech tends to be more indirect than that of men, perhaps in an attempt to soften the message. Eakins and Eakins (1981), and Tannen (1993) report that women's speech is more concerned with interpersonal matters, whereas men are more likely to relate factual information and employ stronger statements. They also note that men interrupt women much less frequently than women interrupt men.

Again, these hypothesized differences do not reflect inferiority; rather, they represent different and often complementary communicative strategies.

Problems of Translation

It is inevitable that human beings will experience some degree of confusion and miscommunication in their business and social interactions. Such is the case because our second order realities, or perceptions, are not always congruent.

These problems become even more significant when speakers of two different languages must rely on the process of translation to communicate with one another.

The mistranslation of words or idioms from one language to the next, to achieve vocabulary or idiomatic equivalence, is often at fault for such miscommunication. However, the problem is often deeper, a matter of conceptual equivalence in that language is not a neutral medium for understanding the world. In fact, each language represents a different way of viewing the world. In the film, *The Primal Mind*, Jamake Highwater discusses the differences in calling a particular water-based foul, a "méksikatsi," versus a "duck." The following is an excerpt from Highwater's 1981 book:

> "The greatest distance between people is not space but culture.
>
> When I was a child I began the arduous tasks of exploring the infinite distance between peoples and building bridges that might provide me with a grasp of the mentality of Native Americans as it relates to the worldview of other civilizations. I had to undertake this task in order to save my life; for had I simply accepted the conventions by which white people look at themselves and their world I would have lost the interior visions that make me an Indian, an artist, and an individual.
>
> This perilous exploration of reality began for me in southern Alberta and in the Rockies of Montana when I was about five years old. One day I discovered a wonderful creature. It looked like a bird, but it was able to do things that many other birds cannot do. For instance, in addition to flying in the enormous sky, it swam and dove in the lakes and, sometimes, it just floated majestically on the water's silver surface. It would also waddle rather gracelessly in the tall grasses that grew along the shores. The bird was called méksikatsi, which, in the Blackfeet language, means "pink-colored feet." Méksikatsi seemed an ideal name for the versatile fly-swim bird, since it really did have bright pink feet.
>
> When I was about ten years old my life changed abruptly and drastically. I was placed in an orphanage because my parents were destitute, and eventually I was adopted by a non-Indian foster father when my own parent was killed in an automobile accident. I found myself wrenched out of the world that was familiar to me and plunged without guidance into an entirely alien existence. I was told to forget my origins and try to become somebody I was not.
>
> One day a teacher of English told me that a méksikatsi was not really méksikatsi. It didn't matter that the word described the bird exactly for me or that the Blackfeet people had called it méksikatsi for thousands of years. The bird, I was told, was called duck.
>
> "DUCK?"
>
> Well, I was extremely disappointed with the English language. The word "duck" didn't make any sense, for indeed méksikatsi doesn't look like the word "duck." It doesn't even sound like the word "duck." And what made the situation all the more troublesome was the realization that the English verb "to duck" was derived from the actions of the bird and not vice versa. So why do people call méksikatsi duck?
>
> As my education in the ways of non-Indian people progressed, I finally came to the understanding what duck means to them—but I could never forget that méksikatsi also has meaning, even though it means something fundamentally different from what duck means."

It can be difficult to achieve accurate translation between languages. However, one technique that helps to discover mistranslation is "back-translation." First, the text written or spoken in the language of origination is translated into another, (i.e., Spanish version 1 to English version 1).

Then, the translated segment is retranslated into the language of origination (English version 1 to Spanish version 2), and the two versions of the original language compared for equivalence, (Spanish version 1 and Spanish version 2).

Most importantly, it must be recognized that when we grow up and function in different cultures, we may experience somewhat different realities, and these differences may appear in our language. It should be noted that language is not a passively acted upon entity as we use language to create cultural reality. Thus the two, language and culture, are inextricably linked and can be likened to two sides of the same coin.

Summary

The focus of this chapter was language and the power of words. It focused specifically on the semantics of language by examining the Sapir-Whorf Hypothesis and the Semantic Differential. We also considered four types of language differences and the problem that exists when we attempt to translate text from one language to another.

In the following excerpt from *Language in Thought and Action*, S. I. Hayakawa offers his views on language as a symbolic process. As you read, note what he has to say about language and *how he says it*. What examples can you find in his words that Hayakawa is a product of a specific time and culture?

Symbols

S. I. Hayakawa

This basic need, which certainly is obvious only in man, is the need of symbolization. The symbol-making function is one of man's primary activities, like eating, looking, or moving about. It is the fundamental process of the mind, and goes on all the time.

Susanne K. Langer

Man's achievements rest upon the use of symbols.

Alfred Korzybski

The Symbolic Process

Animals struggle with each other for food or for leadership, but they do not, like human beings, struggle with each other for things that *stand for* food or leadership: such things as our paper symbols of wealth (money, bonds, titles), badges of rank to wear on our clothes, or low-number license

From *Language in Thought and Action*, 4th edition by Hayakawa. 1978. Reprinted with permission of Heinle, a division of Thomson Learning: www.thomsonrights.com. Fax 800-730-2215.

plates, supposed by some people to stand for social precedence. For animals, the relationship in which one thing *stands for* something else does not appear to exist except in very rudimentary form.[1]

The process by means of which human beings can arbitrarily make certain things *stand for* other things may be called the *symbolic process*. Whenever two or more human beings can communicate with each other, they can, by agreement, make anything stand for anything. For example, here are two symbols:

$$X \qquad\qquad\qquad\qquad Y$$

We can agree to let X stand for buttons and Y stand for bows; then we can freely change our agreement and let X stand for the Chicago White Sox and Y for the Cincinnati Reds; or let X stand for Chaucer and Y for Shakespeare, X for North Korea, and Y for South Korea. *We are, as human beings, uniquely free to manufacture and manipulate and assign values to our symbols as we please.* Indeed, we can go further by making symbols that stand for symbols. If necessary we can, for instance, let the symbol M stand for all the X's in the above example (buttons, White Sox, Chaucer, North Korea) and let N stand for all the Y's (bows, Cincinnati Reds, Shakespeare, South Korea). Then we can make another symbol, T, stand for M and N, which would be an instance of a symbol of symbols of symbols. This freedom to create symbols of *any* assigned value and to create *symbols that stand for symbols* is essential to what we call the symbolic process.

Everywhere we turn, we see the symbolic process at work. Feathers worn on the head or stripes on the sleeve can be made to stand for military rank; cowrie shells or rings of brass or pieces of paper can stand for wealth; crossed sticks can stand for a set of religious beliefs; buttons, elks' teeth, ribbons, special styles of ornamental haircutting or tattooing, can stand for social affiliations. The symbolic process permeates human life at the most primitive and the most civilized levels alike. Warriors, medicine men, policemen, doormen, nurses, cardinals, and kings wear costumes that symbolize their occupations. American Indians collected scalps, college students collect membership keys in honorary societies, to symbolize victories in their respective fields. There are few things that men do or want to do, possess or want to possess, that have not, in addition to their mechanical or biological value, a symbolic value.

All fashionable clothes, as Thorstein Veblen has pointed out in his *Theory of the Leisure Class* (1899), are highly symbolic: materials, cut, and ornament are dictated only to a slight degree by considerations of warmth, comfort, or practicability. The more we dress up in fine clothes, the more we restrict our freedom of action. But by means of delicate embroideries, easily soiled fabrics, starched shirts, high heels, long and pointed fingernails, and other such sacrifices of comfort, the wealthy classes manage to symbolize, among other things, the fact that they don't have to work for a living. On the other hand, the not-so-wealthy, by imitating these symbols of wealth, symbolize their conviction that, even if they do work for a living, they are just as good as anybody else.

With the changes in American life since Veblen's time, many changes have taken place in our ways of symbolizing social status. Except for evening and party wear, fashionable clothes nowadays are often designed for outdoor life and therefore stress comfort, informality, and, above all, freedom from the conventions of business life—hence the gaily colored sports shirts for men and capri pants for women.

In Veblen's time a deeply tanned skin was indicative of a life spent in farming and other outdoor labor, and women in those days went to a great deal of trouble shielding themselves from the sun with parasols, wide hats, and long sleeves. Today, however, a pale skin is indicative of confinement in offices and factories, while a deeply tanned skin suggests a life of leisure—of trips to Florida, Sun Valley, and Hawaii. Hence, a sun-blackened skin, once considered ugly because it symbolized work, is now considered beautiful because it symbolizes leisure. "The idea is," as Stanton Delaplane said in the San Francisco *Chronicle*, "to turn a color which, if you were born with it, would make it extremely difficult to get into major hotels." And pallid people in New York, Chicago, and Toronto who cannot afford midwinter trips to the West Indies find comfort in browning themselves with drugstore tanning solutions.

Food, too, is highly symbolic. Religious dietary regulations, such as those of the Catholics, Jews, and Mohammedans, are observed in order to symbolize adherence to one's religion. Specific foods are used to symbolize specific festivals and observances in almost every country—for example, cherry pie on George Washington's birthday; haggis on Burns' Nicht. And eating together has been a highly symbolic act throughout all of man's known history: "companion" means one with whom you share your bread.

The white Southerner's apparently illogical attitude toward Negroes can also be accounted for on symbolic grounds. People from outside the South often find it difficult to understand how many white Southerners accept close physical contact with Negro servants and yet become extremely upset at the idea of sitting beside Negroes in restaurants or buses. The attitude of the Southerner rests on the fact that the ministrations of a Negro servant—even personal care, such as nursing—have the symbolic implication of social inequality; while admission of Negroes to buses, restaurants, and nonsegregated schools has the symbolic implication of social equality.

We select our furniture to serve as visible symbols of our taste, wealth, and social position. We often choose our residences on the basis of a feeling that it "looks well" to have a "good address." We trade in perfectly good cars for later models, not always to get better transportation, but to give evidence to the community that we can afford it.[2]

Such complicated and apparently unnecessary behavior leads philosophers, both amateur and professional, to ask over and over again, "Why can't human beings live simply and naturally?" Often the complexity of human life makes us look enviously at the relative simplicity of such lives as dogs and cats lead. But the symbolic process, which makes possible the absurdities of human conduct, also makes possible language and therefore all the human achievements dependent upon language. The fact that more things can go wrong with motorcars than with wheelbarrows is no reason for going back to wheelbarrows. Similarly, the fact that the symbolic process makes complicated follies possible is no reason for wanting to return to a cat-and-dog existence. A better solution is to understand the symbolic process so that instead of being its victims we become, to some degree at least, its masters.

Language as Symbolism

Of all forms of symbolism, language is the most highly developed, most subtle, and most complicated. It has been pointed out that human beings, by agreement, can make anything stand for anything. Now, human beings have agreed, in the course of centuries of mutual dependency, to let the various noises that they can produce with their lungs, throats, tongues, teeth, and lips systematically stand for specified happenings in their nervous systems. We call that system of agreements *language*. For example, we who speak English have been so trained that, when our nervous systems register the presence of a certain kind of animal, we may make the following noise: "There's a cat." Anyone hearing us expects to find that, by looking in the same direction, he will experience a similar event in his nervous system—one that will lead him to make an almost identical noise. Again, we have been so trained that when we are conscious of wanting food, we make the noise "I'm hungry."

There is, as has been said, *no necessary connection between the symbol and that which is symbolized.* Just as men can wear yachting costumes without ever having been near a yacht, so they can make the noise "I'm hungry" without being hungry. Furthermore, just as social rank can be symbolized by feathers in the hair by tattooing on the breast, by gold ornaments on the watch chain, or by a thousand different devices according to the culture we live in, so the fact of being hungry can be symbolized by a thousand different noises according to the culture we live in: "*J'ai faim,*" or "*Es hungert mich,*" or "*Ho appetito,*" or "*Hara ga hetta,*" and so on.

However obvious these facts may appear at first glance, they are actually not so obvious as they seem except when we take special pains to think about the subject. Symbols and things symbolized are independent of each other; nevertheless, we all have a way of feeling as if, and sometimes acting as if, there were necessary connections. For example, there is the vague sense we all have that foreign languages are inherently absurd: foreigners have such funny names for things, and why can't they call things by their right names? This feeling exhibits itself most strongly in those tourists who seem to believe that they can make the natives of any country understand English if they shout loud enough. Like the little boy who was reported to have said, "Pigs are called pigs because they are such dirty animals," they feel that the symbol is inherently connected in some way with the thing symbolized. Then there are the people who feel that since snakes are "nasty, slimy creatures" (incidentally, snakes are *not* slimy), the word "snake" is a *nasty, slimy word.*

The Pitfalls of Drama

Naïveté regarding the symbolic process extends to symbols other than words, of course. In the case of drama (stage, movies, television), there appear to be people in almost every audience who never quite fully realize that a play is a set of fictional, symbolic representations. An actor is one who symbolizes other people, real or imagined. In a movie some years ago, Fredric March enacted with great skill the role of a drunkard. Florence Eldridge (Mrs. March) reports that for a long time thereafter she got letters of advice and sympathy from women who said that they too were married to alcoholics. Also some years ago it was reported that when Edward G. Robinson, who used to play gangster roles with extraordinary vividness, visited Chicago, local hoodlums would telephone him at his hotel to pay their professional respects.

One is reminded of the actor, playing the role of a villain in a traveling theatrical troupe, who, at a particularly tense moment in the play, was shot by an excited cowpuncher in the audience. But this kind of confusion does not seem to be confined to unsophisticated theatergoers. In recent times, Paul Muni, after playing the part of Clarence Darrow in *Inherit the Wind,* was invited to address the American Bar Association; Ralph Bellamy, after playing the role of Franklin D. Roosevelt in *Sunrise at Campobello,* was invited by several colleges to speak on Roosevelt. Also, there are those astonishing patriots who rushed to the recruiting offices to help defend the nation when, on October 30, 1938, the United States was "invaded" by an "army from Mars" in a radio dramatization.[3]

The Word Is Not the Thing

The above, however, are only the more striking examples of confused attitudes toward words and symbols. There would be little point in mentioning them if we were *uniformly and permanently aware* of the independence of symbols from things symbolized, as all human beings, in the writer's opinion, *can be* and *should be.* But we are not. Most of us have, in some area or other of our thinking, improper habits of evaluation. For this, society itself is often to blame: most societies systematically encourage, concerning certain topics, the habitual confusion of symbols with things symbolized. For example, if a Japanese schoolhouse caught on fire, it used to be obligatory in the days of emperor-worship to try to rescue the emperor's *picture* (there was one in every schoolhouse), even, at the risk of one's life. (If you got burned to death, you were posthumously ennobled.) In our society, we are encouraged to go into debt in order that we may display, as symbols of prosperity, shiny new automobiles. Strangely enough, the possession of shiny automobiles even under these conditions makes their "owners" *feel* prosperous. In all civilized societies (and probably in many primitive ones as well), the symbols of piety, of civic virtue, or of patriotism are often prized above actual piety, civic virtue, or patriotism. In one way or another, we are all like the brilliant student who cheats on his exams in order to make Phi Beta Kappa: it is so much more important to have the symbol than the things it stands for.

The habitual confusion of symbols with things symbolized, whether on the part of individuals or societies, is serious enough at all levels of culture to provide a perennial human problem.[4] But with the rise of modern communications systems, the problem of confusing verbal symbols with realities assumes peculiar urgency. We are constantly being talked at, by teachers, preachers, salesmen, public-relations counsels, governmental agencies, and moving-picture sound tracks. The cries of the hawkers of soft drinks, detergents, and laxatives pursue us into our homes, thanks to radio and television—and in some houses the sets are never turned off from morning to night. The mailman brings direct-mail advertising. Billboards confront us on the highway, and we even take portable radios with us to the seashore.

We live in an environment shaped and largely created by hitherto unparalleled semantic influences: mass-circulation newspapers and magazines which are given to reflecting, in a shocking number of cases, the weird prejudices and obsessions of their publishers and owners; radio programs, both local and network, almost completely dominated by commercial motives; public-relations counsels who are simply highly paid craftsmen in the art of manipulating and reshaping our semantic environment in ways favorable to their clients. It is an exciting environment, but fraught with danger: it is only a slight exaggeration to say that Hitler conquered Austria by radio. Today, the full resources of advertising agencies, public-relations counsels, radio, television, and slanted news stories are brought to bear in order to influence our decisions in election campaigns, especially in years of presidential elections.

Citizens of a modern society need, therefore, more than that ordinary "common sense" which was defined by Stuart Chase as that which tells you that the world is flat. They need to be systematically aware of the powers and limitations of symbols, especially words, if they are to guard against being driven into complete bewilderment by the complexity of their semantic environment. The first of the principles governing symbols is this: The symbol is NOT the thing symbolized; the word is NOT the thing; the map is NOT the territory it stands for.

Maps and Territories

There is a sense in which we all live in two worlds. First, we live in the world of happenings which we know at first hand. This is an extremely small world, consisting only of that continuum of the things that we have actually seen, felt, or heard—the flow of events constantly passing before our senses. So far as this world of personal experience is concerned, Africa, South America, Asia, Washington, New York, or Los Angeles do not exist if we have never been to these places. Jomo Kenyetta is only a name if we have never seen him. When we ask ourselves how much we know at first hand, we discover that we know very little indeed.

Most of our knowledge, acquired from parents, friends, schools, newspapers, books, conversation, speeches, and television, is received *verbally*. All our knowledge of history, for example, comes to us only in words. The only proof we have that the Battle of Waterloo ever took place is that we have had reports to that effect. These reports are not given to us by people who saw it happen, but are based on other reports; reports of reports of reports, which go back ultimately to the first-hand reports given by people who did see it happening. It is through reports, then, and through reports of reports, that we receive most knowledge: about government, about what is happening in Korea, about what picture is showing at the downtown theater—in fact, about anything that we do not know through direct experience.

Let us call this world that comes to us through words the *verbal world*, as opposed to the world we know or are capable of knowing through our own experience, which we shall call the *extensional world*. (The reason for the choice of the word "extensional" will become clear later.) The human being, like any other creature, begins to make his acquaintance with the extensional world from infancy. Unlike other creatures, however, he begins to receive, as soon as he can learn to understand, reports, reports of reports, reports of reports of reports. In addition he receives inferences made from reports, inferences made from other inferences, and so on. By the time a child is a few years old, has gone to school and to Sunday school, and has made a few friends, he has accumulated a considerable amount of second- and third-hand information about morals, geography, history, nature, people, games—all of which information together constitutes his verbal world.

Now, to use the famous metaphor introduced by Alfred Korzybski in his *Science and Sanity* (1933), this verbal world ought to stand in relation to the extensional world as a *map* does to the *territory* it is supposed to represent. If a child grows to adulthood with a verbal world in his head which corresponds fairly closely to the extensional world that he finds around him in his widening experience, he is in relatively small danger of being shocked or hurt by what he finds, because his verbal world has told him what, more or less, to expect. He is prepared for life. If, however, he grows up with a false map in his head—that is, with a head crammed with error and superstition— he will constantly be running into trouble, wasting his efforts, and acting like a fool. He will not be adjusted to the world as it is; he may, if the lack of adjustment is serious, end up in a mental hospital.

Some of the follies we commit because of false maps in our heads are so commonplace that we do not even think of them as remarkable. There are those who protect themselves from accidents by carrying a rabbit's foot. Some refuse to sleep on the thirteenth floor of hotels—a situation so common that most big hotels, even in the capitals of our scientific culture, skip "13" in numbering their floors. Some plan their lives on the basis of astrological predictions. Some play fifty-to-one shots on the basis of dream books. Some hope to make their teeth whiter by changing their brand of tooth paste. All such people are living in verbal worlds that bear little, if any, resemblance to the extensional world.

Now, no matter how beautiful a map may be, it is useless to a traveler unless it accurately shows the relationship of places to each other, the structure of the territory. If we draw, for example, a big dent in the outline of a lake for, let us say, artistic reasons, the map is worthless. But if we are just drawing maps for fun without paying any attention to the structure of the region, there is nothing in the world to prevent us from putting in all the extra curlicues and twists we want in the lakes, rivers, and roads. No harm will be done *unless someone tries to plan a trip by such a map*.

Similarly, by means of imaginary or false reports, or by false inferences from good reports, or by mere rhetorical exercises, we can manufacture at will, with language, "maps" which have no reference to the extensional world. Here again no harm will be done unless someone makes the mistake of regarding such "maps" as representing real territories.

We all inherit a great deal of useless knowledge, and a great deal of misinformation and error (maps that were formerly thought to be accurate), so that there is always a portion of what we have been told that must be discarded. But the cultural heritage of our civilization that is transmitted to us—our socially pooled knowledge, both scientific and humane—has been valued principally because we have believed that it gives us accurate maps of experience. The analogy of verbal worlds to maps is an important one and will be referred to frequently throughout this book. It should be noticed at this point, however, that there are two ways of getting false maps of the world into our heads: first, by having them given to us; second, by creating them ourselves when we misread the true maps given to us.

Endnotes

1. One investigator, J. B. Wolfe, trained chimpanzees to put poker chips into an especially constructed vending machine ("chimpomat") which supplied grapes, bananas, and other food. The chimpanzees proved to be able to distinguish chips of different "values" (1 grape, 2 grapes, zero, and so on) and also proved to be willing to work for them if the rewards were fairly immediate. They tended, however, to stop work as they accumulated more chips. Their "money system" was definitely limited to rudimentary and immediate transactions. See Robert M. Yerkes' *Chimpanzees: A Laboratory Colony* (1943).

    Other examples of animals successfully learning to react meaningfully to things-that-stand-for-other-things can readily be offered, but as a general rule these animal reactions are extremely simple and limited when contrasted with human possibilities in this direction. For example, it appears likely that a chimpanzee might be taught to drive a simplified car, but there would be one thing wrong with its driving: its reactions are such that if a red light showed when it was halfway across a street, it would stop in the middle of the crossing, while, if a green light showed when another car was stalled in its path, it would go ahead regardless of consequences. In other words, so far as such a chimpanzee would be concerned, the red light could hardly be said to *stand for* stop; it *is* stop.

2. The writer once had an eight-year-old car in good running condition. A friend of his, a repairman who knew the condition of the car, kept urging him to trade it for a new model. "But why?" the writer asked. "The old car's in fine shape still." The repairman answered scornfully, "Yeah, but what the hell. All you've got is transportation."

    Recently, the term "transportation car" has begun to appear in advertisements; for example, " '48 Dodge—Runs perfectly good; transportation car. Leaving, must sell. $100." (Classified section of the *Pali Press*, Kailua, Hawaii.) Apparently it means a car that has no symbolic or prestige value and is good only for getting you there and bringing you back—a miserable kind of vehicle indeed!

3. See Hadley Cantril's *The Invasion from Mars* (1940); also John Houseman's "The Men from Mars," *Harper's* (December 1948).

4. The charge against the Pharisees, it will be remembered, was that they were obsessively concerned with the symbols of piety at the expense of an adequate concern with its spirit.

CHAPTER 6

Non-Verbal Communication

Learning Objectives

After reading this chapter, you should be able to:

- Provide examples of channels of communication.
- Explain why communication is a multi-channel behavior.
- Define and provide examples of paralanguage.
- Define and provide examples of major categories of non-verbal communication: chronemics, cosmetics, costuming, haptics, objectics, olfactics, organismics, kinesics, proxemics, and vocalics.
- Describe the possible relationships between non-verbal and verbal communication.
- Define self-synchrony, interactional synchrony, and asynchrony as these terms apply to communication.

Introduction

One cannot, not communicate. Not answering a friend's text message, leaving one's meal uneaten during a business dinner, or sleeping during class—all send messages, albeit non-verbally, in a most powerful fashion!

This chapter serves as an introduction to non-verbal communication. To set the stage for this content, we will consider how communication is a multi-channel behavior that can simultaneously be expressed via one or more channels (visual, auditory, olfactory, gustatory and/or tactile). Next, we will present non-verbal communication as one of three types of communication codes.

Communication Channels

Let us consider what is meant by the term *channel*. A channel can be defined as "a vehicle or medium through which signals are sent" and received by sensory organs (DeVito, 1991). The five major sensory channels used for communication are the visual, auditory, olfactory, gustatory and tactile senses. The pervasiveness of these modalities in our communicative repertoire is evidenced by the use of many sensory-based predicates (Foxman, 1988). For example:

Visual: "I can picture that"

Auditory: "Stop and hear the music"

Olfactory: "The sweet smell of success"

Gustatory: "I can just taste it!" (i.e., victory)

Tactile: "Reach out and touch someone"

It is rare that we use one channel exclusively. For example, in our face-to-face communication, we speak and listen (the auditory channel), use facial expression and gestures, and note these in our communication partners (the visual channel). We may also receive and emit odors (olfactory channel) and be touched or touch others (the tactile channel). Thus, communication is a multi-channel behavior.

Carol Foxman (1988) president of a communication skills training company, advised that each of us has a preferred sensory-based communication style, and that it is advantageous for a speaker to match their communication style to that of their listener. Three major communication styles are as follows:

> *Visual:* Visually-based individuals, ("visuals") are best influenced by pictures and will generate mental pictures that correspond to what you are saying. Their vocabulary may contain phrases like, "I see," or "I can envision that." Foxman advises helping "visuals" to "see what you mean" by using pictures, graphs, charts and other visual examples, and by dressing well to make a good visual impression. She includes visual predicates ("I see what you mean") when communicating with "visuals."

> *Auditory:* Individuals who rely primarily on auditory information attend to a speaker's voice quality and rate of speech, and function best in a quiet, distraction-free environment. According to Foxman, "auditories" will often respond favorably to a telephone call, whereas "visuals" need to see the speaker in person. She recommends using auditorally based vocabulary predicates (e.g., "I hear you," "hear me out") to best communicate with "auditories."

> *Tactile:* The kinesthetically-based individual ("kinesthetics") tends to respond favorably to experientially based programs, in which he/she can feel, manipulate, or experience pertinent material. This type of individual often needs to pick up and feel items before purchase. Sensory-based, kinesthetic vocabulary words include: "feel," "soft," "hot," "firm," and "support."

This suggests that sensory-based perceptual abilities may influence our response to verbal stimuli. To achieve optimal communication, we should attempt to match our own communication style to that of our listener

Communication Codes

Another way of viewing communication channels is to separate them into carriers of the verbal and non-verbal codes of communication. Many in the communication field prefer to consider three communication codes:

> *Verbal:* words we say, read or write, and American Sign Language

> *Paralanguage:* vocal behavior which is non-verbal, including use of pauses and silence, vocal qualities (pitch, voice quality, and loudness), intonation, and non-

speech noises (coughing, sneezing, snoring, laughing, and crying.) Sometimes par-alanguage is categorized as vocalic, non-verbal communication.

Non-verbal communication: non-linguistic forms of communication such as chrone-mics, cosmetics, haptics, objectics, olfactics, organismics, kinesics, proxemics and vocalics. These terms will be described later in this chapter.

Leeds-Hurwitz (1992) cautions that verbal and non-verbal communications co-occur and should not be studied separately. Moreover, these must be considered as they occur in a particular:

Context (e.g., a conversation between a physician and a patient; a funeral; a class-room discussion, etc.);

Temporal reality (e.g., two close friends who have known each other ten years have a drink together on December 24, 2007; two people just met in a bar)

Culture (dinner in a military academy; Thanksgiving dinner at a relative's house)

Researchers estimate that non-verbal and paralinguistic communication carry much more information than verbal communication. Therefore, in the following section, we will consider these non-verbal codes in greater depth.

Non-verbal communication refers to those aspects of communication other than the use of words. Mention the phrase "non-verbal communication" and most of us think of body-language, eye-contact, or physical attractiveness. However, non-verbal communication encompasses much more than these very visible characteristics. In fact, some of the non-verbal communication that is most significant to human interaction cannot be seen at all! The following are categories of non-verbal communication that are important in our daily lives.

Categories of Non-Verbal Communication

Chronemics: The Use of Time to Communicate

Health care providers are aware that the amount of time a patient waits in a physician's office can influence the patient's perception of the physician's competence and caring, especially if the delay greatly exceeds a half-hour. The patient's use of time may be similarly communicative to the physi-cian. The patient who arrives an hour early for an appointment may be demonstrating anxiety, or possibly illness and confusion. In contrast, another patient's perpetual lateness may signal avoid-ance, a lack of commitment to treatment, or disrespect for the physician.

The expected degree of promptness is dictated by the status relationships of the participants. While it is acceptable for lower status individuals to be kept waiting by those of higher status, the reverse is not true.

Cultural expectations also influence chronemic communication. In South America, for exam-ple, it is not unusual to wait many hours past the scheduled time for a business appointment. Even more significantly, religious beliefs relative to the importance of historical events in understand-ing current situations, or a strong belief in the existence of an "afterlife" may influence one's phi-losophy of communication.

Chronemic communication is also affected by our personal view of time. Individuals with a predominately *"past-historical orientation"* view current and future events relative to those that occurred previously. Individuals with a *"present orientation"* disregard lessons of the past and do not plan for the future; present satisfactions are paramount. Delaying gratification and "living for tomorrow" are characteristics of a predominately *"future orientation."* Most individuals, however, maintain a well-integrated "time-line," such that they are able to learn from the past, live in the present, and plan for the future.

Cosmetics: The Use of Applied Cosmetics or Plastic and Reconstructive Surgery to Alter Physical Appearance

Upon entering the first floor of a major department store, one typically encounters the numerous cosmetic displays that fuel a multi-billion dollar industry. Applied cosmetics are a type of "silent" non-verbal communication, and include the facial make-up and hair color products used by both sexes.

The degree and type of applied cosmetic use is communicative in our society. For instance, the perceived overuse of facially applied cosmetics may negatively affect others' impressions of the wearer's competence and character. Failure to use makeup in certain contexts also has communicative value, which may be positive ("She is a natural beauty," or "She is an unassuming individual."), or negative ("She really should wear some make-up." or; "She looks too plain."). The recent movie, *The Devil Wears Prada*, contains numerous references to the communicative role of both cosmetics and clothing.

In addition to the use of applied cosmetics, surgical or dental cosmetic intervention such as rhinoplasty, facelift, or orthodontic treatment can result in favorable changes in physical appearance, and subsequently, in the patient's body image. Sometimes this surgery is reconstructive to repair a congenital malformation such as a cleft lip, or to revise scar tissue after an injury.

Costuming: The Use of Dress to Communicate

Often, individuals will convey membership in an occupational group by virtue of their dress. The researcher's lab coat, nurse's uniform, banker's suit, and military officer's uniform are examples of expected professional dress. (For further reading in this area, refer to John Malloy's books on this topic.)

The expectations for appropriate dress are also influenced by one's age, cultural or religious group, climate and geographic factors, gender, and socioeconomic status. Consider, for example, the non-verbal communicative value of the "hospital gowns" worn by hospitalized patients. The various ways in which hospital employees dress in different departments (e.g., security guards, food service personnel, social workers, administrators, escorts, volunteers, pharmacists) are also fascinating to observe and compare.

A classic article by Davis (1989), *Of maids' uniforms and blue jeans: The drama of status ambivalences in clothing and fashion*, describes how fashion projects gender, sexuality, ethnicity, nationality, and age. Clothing can also serve as a "prop" to project our attitudes and even our ambivalence about our desired or actual identities. For example, consider the wealthy individual who "dresses-down," but does so while wearing an expensive, but understated piece of clothing or jewelry that may only be recognized by a similarly wealthy or fashion conscious individual. This may represent the wearer's concerted effort to appear well-to-do but not "ostentatious," thus detaching themselves somewhat from their "well-to-do role." This consciously subtle 'dressing-down' may represent an even more dramatic signal of their affluent status than if they were to actually "dress-up."

Haptics: The Use of Touch to Communicate

The use of touch in communication is a complicated area to study because there are so many variables to consider. For example: Who is touched and by whom? What is the relationship of the participants? What area of the body is touched? What is the duration and intensity of the touch? What is the context (e.g., on the football field, in the office)? What are the specific cultural expectations for touch?

Despite the complexity of haptic communication, simply "reaching out to touch someone" can be powerful medicine. The health care professional who lightly touches an ill patient's arm to convey comfort, and the volunteer in the neonatal intensive care nursery who cuddles a premature infant, are both engaging in potentially therapeutic non-verbal communication.

Objectics: The Use of Objects to Communicate

The choice and display of objects in our environment constitutes non-verbal communication. This includes our choice of furnishings in the home and office and even how the books and papers on our desk are organized (or, disorganized).

The use of objects in the environment is also indicative of status, as in a family member's predictable seat at the dinner table, or the corporate chief executive officer's seat at the head of the board table.

Examples of objectics in the health care setting are the displaying of diplomas and professional licenses in the medical office or pharmacy. The furnishings, artwork, and even the magazines that are available in a hospital, physician's or dentist's office are often consciously selected to appeal to the target consumer population. You might, for example, compare and contrast the furnishings in a pediatrician's versus an internist's office. It is also fascinating to compare the decor of the lobby areas in major corporations.

We may also use objects to enhance or adorn our appearance. Such objects, termed "artifacts," may include jewelry, sunglasses, wigs, and hairpieces.

Oculesics: The Use of the Eyes to Communicate

Can you think of someone who uses too little eye contact? Or one who stares so relentlessly that the object of the gaze becomes uncomfortable? Have you ever noticed that pupils constrict when we become distressed, and dilate when we are pleased by what we are seeing or hearing?

Ocular non-verbal behavior is very communicative in both obvious and subtle ways. It is used to seek feedback from others, to signal the nature of the relationship, and to let others know when they can speak.

Olfactics: The Use of Smell to Communicate

While olfactory communication is perhaps the least studied category of non-verbal communication, it is one of the most primitive and powerful. We possess strong "olfactory memories," though we do not usually think about what we smell unless it strikes us as particularly positive or negative.

Oftentimes the olfactory sense is targeted to evoke a particular memory, perception, or emotion. Common examples of olfactory manipulation include: baking an apple pie when a house is being shown for sale, venting the scent of fresh bread baking to attract customers to a bakery, and spraying "new car scent" in used cars. In fact, unbeknownst to most, hosiery, underwear, socks, cosmetics, paper, and rugs are perfumed to enhance our acceptance of these products.

Personal scent manipulation is also practiced in the United States. This takes the form of toothpaste, mouthwashes, deodorant, shampoos, fabric softeners, razors (to shave off hairs which retain odor), and colognes and perfumes (Hickson and Stacks, 1985). Examples of olfactory manipulation can also be found in the health care setting, as in the use of antiseptic-like cleaning agents to convey a sense of sterility and powerful exhaust systems to eliminate food smells in patient or administrative areas.

Organismics: The Effect of Unalterable Body Characteristics on Communication

Organismics refers to unalterable, or difficult to alter body characteristics such as sex, age, eye color (except for colored contact lenses), skin color, height, weight and body shape. There is considerable evidence that one's personal appearance plays a major role in shaping self-image and social identity. Individuals who are physically attractive are perceived as being more credible, sociable, and warm than those who are less attractive.

Organismic non-verbal characteristics are readily visible, and often have a high impact in U.S. society. Research indicates that in some business settings, taller individuals enjoy higher salaries than their shorter, but similarly capable colleagues. Persons might be treated less equitably because of their skin color, age, gender, and/or weight.

Kinesics: The Use of Body Movement to Communicate

Kinesic communication includes facial expression, posture, gestures, and rate of walking to communicate. The nature of these movements may be influenced by status, cultural background, and gender.

A person's emotional state is often reflected in kinesic activity. Visualize, for example, the slumped posture, bland facial expression, and slow movements of a depressed individual. Contrast this with the kinesic activity of the agitated and anxious person, or the confident and happy individual. Contrast the kinesic communication evidenced by college during a boring class lecture; a dynamic class discussion; or a challenging multiple choice examination

The quality of an interpersonal relationship can also be revealed by observing kinesic cues. Compatible individuals typically display synchronous body movements and similar postures.

Professionals in the health care setting, attorneys in the courtroom, and public relations executives may all derive much information by astute observations of kinesic behaviors.

Proxemics: The Use of Space to Communicate

Much like kinesic behavior, the use of space to communicate is influenced by status, cultural background, and gender. For example, Americans (a "non-contact" cultural group) will go to great lengths to avoid spatial violations, as opposed to individuals from Arab countries ("contact cultures"). Females in the United States tend to be more tolerant of interpersonal proxemic intrusion than males.

The study of proxemics includes both personal space and territory. Personal space refers to the invisible bubble that surrounds us as a body buffer zone. There are four personal distance zones in the United States:

1. Intimate distance: 0–18 inches;
2. Personal distance: 18 inches–4 feet;

3. Social distance: 4–10 feet; and
4. Public distance: 10 feet or greater.

When our personal space requirements are violated, we may experience adverse psychological and even physiological effects.

Humans maintain several types of territory, including territories at work, at play, and at home. The amount or location of the territory may be an important indicator of status. Indeed, a spacious air conditioned office with a private bathroom on the highest floor of a bank connotes more status than a poorly ventilated partitioned work area in the basement.

Vocalics: The Use of the Voice and Silence to Communicate

We generally possess certain vocal characteristics which others use to stereotype us, though we can, on occasion, alter our true speaking voices. There are many aspects of non-verbal vocal behavior that are communicative, including loudness, pitch, speaking rate, intonation, and nasality. We expect the voice that we hear to be consistent with an individual's age, sex, and body shape.

The amount that we talk is highly communicative. While it is commonly assumed that females talk more than males, Hickson and Stacks (1985) dispute this:

> "A significant body of research now indicates that men not only speak longer, use more words in total interaction, participate more in group discussions, but also talk more than do females."

More recently, a study published in *Science* reported no gender differences. Mehl and colleagues (2007) outfitted 396 college students with devices that automatically recorded their talk every 12 and a half minutes, capturing approximately 4 percent of their daily utterances. The research team learned that women speak slightly more than 16,000 words a day, and men, slightly less than 16,000 words a day. The difference was not statistically significant.

The use of pause and silence are two very important aspects of non-verbal behavior. Pauses serve as "non-verbal punctuation" in our conversations. They tell others when we wish to "keep the floor," when we are finished speaking, and when we will yield our speaking turns (Hickson and Stacks, 1985).

Silence has many possible communicative functions. It can be used to hurt others, as when we "give someone the silent treatment." Silence also allows the speaker time to think, to communicate an emotional response, and even to isolate oneself. Like other aspects of non-verbal behavior, the use of silence differs between cultures.

Role of Non-Verbal Communication

Non-verbal communication has many different functions. It expresses emotions, provides information, and enables us to exercise social control.

The relationship of non-verbal communication to verbal communication is complex. Non-verbal communication can contradict the verbal message, emphasize what has been said, substitute for words, and regulate the conversation. In many instances, non-verbal communication is ambiguous, and the verbal message is needed to complete the meaning.

Now that we have defined some of the categories of non-verbal communication, and the need to interpret it as it all applies to a specific occasion and culture, read, "The Pious One," by Harvey

Arden, an article filled with examples of culture-specific, non-verbal communication. The article takes an ethnographic approach to describing communication within an ultra-orthodox Hasidic community in the Williamsburg section of Brooklyn, New York. Consider how this culture dictates virtually every aspect of non-verbal communication, including costuming, chronemics, haptics, objectics, and so on.

Significance of Non-Verbal Communication

It has been estimated that non-verbal communication accounts for between 65 percent and 93 percent of the communication we experience in face-to-face interactions (Hickson and Stacks, 1985). Mehrabian (1981) examined the total message in two-person communication and discovered that:

Thirty-eight percent of the meaning of the message is expressed **vocally.**

Fifty-five percent of the meaning of the message is expressed **facially.**

Seven percent of the meaning of the message is expressed **verbally.**

This research confirms the old truism that "it's not what you say, but how you say it!"

Non-verbal communication is so pervasive and significant in human society that every student reading this will already have developed much expertise in the area. In fact, you are most likely well aware of what non-verbal behaviors are acceptable in our society. Much of the time, commonly performed non-verbal behaviors are not consciously considered unless some irregularity in non-verbal behavior has occurred. Consider, for example, how often you might be concerned with:

- How close you are standing to a colleague.
- Whether your eye contact is appropriate.
- If you are walking in synchrony with your companion.
- If your clothing is appropriate.
- If your height or weight attracts attention.
- If your voice sounds confident.
- If your "business handshake" is firm, non-sweaty, and of proper duration.
- If you are wearing too much perfume or cologne.
- If you are using the proper fork at lunch.

Attention to non-verbal communication often occurs in an anxiety-producing situation when one feels his/her performance is being closely evaluated. Conscious concern about non-verbal communication may also emerge when one is unfamiliar with the norms of the culture or small group. For example, a first dinner experience with the family of one's partner or future spouse may elicit the guest's concern about where to sit, knowledge of table manners, what to wear, how much affection should be demonstrated in public, and even whether to bring a gift of flowers or candy. With greater familiarity with the family and their culture, one is better able to predict and conform to the "non-verbal norms" of the new group.

Some aspects of non-verbal communication, such as costuming (i.e., the clothes we wear); cosmetics and hair care; organismics (e.g., body weight); and olfaction (which encompasses cleanliness and the use of deodorants, after-shave lotions, perfumes, or colognes) receive daily attention in our society. In fact, they are the basis of multi-billion dollar industries. Best-selling etiquette books and highly paid "image makers" are also testimony to the importance of non-verbal communication.

It is interesting to consider how we learn all the complexities of non-verbal communication. Are we genetically programmed to absorb the non-verbal codes of our culture? Does the aptitude for this type of learning differ for females versus males and/or between individuals? What part does direct teaching play in the acquisition of this body of knowledge? Are there developmental stages or critical periods of learning for the acquisition of non-verbal behaviors?

A discussion of this topic area would be incomplete without reminding the reader that non-verbal communication is an integral function of the arts, such as instrumental music, mime, dance, painting, sculpture, and even photography. Clearly, mastery of each of these forms of non-verbal communication requires aptitude, and in most cases, direct instruction or modeling.

Relationship Between Non-Verbal and Verbal Communication

The nature of the relationship between non-verbal and verbal communication in a given communicative interaction may assume one of the following scenarios:

1. Non-verbal communication may **accompany** speech but have no meaning.
   Example: A non-meaningful ritual with cigarettes, glasses, hand movements, or head ticks.

2. Non-verbal communication may **repeat** verbal communication.
   Example: The airport security officer instructs you to "move through the scanner," and then motions for you to do so.

3. Non-verbal communication may **supplement** verbal behavior.
   Example: The piano teacher tells the student to replay the music, and then demonstrates the correct phrasing.

4. Non-verbal communication may **substitute** for verbal behavior.
   Example: The pharmacist communicates to a coworker that the patient on the telephone is difficult to satisfy by pointing to the telephone, while continuing to politely counsel the patient.

5. Non-verbal communication may **reinforce** verbal communication with an added degree of feeling, or add **communication redundancy.**
   Example: The minister gently touches the man's shoulder, saying: "I am so saddened to hear of your loss."

6. Non-verbal communication may **contradict** verbal communication.
   Example: Using slow, reluctant speech, the employee says, "I don't mind redoing the report, it's only the third time." An extreme example of contradiction often involves non-verbal communication and was described by Bateson (1972) as a *double bind situation.* This occurs when a person is expected to do things which are incompatible. For example, a child would be in a double bind situation if the parent verbally demands a hug, but non-verbally tenses up and steps back from the child.

7. Non-verbal communication may **regulate** verbal communication, in one of the following ways:
   Turn yielding: The speaker non-verbally tells the listener, "It's your turn to talk."
   Examples: Volume decreases, speech slows, posture is relaxed, pitch rises at end of statement and trailers may be used, such as "you know?"

Turn maintaining: The speaker non-verbally tells the listener, "I do not want to give up my turn to talk." Examples: the speaker uses increased rate and volume of speech, filled pauses such as "er . . . er" or "I . . . I," and avoids eye contact with the listener.

Turn requesting: The listener non-verbally indicates the desire to talk.
Examples: Forward leaning, tense posturing, audible inspiration of air, interrupting without eye contact, speaking loud and fast to avoid counter-interruption, pretended or pseudo agreement and fast and rhythmic head nodding, raised finger.

Turn denying: Listener indicates no desire for a turn to talk.
Examples: Silence, relaxed posture, smiling, no change in facial expression or eye contact.

Communication Metaphors

Metaphors (i.e., extended comparisons of the aspects of two systems) have been used to better understand the process of human communication, especially as they relate to the relationship between non-verbal and verbal communication, is an extended comparison of the aspects of two systems.

In the *Telegraph Metaphor,* communication is viewed as a process like that of telegraph transmission; wherein person 1 sends a message to person 2, and the, if desired, person 2 sends a message back to person. However, the workings of the telegraph are not analogous to that of the full-blown interpersonal conversation. Can you recall, for example, a face-to-face conversation in which the listener did not intentionally or unintentionally communicate non-verbally to the speaker?

Leeds-Hurwitz (1992) presented the *Orchestra Metaphor* as a substitute for the traditional Telegraph Metaphor. The Orchestra Metaphor is a more complete, and nuanced metaphor for communication, and includes the following concepts:

1. The conversation, like the live symphony, is transmitted via several channels. For example, if you attend a performance of a symphonic orchestra, you will both see and hear the performance. You also might feel the vibration of the music.
2. Both the orchestral work, and the conversation are comprised of a large number of behaviors or notes. Each act is a single note within the same musical or verbal symphony.
3. These behaviors might be more rehearsed in the case of the orchestral performance, although aspects of the communicative act may be pre-rehearsed or follow certain social rules.
4. Both an orchestra and a communicative interaction have emergent meaning, in that the meaning becomes more evident as the orchestral or communicative event progresses.
5. Intrapersonal communication occurs both for members of the orchestra and audience, and the participants in a conversation.
6. There is interaction between the participants in a communicative act during the conversation. There is also interaction between the orchestra and the audience, such as applause, coughing, verbal cues, etc.
7. The activities of "the actors" in a communicative episode, or in an orchestral performance, must be coordinated. For example, the participants in a conversation can't talk at the same time, interrupt one another, or talk about different things at the same time. Similarly, the members of the orchestra must play the same piece.

The Dance Metaphor is another interesting communication metaphor that recognizes the importance of non-verbal communication (Leeds-Hurwitz, 1992). This metaphor considers the significance of verbal and non-verbal synchrony, both in dance, and in spoken conversation:

1. *Self-synchrony:* The degree of synchrony within one's self. In the speaker, this refers to the synchrony between our movements and our speech.
2. *Interactional synchrony:* This refers to the rhythms of movements and speech between ourselves and others, in speech or in dance. In conversation, this can refer to turn-taking, or interactions over long time periods.
3. *Asynchrony:* This occurs when people do not move in ways that are in synchrony with themselves or others.

Thus, it can be seen that communication is a complex behavior during which information is transmitted continuously over multiple channels, within a specific context.

Summary

This chapter provided an overview of the importance of the non-verbal elements of communication. Following a discussion of the categories of non-verbal communication, we presented two metaphors that Wendy Leeds-Hurwitz uses to illustrate the relationship between verbal and non-verbal communication. This chapter ends with a reading by Arden and Benn called *"The Pious Ones,"* from *National Geographic.* Not only is this article a good ethnographic study of the Hasidic Jewish community in Brooklyn, it is a nice text for exploring the importance of non-verbal communication in culture.

The Pious Ones

Harvey Arden

Maybe we should have parachuted in. That would have seemed much more appropriate somehow for two travelers dropping out of one world into another. Instead, mundanely, photographer Nathan Benn and I took the subway, boarding on Manhattan's lower East Side and emerging ten minutes later into a setting that looked for all the world as if some errant stagehands had mixed the scenery for two different plays—one about a decaying tenement neighborhood in today's Brooklyn, the other about a pre-World War II rural Jewish village, or *shtetl,* of eastern Europe.

"Welcome to Williamsburg in Brooklyn," Nathan said. "Or to Satmar in old Hungary. It depends on how you look at it."

Passing shopwindows hieroglyphed with square-block Hebrew letters we entered the extraordinary world of Williamsburg's Hasidic Jews, or Hasidim—meaning "pious ones." Here, wedged amid Brooklyn's ethnic hodgepodge, sprawls a 40-block enclave of ultra-orthodox Judaism, where most of the men wear flowing beards and dangling earlocks in accordance with God's command in the Book of Leviticus 19:27: "Ye shall not round the corners of your heads, neither shalt thou mar the corners of thy beard."

Their clothing, derived from styles long worn by Jews in eastern Europe, is a striking study in monotone—black or dark-toned suit, wide-brimmed black hat, white shirt buttoned at the neck, no tie. "It may seem plain to you," one Hasid told me, "but to me it's beautiful!" On Sabbaths and holidays the married men don great sable-trimmed hats called *shtreimels,* giving them a noble, almost regal air as they stride along.

The women, not limited to their menfolk's color scheme, wear modish but distinctly modest garments as they push their baby carriages and strollers along Lee Avenue (page 295). Only after you've been told are you likely to notice that most of them are wearing wigs. Often styled in the latest coiffure, these are worn to conceal their real hair—which is cropped after their wedding and henceforth hidden from men's eyes as prescribed by a centuries-old tradition.

Here, a single subway stop from Manhattan, children learn Yiddish as their native tongue, and rarely if ever see a television show or movie, or read a novel. Nor for that matter are they likely to drift into delinquency, experiment with drugs, or rebel against the value system of their elders.

For here the *mitzvahs,* or commandments, which God on Mount Sinai charged His chosen people to obey, are honored as rules of living with a devotion so vibrant that the tablets of the law might have been carried down by Moses to Lee Avenue this very morning.

To these Brooklyn streets after World War II came several thousand Hasidim, remnants of a widespread movement within Judaism that flourished in eastern Europe from the mid-1700's until—but only until—the Nazi catastrophe. The survivors arrived in America and Palestine with blue concentration camp numbers tattooed on their forearms and the searing horror of Hitler's death camps branded on their souls.

Hoping to get a glimpse of the famed Hasidic *tzaddik,* or spiritual leader—the Satmar Rebbe, Yoel Teitelbaum—Nathan and I hurried to reach the Satmar *bes medresh,* or house of study and prayer, before sunset. Already a fireball sun had tangled itself in the cables of the nearby Williamsburg Bridge. Before us stretched an almost surreal perspective of venerable Brooklyn brownstones, their storefronts already shuttered against the gathering blue dusk of this fast-approaching Rosh Hashanah, the Jewish New Year.

"A few minutes more on the subway and we'd already have broken the law," Nathan said. "The *Jewish* law, that is, against traveling or working on a Sabbath or religious holiday. For an Orthodox Jew to ride a subway or even to push the buttons on an elevator is forbidden. And put on your yarmulke, too." He referred to the skullcap traditionally worn by Jews. "The Hasidim wear them all the time—even when they're sleeping."

I later inquired of a Hasidic acquaintance why he wore his yarmulke even when he went to bed.

"Because a Jew covers his head as a sign of his respect for God," he answered." And—tell me, please—am I not still a Jew when I'm sleeping?"

From the pocket of my coat I extracted a black skullcap and stopped before a shop-window to position it on my head. At that moment a Hasidic lad, a beardless copy of his dark-clad elders, came to a sudden halt in front of me, eyebrows raised.

"You should be ashamed!" he admonished, his earlocks quivering. "Do you mean that you put on your yarmulke only after you've gotten here? Are you a Jew only when you're in Williamsburg?" Eyes flashing darkly, he hurried off down Lee Avenue. I shrugged with a sense of utter helplessness. It would not be the last time that the admittedly unorthodox quality of my own Jewishness would be brought into open question by zealously observant Hasidim.

Though I had become bar mitzvah—a "son of the commandment" or a "man of duty"—at age 13, I had only occasionally attended a synagogue since then. Certainly I had no sense of obligation to follow all of the multitude of mitzvahs, or commandments, that God had charged the Jews of Moses' time to obey in fulfillment of their covenant with Him. To the Hasidim, however, these mitzvahs are as important today as they were in ancient times.

No fewer than 613 such mitzvahs are enunciated in the five books of Moses comprising the Torah, or Pentateuch. They range from the Ten Commandments and such sublime moral precepts as "thou shalt love thy neighbour as thyself" to so technical a regulation as "neither shall a garment mingled of linen and woollen come upon thee."

These latter two mitzvahs, seemingly worlds apart in significance, appear in consecutive verses of the Book of Leviticus (19: 18, 19). The Hasidim hew as strictly to the latter as to the former. To heed and safeguard the 613 mitzvahs, plus literally thousands of other laws and traditions that have evolved from them over the millenniums, becomes the very fulcrum of their daily existence.

Reaching the Satmar bes medresh, Nathan and I elbowed our way through a dense crowd of Hasidim toward a large inner doorway. Squeezing up as far as we could, we stood on tiptoe and peered into the main prayer hall, a great room into which, I later learned, some seven thousand people had been packed. All were utterly absorbed in prayer, faces adrip with mingled sweat and tears of ecstasy, lips murmuring impassioned prayers at a furious pace, bodies rocking and swaying and trembling with emotion—turning that huge prayer hall into an echo chamber of the spirit reverberating with passion for God.

The Satmar Rebbe himself, leading the prayers at the front of the room, was completely blocked from our view by adoring crowds of Hasidim. A Hasid later explained to me why he tries to get physically near the Rebbe: "The Rebbe's soul," he said, "is closer to God than other men's. We get as near to him as we can so that our prayers will be carried Up to heaven with his, like sparks rising up with a great flame."

Not until my next visit to Williamsburg did I actually get a clear view of the Rebbe. This was at the annual celebration of his escape from the Nazis, an observance combined with a fund raising for the Satmar parochial school system, which serves thousands of Hasidic children.

Once again I found myself in the midst of a great crowd of Hasidim. All were amurmur with expectation of the Satmar Rebbe's arrival. A sudden commotion erupted around a side entrance of the hotel ballroom where the celebration was being held. All eyes turned in that direction.

Preceded by aides, who created an aisle for him through the vast throng, the Rebbe himself now entered—a slender patriarch with flowing white earlocks and a graceful tuft of white beard curled on his black-suited breast like new-spun silk. His face, untouched by the pandemonium around him, radiated an almost visible glow of spirituality that seemed to be reflected in the faces of his disciples.

At the sight of the revered tzaddik, the entire congregation rose to its feet in a single body and exploded into a rhythmic wall-rattling chant, which crescendoed until it seemed the room could contain not another decibel. At this point the Rebbe, with the slightest batonlike motion of one index finger, brought the runaway chorus of thousands to an instantaneous halt. Even the echoes seemed to die at once.

Now, through the loudspeakers, came the Rebbe's voice—the merest pin-scratch on a slate of silence. Yet that parchment-thin, otherworldly voice was instantly compelling. His disciples, many rocking and swaying as if in prayer, hung on each word as he thanked God for liberating him from the Nazis and for enabling him to be here with his beloved Hasidim. He spoke of the crucial importance of educating their children in Hasidic schools and reminded them that charity, which made such education possible, was one of the noblest of virtues. He then sat back, a benign expression lighting his face, and allowed his aides to take over the fund-raising activities (following pages).

There was a time, before a stroke weakened him some years back, when the Rebbe—now approaching 90—would have discoursed at greater length. His disciples recall how, on the Festival of Simchas Torah—"Rejoicing in the Torah"—he would dance for hours through the night with the holy Torah scroll cradled in his arms.

"He's as famed for his scholarship as for his saintliness," one Hasid told me. "Once, when I was a boy, I climbed a tree outside his window to see if it was true he often studied all night long. Well, there he was, in the middle of the night, bent over a volume of the Talmud, his finger at his temple, studying. A true saint he is!"

If the adulation of his devotees seems somewhat extreme to the outsider, one must understand the pivotal importance of this charismatic man in both their private lives and their collective history.

Long before World War II he was already a famed tzaddik in eastern Hungary, becoming spiritual leader of a Hasidic community centered in the town of Satmar—today a part of Romania, and spelled Satu Mare. This region came under the Nazi jackboot late in the war, by which time the vast majority of eastern Europe's Hasidim—perhaps 500,000 or more, no one knows even roughly how many—had been systematically annihilated with millions of other Jews. Then, in 1944, the Satmar Rebbe and his followers, along with most of the rest of Hungarian Jewry, were dispatched to death camps.

Even in that living hell he and his Hasidim strove to fulfill what mitzvahs they could. One of the first cruelties inflicted by the Nazis was the shearing off of their beards and earlocks. The Rebbe, it is told, pretended to have a toothache and concealed both beard and earlocks beneath a large bandage. Miraculously, the Nazis took no notice.

The bribing of Nazi officials enabled a trainload of Jews, including the Satmar Rebbe, to escape to Switzerland. Soon after, the Rebbe went to Jerusalem. There, however, his ideas failed to jibe with those of the Zionists who were working to set up the yet-unborn State of Israel. The government of the Promised Land, the Rebbe adamantly insisted, must be founded not by men but by the Messiah himself. To this day he declares that the present State of Israel usurps the soil of Zion and actually delays the coming of the Messiah.

Such a militantly anti-Zionist attitude—not shared by all groups of Hasidim—has raised the blood pressure of many Israelis and pro-Zionist American Jews.

Leaving Jerusalem in 1946, the Satmar Rebbe came to the Williamsburg neighborhood of Brooklyn, already a bastion of American Orthodox Jewry that had become a haven for displaced European Jews after the war. Though many of Williamsburg's newly arrived Hasidim had not been the Rebbe's immediate disciples before the war, they found in his presence a spiritual magnetism that could pull together the shattered pieces of their lives.

"When we arrived," one Hasid told me, "we had nothing. We were dazed, hopeless, without any direction or center in our lives. The Satmar Rebbe, may he be forever blessed, gave us that direction, gave us a center. He instilled in us a new hope and restored our belief in the world—and in ourselves."

Starting from scratch, the Rebbe laid the foundations of a new Satmar Hasidic community; its membership today numbers in the tens of thousands. Other Hasidic rebbes, too, settled in Williamsburg and nearby Brooklyn neighborhoods—most notably the Lubavitcher Rebbe, whose following in Crown Heights has attracted thousands of American Jews. These Brooklyn communities and the various groups in Israel comprise the largest concentrations of Hasidim in the world.

Transplanted to America, a new tree of faith began growing—and blooming—in the streets of Brooklyn.

I once asked my Satmar friend Moishe Green: "Who will take the Rebbe's place when, God forbid, he leaves this world?"

He answered: "We don't think about it. Only the Messiah himself can replace so great a tzaddik as the Rebbe. My own belief is that, before the Rebbe leaves us, the Messiah will come to Brooklyn and lead us home to the Promised Land."

Such deep-seated belief in the redeeming powers of Hasidic rebbes traces back to the 18th century to the founding father of Hasidism, Israel Baal Shem Tov, one of the most extraordinary and luminous figures in the millenniums-long history of Judaism. A poor and unpretentious man, a native of the Carpathian Mountain region, he brought to the poverty-wracked, pogrom-plagued, Jewish masses of Poland and the Ukraine a spiritual message of transcendent joy and hope.

Inveighing powerfully against the often-arid emphasis on religious scholarship that had come to dominate Jewish spiritual life in his time, he proclaimed that even the most unlearned Jew could experience a direct communion with God through ecstatic worship and a truly joyful keeping of the mitzvahs. What mattered was not so much the loftiness of one's intellect as the purity of one's soul, however humble. Love of God, he taught, could be expressed as well through spontaneous singing and dancing as through formal prayer and scholarship.

For a time this passionately mystic approach to religious life aroused the bitterest opposition of the Orthodox establishment. Some of the early Hasidim were excommunicated. Yet the movement spread like holy wildfire, inflaming the hearts and minds of vast numbers of east European Jews, learned and unlearned alike. It was a genuine democratization of Jewish religious life, making the deepest spiritual experience accessible to the many as well as to the few.

After the death of the Baal Shem Tov—a title meaning, roughly, "Master of the Good Name"—his closest disciples established a number of Hasidic communities, where the fervor of his teachings continued to burn bright. These leaders became known by the title *rebbe*—a designation not to be confused with *rabbi*, though both mean "my master" or "my teacher." Any pious and learned man may become a rabbi, but only the rarest of individuals has the transcendent qualities required of a rebbe.

In time—and this has often been criticized by outsiders—the leadership of Hasidic communities became largely dynastic, usually being passed from a rebbe to one of his sons. The community's loyalty to the rebbe is easily transferred to the offspring. On some occasions, in the absence of a suitable direct heir, a son-in-law or an especially eminent disciple is chosen.

The modern Jewish writer and philosopher Martin Buber devoted a great deal of his life's work to collecting tales concerning the various Hasidic rebbes. His two-volume *Tales of the Hasidim*, a monument of scholarship, mirrors both the charm and the profundity of Hasidic thinking.

Though Hasidism has unquestionably evolved since the time of the Baal Shem Tov, becoming more formalized in its rituals—some critics would even say rigidified—I found its original message of joyful communion with God still ringing loud and clear in the streets of Brooklyn.

I recall one night being swept up in the ecstatic revels of a group of rabbinical students. For hours, to the sour strains of an improvised trumpet-and-accordion band, they snake-danced in a great writhing, singing, chanting mass that seemed to become more and more energized as the minutes throbbed along. Joining in, somewhat reluctantly at first, I put my hands on the shoulders of the Hasid in front of me and allowed myself to be swept along on that mounting black wave of communal ecstasy.

At one point I found myself swaying beside Moishe Green, whose forehead was pearled with sweat. His eyes glowed. "You see," he breathed, "we aren't just dancing. We're soaring to God!"

Even in a milieu where the spiritual predominates, the rent must be paid and groceries bought. The Baal Shem Tov himself often worked at humble jobs, and his followers in Williamsburg frequently do likewise.

The Hasidic mode of life, with its wide range of behavioral and educational restrictions, makes holding many kinds of well-paying jobs extremely difficult. You often see bearded Hasidim with dancing earlocks and sweating brows driving pickup trucks, heaving crates, working as clerks or storekeepers. Many work in Manhattan as diamond cutters and merchants—bringing much-needed cash into the financially pinched Williamsburg community. Hasidic women as well as men work in the "needle trades," manufacturing garments for firms often owned by Orthodox Jews.

"We are part of the capitalist society," Rabbi Albert Friedman, a community leader said. "We take jobs that do not interfere with our way of life. Yes, we have some wealthy men whom God has blessed with financial success, and they share—are expected to share—with the others."

A great many Hasidim work in jobs that fill the exacting and specialized needs of the community. Meat, for instance, must not be simply kosher but *glat* kosher, that is, kosher beyond any conceivable question. The Hasidim frankly distrust any food that they themselves have not subjected to the most rigorous conformance with Jewish dietary law.

Hence, most of the food consumed by the Hasidim is prepared with fastidious care within the community itself. Ritual slaughterers dispatch cattle and chickens according to ancient laws. Stores feature "Jewish milk" from dairies supervised by observant Jews. Wheat for the Passover matzo, or unleavened bread, is guarded with unceasing vigilance from the time it is harvested and milled until it comes piping hot and crisp from glowing bakery ovens in Williamsburg. If so much as a single drop of water comes in contact with the flour before it is used—hence allowing it to leaven however slightly—the entire batch is rendered useless for Hasidic consumption. This extraordinary care in food preparation has great appeal for other Jews, and some non-Jews as well. Outsiders' purchases of Hasidic foodstuffs help buoy the community's economy. You'll find no doctors or lawyers among the Satmar Hasidim, since they don't acquire the education needed for the professions. Besides, going to college is frowned upon—a waste of time in a life devoted to the study of the Torah and its vast exposition, the Talmud.

At the age of 3, a boy has his first haircut, leaving him with shaven crown and untouched earlocks. Next he is taken to the bes medresh. There a dab of honey is placed on an aleph—first letter of the Hebrew alphabet—in the Torah; his finger is placed on this, and then on his lips, to show him that the study of God's law is sweet. Thus begins a lifetime "toiling in the Torah."

Teenage boys often arrive at their school, or *yeshivah*, to begin study at five in the morning and, what with a day of study and prayers, don't arrive home until eight in the evening. A few hours in the afternoon are spent on what the Hasidim call "English"—meaning not just the English language, which many children first learn in school, but all the curriculum required to meet minimal New York State educational requirements, subjects such as math, history, and geography.

"The plain fact is," I was told, "many parents would rather their children didn't learn any more 'English' than necessary."

Said another Hasid: "Constant study of the Torah and Talmud sharpens the mind to a phenomenal degree. Some of our boys have become computer programmers—a profession requiring keen logical skills."

You see them studying, usually in pairs, the great tomes of the Talmud spread before them on desks or tables. Rarely do they use a pencil while studying, instead storing in their minds endless passages of Jewish law and tradition. Some go on to be ordained as rabbis, but, in actual fact, relatively few of Satmar's scholars are needed for rabbinical posts. Most marry in their late teens or early 20's, study for a final year or so full time—if the family can afford it—then find a job. For the rest of their lives they will spend much of their free time on Torah study.

"Think what they might do if all that study were directed to some worldly purpose," I remarked to a non-Satmar Hasid knowledgeable about the outside world.

"I suppose so," he said. "After all, look at Freud, Marx, Einstein—all Jews who made their mark on the non-Jewish world. To me, however, they would have been much better off studying in a yeshivah. What a waste of three fine Talmudic minds!"

Hasidic girls get a much more rounded education, by American standards, than the boys. Not encouraged to study the Talmud, they need learn only the traditional practices required of a Hasidic housewife in running a completely orthodox home. Hence, they have vastly more time for worldly studies, and in speech, manner, and, appearance often seem more Americanized than the men.

The pivot of their lives is the home, which in Williamsburg usually means modest quarters in an elderly apartment building, a brownstone, or a housing project. Even in the dimmest basement apartment, there shines an inner sunlight, a glow of *Yiddishkeit*. To this sanctuary of feminine order and arrangement, the men and older boys often come rushing home from work or study for a hastily gulped meal with the family, then fly out again into the night for evening prayers at the bes medresh.

On the Sabbath, of course, all this hubbub comes to a serene standstill, and the woman's role as queen of the household comes to the fore. As wife and mother she lights the Sabbath candles—an act of utmost sanctity that leaves no doubt as to her vital position in the family. Often, when not tied down to little ones, she takes a job to supplement the family income. On the occasions when women attend the bes medresh, the balcony is set aside for them. A latticed screen separates them from the menfolk, who are not supposed to be distracted from their prayers by the presence of the opposite sex.

If their lot seems a far cry from women's liberation, I found few complaints. "Nothing is more satisfying than a Jewish life lived in the Hasidic way," one housewife told me.

With Nathan Benn one afternoon I knocked at the door of the basement apartment of a Hasidic friend, a rabbi—and thoughtlessly extended my hand in greeting to his wife.

"Oh, no," she said, stepping back. "I can't shake hands, I'm sorry. Please take no offense." I had forgotten that Hasidic women do not touch men other than their husbands and close relatives. Even between a man and wife, it is exceedingly rare to see an overt display of affection.

Later we sat down with the family to a wondrous meal of chicken soup and gefilte fish, boiled chicken and whitefish, potato *kugel*, and so on—an archetypal Jewish feast. The rabbi intoned a sequence of blessings in a marvelously moving cantorial tenor. As we ate, we imbibed deep draughts of Talmudical lore along with frequent glassfuls of fruit-flavored Mayim Chaim—a brand of kosher soda pop whose name means "water of life" or "living water."

At one point in the meal, Nathan poured himself a glass of Mayim Chaim. Seeing my glass nearly empty to his right, he swiveled the bottle around and started to fill it. The entire family gasped.

"That is not done, Nathan!" admonished the rabbi. "It is simply not done!"

"But what did I do!" Nathan asked.

"Oh . . . well . . . after all, Nathan, how could you know?" said the rabbi evasively.

"Know what?" Nathan pleaded.

"Please," said the rabbi, "we talk no more about it. The subject is finished."

With that, he lapsed into Yiddish, refusing to discuss the matter further.

Later, recalling the incident to another Hasid, I demonstrated how Nathan had poured my glass of Mayim Chaim.

"Stop!" he cried. "Don't do that!"

"Do what?" I asked.

"The way you're pouring the bottle, turning your hand backward like that . . . it's how one performs the ablutions when washing the dead! We never make such movements in normal situations."

Once again I had run headlong into the multifarious rituals that at times seem to surround the Hasidic way of life like a spear-point fence, making entrance difficult for outsiders, and egress no easy thing for the Hasidim themselves. Yet, in the eyes of the Hasidim, each spearpoint in that fence safeguards the fulfillment of their holy covenant with God. Their adherence to every last punctilio of religious law is no mere rote act but a conscious fulfillment of God's command, bringing about the sanctification of even the smallest acts of everyday life.

With the outside world, the Satmar Hasidim seemed to me to live not so much side by side as back to back. I recall one afternoon approaching on the street a Roman Catholic nun whose church, with a largely Spanish-speaking congregation, stands almost incongruously in the middle of Williamsburg's Hasidic neighborhood. When I asked her about her experiences with the Hasidim, she simply shook her head. "I have lived in this parish for 13 years," she said, "but never has a Hasid come up and spoken to me. Not once. They don't even catch your eye."

Police detective Nino Marano, whose beat has been Williamsburg for years, told me: "The Hasidim rarely bother other people, and would just as soon other people didn't bother them. We've had periodic trouble—fights between Hasidim and other ethnic groups. But you rarely see a Hasid who starts the trouble—though they often seem to attract it just by being so different and stand-offish. Once a Hasid made insulting remarks when I ticketed his truck for a parking violation. Another Hasid reported the man's conduct to the *bes din,* the religious court, where the Hasidim prefer to handle their own civil infractions. Hearing the case, the rabbis berated the man and he apologized. I was much more satisfied than if he's been hauled before a civil judge."

Nearly all Hasidim take pride in becoming American citizens, which allows them to vote. "We are often the swing vote in local elections and political affairs," Rabbi Friedman told me.

Although the Satmar Hasidim share to some degree in community funds made available by various government agencies—they pay taxes, after all, like everyone else—they prefer self-help to reliance on outsiders. They not only run their own school system out of Satmar funds, but also operate a walk-in clinic, a nursing service, an emergency first-aid and ambulance service, a private community bus service, a summer camp system, an employment agency, and a free-loan society. They very definitely care for their own.

Recently they have also established a small self-contained community for a few hundred Hasidim at Monroe in New York's Orange County—about an hour's drive up-state. Does this signal a mass exodus from the inner city? Probably not, at least for the near future. Immediate plans for the Monroe complex envisage a community of perhaps 250 families. "We are not running away," Rabbi Friedman explained. "We are simply growing."

While I toured a Satmar school for girls, the principal, Rabbi Naftali Hertz Frankel, pointed out how reverently the children repeat the Pledge of Allegiance.

"Almost all of them are the grandchildren of concentration camp survivors," he said. "They *know* how much America and its freedom means. To them, the Pledge of Allegiance is almost a kind of prayer."

Taking leave of Williamsburg, I stopped off to say good-bye to a bearded old Hasidic friend at the tiny Xerox shop he manages on Lee Avenue.

Between running off copies for customers, he spoke of his first family—all killed in the concentration camps—and of the blessings of raising a second family in "a nice Yiddish place like Williamsburg."

The green light of the Xerox duplicator flickered on his gray beard and earlocks. I recalled an old Jewish tale I had heard about Hanoch the shoemaker, as one of the 36 legendary "secret tzaddikim," or holy men, who—unbeknownst even to themselves—help sustain the universe with their piety.

Hanoch, goes the legend, uttered praises of the Lord with each stroke of his tack hammer. Watching my Hasidic friend reel off another batch of Xerox copies, I conjured up the image of him, too, as one of the secret 36, uttering praises to God each time he pushes the "print" button on the Xerox machine for another copy.

It was one last indelible image to carry with me as I took the subway from Williamsburg to that other world in Manhattan.

CHAPTER 7

Listening and Empathy

Learning Objectives

After reading this chapter, you should be able to:

- Describe the extent to which listening is an important aspect of communication.
- Discuss how hearing and listening differ.
- Defend the statement, "listening is not a passive activity."
- Define "selective attention."
- Explain what is meant by "redundancy" and how speakers can use it to help listeners remember information.
- Provide an example of a situational obstacle to listening.
- Define what is meant by "internal obstacles" to listening.
- Define the types of listening: pleasurable, discriminative, critical, and therapeutic/empathic.
- Define empathy.
- Describe client-centered counseling.
- Differentiate between empathy and projection.
- Contrast empathy and sympathy.
- Discuss why empathy is not the same as agreement.
- Provide an example of: behaviors that: elicit information, affirm content, and affirm the person.
- Describe how voice quality may or may not contribute to the perception of empathy.

Introduction

The conversation at Sunday dinner was progressing well. As usual, the ten of us had jumped from topic to topic, some serious, some humorous, some sparking debate. I thought that I was engaged, or at least adequately feigning participation. That illusion shattered the moment I asked the question. "So how's Sally? I haven't heard anything about her for awhile." All conversation stopped. All eyes were on me. Finally my wife said, "Where were you five minutes ago when we were talking about her?" The message was clear. I was not listening.

Students are often times surprised to learn that listening is considered to be an absolutely vital part of communication. According to the following often quoted surveys, however, we see that listening is not only an important aspect, but the most important aspect of communication.

	1926 STUDY	1981 STUDY
Writing	11%	14%
Reading	15%	17%
Speaking	32%	16%
Listening	42%	53%

—Source Rankin (1926), Barker (1981) quoted in Tubbs & Moss

Both the 1926 and the 1981 studies indicate that of all the time we spend in some form of communication, *at least half* of that time is spent listening. As we shall see, however, listening, like any other skill, is not something that humans simply do. Instead it requires intentionality and practice.

In this chapter we will distinguish listening from hearing, discuss the skills associated with listening, and examine some specific types of listening. This final topic will be a detailed discussion of empathy as a specialized type of listening.

Listening vs. Hearing

Kaitlin: Are you listening?

Tyler: Yeah, yeah, I hear ya.

"Most people tend to be 'hard of listening' rather than 'hard of hearing'."

—online Student Handbook, University of Minnesota, Duluth

Is there a difference between listening and hearing? Indeed there is. But seldom have two concepts been more often but more wrongly confused. We must begin our discussion, then, with an attempt to detangle the two.

Hearing is the physiological process that occurs when we receive aural stimuli. It is passive and involuntary. For example, you really have no choice as to whether or not to hear your roommate's stereo blasting from his or her side of the room, just as you have no choice as to whether you hear the siren from the passing fire truck, or hear your professor's lecture. You do, however, have a choice as to whether to listen to any or all of these stimuli.

Listening is an active process that that takes us well beyond the often passive experience of hearing. When you listen you mentally turn toward the other person and you are being *intentional, attentive, and retentive.* Let's examine this threefold process more closely.

Three Processes Associated with Listening

Intention

As we said earlier, listening doesn't just happen. It requires intentionality and effort on the part of the would-be listener. Kay Lindahl writes of a time when she became aware of the intentionality associated with listening.

"Listening is not a passive activity. It's not about being quiet or even hearing the words. It is an action, and it takes energy to listen. The first time I became aware of the energy factor was at an international gathering, where I was part of a small group of eight people. We were from four different continents, spoke four different languages, and worshiped in four different faith traditions. Our task was to make recommendations for one part of a document we were creating as a large body. For two days, I went to bed exhausted. I couldn't imagine why I was so tired because I was getting enough sleep and had not been physically active. All we had been doing was sitting around talking and listening. Then it occurred to me that it took a lot of energy to listen with such intention. I was acutely aware of each person as he or she spoke and was committed to understand each contribution. It was quite a workout!" (in Stewart, p. 189.)

Attention

The human mind can process between 300 and 600 words per minute, whereas the average person speaks about 100 and 160 words per minute. As you can see, this leaves the listener with a great deal of time to attend mentally to other things. I might spend the extra time creating a shopping list, anticipating my next comment, or following the action on the television running in the background. At any given time there are many things vying for our attention.

Listening requires us to filter out all other distractions and focus on the source of the stimuli that is important at the moment. This process is referred to as **selective attention.** It implies that human beings have considerable control, not so much over what we hear, but over what we will listen too.

Retention

Remembering (or retaining information) is the third process associated with listening. Researchers like Barker tell us that we forget half of the information we hear as soon as we hear it. If asked about the message after 8 hours, we can only recall about one-third of it.

Public speakers are typically aware of this fact so they live by the mandate to "tell your audience what you are going to say, say it, then tell them what you said." In other words they build **redundancy,** saying the same thing multiple times in multiple ways, into their speeches. But speakers can only do so much to help listeners remember information. At some point the listeners themselves must take an active role. Some common practices that listeners employ include repeating the information or relating the information to other things. Notice how Jamar utilizes both of these devices in the following conversation.

Peggy: Jamar, I'd like you to meet my cousin Philip.

Jamar: Hi Philip.

Philip: How ya doin'?

Jamar: So Philip, where ya from?

Philip: Chicago.

Jamar: Chicago. Do you get to many Cubs' games?

As a result of his active involvement in the interaction, Jamar stands a greater chance of being able to recall Philip's name should they meet weeks later.

Obstacles to Effective Listening

As I have already suggested there are at least two general types of obstacles (noise) that hinder listening. They are situational obstacles and internal obstacles (Wood, 2006).

1. *Situational Obstacles* are conditions that are created by or specific to the situation. These might include information overload, an inadequate PA system for the speaker, audience members talking while the speaker is talking, or extraneous background noise. Many semesters when I teach the introductory communication class we find ourselves in a split auditorium next to an Introduction to Music class. Because of the room divider between us, it is often the case that we are treated to the music from next door. Normally music is a welcomed source of noise, but when it competes with my efforts to lecture and the students' efforts to listen, it can become quite a distraction. In those instances, my students must try extra hard to listen.

2. *Internal Obstacles* are much more person specific. By that I mean that the obstacles to listening are rooted in the thoughts, feelings, and past experiences of the individual listener. For example, if you and your roommate had an argument about the electric bill right before you walked to class, your ability and desire to listen to the lecture might be greatly reduced. Instead you spend the entire period rethinking the argument and planning your responses for the next encounter.

Another example of an internal obstacle might be the negative stereotype you have of New Englanders as aloof and impersonal. If, at a party, you are introduced to someone from Boston, your desire to listen might end before she or he even begins to speak.

Types of Listening

When it comes to listening, it is not only important to distinguish it from hearing, but to recognize that not all listening is the same. You do not, for example, listen to your favorite radio station with the same intensity that you listen to your opponent in a debate. Different situations require different types of listening. In their text, *Human Communication* (2000), Tubbs and Moss discuss four types of listening.

1. **Pleasurable listening** is the listening that occurs when we turn on the stereo or flip to our favorite television show. It also is the listening we experience in many of our "So how was your day?" conversations. In each of these cases the content may be much less important than the listening experience itself. Listening in these situations provide enjoyment, familiarity, and pleasure.

2. The second type of listening, **discriminative listening,** is "primarily used for understanding and remembering" (Tubbs and Moss). You use discriminative listening most often in lectures or when talking on the phone with someone who has not yet mentioned their name. In this latter instance, you attempt to discern important pieces of information or vocal qualities that will help you identify the mystery caller.

3. **Critical listening** is a skill we associate most often with lawyers and debaters. It enables one to listen for inconsistent information or illogical arguments. Your significant other demonstrates critical listening skills when s/he says in the midst of your explanation of where you were last night, "Wait a minute! You said earlier that you were at the library all evening. How, then, did you get to talk to Pat?"

4. The final type of listening is **therapeutic or empathic listening.** It suggests a means of understanding another that takes us beyond his or her words and into the world of that other. Because empathy is such an important type of listening and because it has been greatly misunderstood over the years, the next section of this chapter will explore the experience of empathy.

Empathy

"You know," says Pat, "I've been doing a lot of thinking about my future."

"Really?" you say.

"Yeah" says Pat. "I'd really like to drop my Business major and pick up Theatre, but I'm afraid."

Knowing that your response will direct the flow of the conversation, and potentially Pat's future, what do you say?

This portion of the chapter deals with the often referenced but little understood experience of *empathy*. After defining *empathy* and distinguishing it from some related but distinct experiences, we will discuss some of the behaviors associated with the experience of empathy.

Pick up any one of a hundred textbooks on communication, nursing, health science, or education and you will see writer after writer stating the importance of empathy and the need for practitioners in their discipline to demonstrate it. But after an often overly generalized definition, the text says little else about what empathy is or how it is to be accomplished. The mindset seems to be best described by David Aspy's 1975 article in which he says in essence that we all know what empathy is so "let's get the hell on with it." But I wonder, do we really know what empathy is?

In the same year that Aspy offered his take on empathy, psychologist Carl Rogers published his ground breaking article, *Empathic: An Unappreciated Way of Being*. In it, Rogers describes the basic tenet of his then revolutionary "*client centered counseling.*" This tenet states that if a client is to feel accepted and understood, the counselor must attempt to enter "the private perceptual world of the other and become thoroughly at home in it" (Rogers, 1975, p. 4). This way of knowing another involves laying the self aside temporarily and living in the other's world *as if* it were one's own, without ever losing the *as if* feeling. Rogers described this experience in his now famous dialogue with Martin Buber. He says:

> "I think in those moments I am able to sense with a good deal of clarity the way his (her) experience seems to him (her), really viewing it from within him (her), and yet without losing my own personhood or separateness in that. Then, if in addition to those things on MY part, my client or the person with whom I'm working is able to sense something of those attitudes in me, then it seems to me that there is a real, experiential meeting of persons, in which each of us is changed. I think sometimes the client is changed more than I am, but I think both of us are changed in that kind of an experience." (Buber, 1965, p. 170, emphasis in original, parentheses inserted by Gareis).

From Rogers' statement it is clear that there are two necessary components of empathy. They are: genuinely understanding the other and never losing sight of the fact that it is this other's world and not my own that is the point of focus. With that in mind, then, we will look next at some related but not synonymous experiences with which empathy is often confused.

What Empathy Is Not

1. Empathy is not **projection.**

In the best sense, projection is "assuming that others do, think and feel in the same way as you." It implies that in order to understand how another feels in a particular situation, I simply visualize myself in the situation and see how I would respond. On one hand it, perhaps rightly, assumes a level of similarity between and among members of the same culture. On the other hand, it disallows individuality and difference on the part of the other. Projection can best be seen in statements like, "You shouldn't (or really don't) feel that way." If, however, the person does in fact feel that way, what he or she may need is empathy, not correction.

2. Empathy is not **sympathy.**

In her extensive work, *On the Problem of Empathy* (1970), Edith Stein discusses a second phenomenon that is often confused with empathy. That phenomenon is *sympathy*.

Stein contrasts the two phenomena by first distinguishing between primordial and non-primordial experiences. *Primordial experiences* are those that come to me as mine, while non-primordial experiences are those that come to me as an Other's. Sympathy is a primordial experience that involves my "feeling with" the other. Empathy, on the other hand, is a *non-primordial phenomenon* in which I experience (feel into) the other's consciousness.

The implication of this distinction is that far from feeling "the same as the other," to be empathic I must perceive and understand the experiences or the feeling **as the other.** As Stein says, "Empathy in our strictly defined sense as the experience of foreign consciousness can only be the non-primordial experience which announces a primordial one" (1970, p. 14).

3. Empathy is not **agreement.**

Very early in my study of empathy, I asked a group of about 200 undergraduates, (via survey), to describe a situation in which empathy had occurred and to explain what signaled its occurrence. While I no longer have the exact figures (a slip I have lamented several times since), I remember that one of the recurring responses from the students was that empathy was known to have occurred because, "S/he AGREED with me." I was reminded of those comments when a similar response showed up on a few of the surveys used in the study upon which this chapter is based. Add to this the ever-growing national sentiment that if "others are not for us (agree with us), they are against us" and one could easily conclude that there is a direct connection between empathy and agreement. The assumption seems to be that whether the interaction is between a parent and a child, an instructor and a student, or a nation and a nation, if I state my position loud and long enough, you WILL understand (i.e., agree with) me.

While this may be the prevailing cultural expectation, however, it is not supported by the literature. In the article by Laing, Phillipson, and Lee (Chapter 4), for example, we see that it is indeed possible to understand (empathize with) another and still disagree. For example, I may understand well how someone can become so frustrated with conditions in their life that they feel like taking a group of school children hostage. That, however, does not mean that I agree with their course of action. Empathy does not require nor is it necessarily agreeing with the other.

Behaviors Associated with Empathy

Everyone agrees that empathy is important, but how do we do it? In this section we will explore the four categories of behaviors that are associated with the experience of empathy. These categories are: *Behaviors that Elicit Information, Behaviors that Affirm Content,* and *Behaviors that Affirm the Person.* What follows is a description of these categories.

1. **Behaviors that *elicit information*** are used to "maintain and/or direct the content flow in the interaction" (Gareis, 1991, p. 68). When used effectively, they suggest that the empathizer is sensitive to the choices and the willingness of the other to disclose. Gentle probes like "Oh?,"

"What did you do then?," and "How did you feel?" or well-timed silence and eyebrow flashes signal a willingness to allow the other to initiate topics and explore issues in greater depth.

2. **Behaviors that *affirm content*** "indicate recognition and understanding of the other's message or experiences" (Gareis, 1991, p. 69). They can be as simple as nods, repeating a word or label, or saying something like "I see," or as complex as a mirroring of expressions or providing a meaningful label for the other's experiences or emotions he or she cannot or has not identified. Labeling serves a very important function by way of affirming content. Not only does a label provide common ground for the interacters, it also gives us a means of calling things not immediately present into awareness and serves a demystifying function. By "demystifying" I mean that once a label is given, "it" can then be addressed and in a rhetorical sense, controlled.

   Another content affirming behavior of note is "sharing a similar story." Says Gareis: "Unlike verbal statements of understanding or labeling the other's feelings, a story from the empathizer shows a very personal affirmation of the other's message. A similar story says, in effect, 'I not only understand, I have been there'" (1991, p. 113).

3. The third category associated with empathy includes **behaviors that *affirm the person.*** As the label suggests, these behaviors are used to signal awareness of and positive regard for the person or character of the other and includes "any movement or act that lessens the physical and/or psychological distance between the self and the other" (Gareis, 1991, p. 69). Examples might be the sharing of physical items like seating or food, suggesting availability, maintaining eye contact, touching the other, or laying aside work or similar distractions.

   Without a doubt one of the most distracting potential interruptions to an ongoing conversation is a ringing telephone. And in this culture it is nearly an unforgivable taboo to ignore a ringing phone. It is a phenomenon that seems to create stress, not only for the person whose phone is ringing, but for others in the room. That is why I will often say to a person with whom I am engaged in conversation, "I'll just let the machine get it." Not only does that simple statement arrest the concerns of my conversational partner, but it signals to that person that he or she has my undivided attention. As you can see, anything said or done in the course of the interaction to signal the worth of the other as a person is a Person Affirming Behavior.

4. **Other Behaviors.** The only significant behavior in this category that affects the experience of empathy either positively or negatively is tone and/or volume of the empathizer's voice. Some respondents reported that the empathizer had a "pleasant" tone suggesting that they could listen to it easily. Others stated that the empathizer sounded "uncaring," "tired," or "bored."

   As I concluded in the original study: "Generally, it appears that vocal variance and an appropriate volume are judged to be more empathic while anything different is considered nonempathic" (Gareis, 1991, p. 130).

Conclusions

To end this section, let me offer two conclusions regarding the experience of empathy in interpersonal exchanges. They are drawn from the 1991 study, *Characteristics of Empathic Exchanges in Human Interactions.*

1. **While the behaviors mentioned are considered extremely important to the experience of empathy, none of these behaviors individually or collectively can cause empathy.** Here the

findings seem to indicate that, while it is never less than the behaviors we exhibit in the presence of another person, empathy is always something more. The behaviors mentioned simply reflect our presence in that world that is never our own.

2. **Some behaviors associated with empathy have a curvilinear effect.** In other words, there are some behaviors associated with empathy that are effective only to a point. Once that point is reached, the same behavior may actually have a negative effect. One example is eye contact. Normally considered to be a positive behavior in the experience of empathy, it "has its limits and must be done with ease and moderation" (Gareis, 1991, p. 127). As Gladstein says in relation to the possible negative effects of eye contact: "It is important to avoid staring, glancing, or giving cold eye responses" (1987, p. 126). What exactly differentiates staring from positive eye contact is difficult to say. There does, however, appear to be a point at which an individual becomes uncomfortably aware of another's gaze. I remember one counselor who intentionally kept a box of tissues behind her. When a client became emotional, the counselor had to intentionally turn to retrieve a tissue. When asked about it, she replied that it was her way of giving a client a moment of "space." In my opinion, she was guarding against the possible negative impact of too much eye contact.

Summary

In this chapter we have discussed the difference between hearing, a physiological process and listening, an active discriminating process. Listening involves the three necessary processes of Intention, Attention, and Retention. After discussing two types of obstacles to listening and the types of listening, we focused our attention on the popular but largely misunderstood experience of empathy. There we concluded that while empathy is always more than the sum of its behavioral parts, it is never less than the behaviors we exhibit to indicate to the other that we have purposely entered their world "as if" it were our own, but without losing the "as if" feeling. The behaviors associated with the experience of empathy are behaviors that elicit content, behaviors that affirm content, behaviors that affirm the person, pleasing vocal variance and an appropriate volume.

CHAPTER 8

Communication and the Self

Learning Objectives

After reading this chapter, you should be able to:

- Identify the four quadrants of the Johari Window and explain the meaning of each.
- Describe an improved Johari window.
- List common principles of self-disclosure in our society.
- Define what Goffman meant by the terms dramatic realization, performance disruptions, dramaturgical loyalty, dramaturgical discipline, and dramaturgical circumspection.
- Define and give examples of: identity negotiation, working consensus, surface acting, deep acting, and family paradigms.
- Discuss whether working consensus is a public or a private reality.
- Describe what is meant by "feeling norms" and discuss how they are formed.
- Describe how institutions accomplish emotion management.
- Discuss how communication constructs gender.
- Reflect upon your beliefs concerning the role of intrapersonal communication in determining your choices and successes.

Introduction

Our final chapter focuses on "the self"—how we view ourselves, and how that influences our communication with others. As we said in the start, this presentation schema runs counter to the approach of other introductory texts; most early on, write about "the self." Why do we diverge from the traditional approach and save "the self," for last? Because, despite society's focus on the importance of "our own" personal communication (e.g., personal e-mail account, blog, cell phone number, and facebook.com site) communication, as we envision it, is *not* "all about me." Our perceptions and communication products are immeasurably shaped and influenced by multiple external factors. These include: the larger physical environment, our biology, culture, family, and peers. Indeed, these influences begin long before conception. With that in mind, let us now consider "the self," and how an individual's communication interacts with these influences.

Communication: A Basic Life Process

Communication is central to each of our lives because it functions as a basic life process:

> "Just as animal and human systems take in oxygen and foodstuffs and transform them into materials necessary to their functioning, they also take in and use information. In the most basic sense, communication is the essential life process through which animal and human systems create, acquire, transform and use information to carry out the activities of their lives" (Ruben, p. 65).

These concepts are contained in the Systems Theory of communication. This theory is useful in clarifying the nature of communication and its fundamental relationship to behavior. A system is defined as "any entity or whole that is composed of interdependent parts." By definition, a system possesses characteristics and capabilities that are distinct from those of its separate parts. An example of a system is a pizza, which, while composed of flour, yeast, water, tomato sauce, and cheese, is far different in appearance, consistency, and taste than any of its component ingredients. Systems can also be living, taking the form of plants, animals, and humans.

As we progress up the scale of life from plants to animals to humans, it becomes clear that the nature of the relationships between the "system" and the environment becomes more and more complex. The very survival of animals depends upon their ability to acquire and use information to accomplish nearly all of life's activities, including courtship and mating, food location, and self-defense.

Communication is particularly critical to the survival of humans, as we are among those animals whose survival directly depends upon our relationships with nurturing adults. Consider, for example, the newly born infant whose main existence is comprised of sleeping, eating, waste elimination, and crying. Babies are unable to engage in locomotion, food gathering, or self-defense. Without a nurturing adult, the baby would not survive. Yet, babies are generally competent in communicating their needs via crying, which serves to alert the caretaker to feed, cuddle, burp, clean, or rock the tot to sleep. Just about the time a caretaker become fatigued and discouraged with the nurturing process, (around six weeks of age), the baby "rewards" the adult with "a smile." And, sometime between nine and twelve months of age, typically developing babies will produce a "first word," often "mama" or "dada." This represents another tremendously rewarding event for the caretaker.

A second collection of theories that explains why communication is central to our lives is Need Theories. These theories are based upon the premise that as a human being grows and matures, so does the range of needs that must be met for the individual to develop into a physically and emotionally healthy person. Perhaps the best-known theory of human needs was developed by Abraham Maslow from his observations of personality development (Maslow, 1970).

Maslow theorized that humans have five different types of needs, and that these exist in a hierarchical arrangement. According to Maslow, the needs are activated in a specific order, so that a higher order need cannot be realized until the next-lower need has been fulfilled. Maslow's hierarchy follows, presented from the highest order need, to the lowest order need:

Self-Actualization Need—The need to fulfill one's highest potential in life.

Esteem Need—The need to be valued and appreciated by others. This includes pride, self-esteem, and prestige.

Social Need—The need to have love, companionship, and a feeling of belongingness to one or more groups.

Safety Need—The need to be free from harm and fear. In a society, this would translate into having a job and financial security, and living and working in a safe neighborhood.

Physiological Need—This need relates to the satisfaction of one's biological requirements for air, food, water, sleep, sex, and protective clothing and shelter (Hamilton and Parker, 1970).

It is important to remember that every "theory" must be tested, and Maslow's is no exception. Maslow's theory has failed to gain total acceptance because of evidence that the needs he identified do not have to be activated in a specific order. In addition, some theorists do not accept that there are as many, or few as, five needs.

An alternative theory has been proposed by Clayton Alderfer (1969). His ERG theory, specifies only three needs:

1. *Existence Needs* (correspond to Maslow's Physiological Needs)
2. *Relatedness Needs* (correspond to Maslow's Social Needs)
3. *Growth Needs* (correspond to Maslow's Self-Actualization and Esteem needs)

It might be said that Alderfer's ERG theory and Maslow's Need theory are similar, despite differing classifications of needs. However, there is one major difference between the two theories. While activation of needs follows a strict hierarchical sequence in Maslow's schema, ERG theory specifies that needs are not necessarily activated in a specific order (Baron, 1986).

It is evident that communication is primary to the satisfaction each of the identified human needs, whether they are as "concrete" as the need to obtain food via a trip to the grocery store, or as "abstract" as the achievement of self-actualization via enrollment in an institution of higher education.

The Johari Window

One of the most interesting models of interpersonal communication, the Johari Window, was developed by two psychologists, Joseph Luft and Harry Ingham (Luft, 1969). The Johari Window is traditionally included in introductory communication and psychology courses to illustrate concepts of self-awareness and self-disclosure. It is included in this particular chapter to illustrate the multiple realities that are constructed by communication with others and ourselves.

	KNOWN TO SELF	NOT KNOWN TO SELF
KNOWN TO OTHERS	Open 1	Blind 2
NOT KNOWN TO OTHERS	Hidden 3	Unknown 4

Figure 1   An example of a Johari window for a shy, withdrawn individual.

The Johari Window consists of four quadrants, as seen in Figure 1. The open quadrant represents information about a person that is available both to themselves and to others. For example, both you and I know that you, a reader of this textbook, are likely to be a student, or are somehow interested in the conduct of communication studies.

The blind quadrant includes information that someone knows about another person, but they themselves do not know. Information of this sort might be that a person is unaware they have a terrible singing voice, or that they tell bad jokes.

The hidden quadrant consists of knowledge that we have about ourselves, but do not disclose to most others, such as our medical conditions, sexual history, and salary.

The unknown quadrant contains information about a person that not known by others nor by the person. This would include undiagnosed medical or psychological conditions, unknown skills or abilities, and one's ultimate requirements to achieve self-actualization.

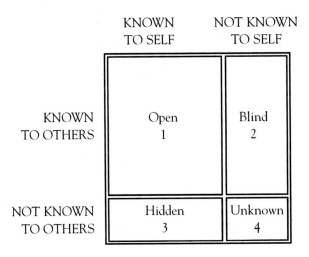

Figure 2   An improved Johari window.

The Johari Window is thus composed of four sometimes conflicting, sometimes congruent personal realities. The Johari Window is not, however, a static entity. Communication with ourselves and with others can change the relative relationships of the four windows, as shown in Figure 2, an improved Johari Window (Tubbs and Moss, 1994). In this altered version of the window, the individual has achieved greater self-knowledge. More about this person is known to others than in the first Johari Window. However, it could be argued that increasing the open quadrant is not always desirable, especially if there are things about ourselves that would be damaging for others to know. Moreover, self-awareness of some types of knowledge might be upsetting and counterproductive.

Through the communication of self-disclosure, we create new realities for ourselves and for others. In our society, there are implicit rules for self-disclosure, such as:

Rule: Self-disclosure should occur in a gradual manner, with more intimacy occurring as the relationship progresses.

Rule: Self-disclosure, unless it is with a trusted therapist, should occur in a reciprocal fashion between two people.

Rule: Self-disclosure about how one feels about the other should not be delivered in a cruel or a damaging fashion.

Rule: Self-disclosure should not be engaged in if it places one in a vulnerable or unsafe position.

Rule: Disclosure about another's unknown quadrant should occur in the spirit of ethical communication.

Thus, the construct of the Johari window shows how we may project multiple identities or realities, and that these might differ depending upon the intended audience.

Impression Management and Identity Negotiation

Erving Goffman, in his 1959 classic book, *The Presentation of Self in Everyday Life*, likens our everyday communication to dramaturgy, or "performances" in which we practice impression management and control the images that others receive about us. Relating this to the Johari Window model, we manipulate the nature and size of our *open quadrant*. In fact, the size and information contained in the open quadrant will vary according to our audience, and what we feel is important for them to know about us. When, for example, we wish for others to become aware of previously unknown facts about us, Goffman believes that we engage in *dramatic realization*. This is accomplished by highlighting selected information, (e.g., "I really like to ski"), thus changing the way others view us. Charles Horton Cooley, (1994) makes the point that while children and adults both engage in *impression formation*, the adult attempts to do so less directly:

"A child obviously and simply, at first, does things for effect. Later there is an endeavor to suppress the appearance of doing so: affection, indifference, contempt, etc., are simulated to hide the real wish to affect the self-image. It is perceived that an obvious seeking after good opinion is weak and disagreeable."

Whether we are children or adults, our personal realities evolve as a result of our communication with others. In fact, our behavior and status in a communicative encounter is most often arrived at as a result of subtle negotiation. For example, when first meeting someone, mutually arrived at decisions are made as to how the interaction will progress. Will the interaction be social, or business-like? Will one communicative partner attempt to diminish the status of another? Who is allowed to interrupt the other? *Identity negotiation* is the process by which two people negotiate and agree upon the identities that each will assume in an interaction. Though this may be done either implicitly or explicitly, skilled communicators attempt to do so in an understanding, non-confrontational way.

When the two actors in a communicative scene finally arrive at this understanding, it can be said that they have reached a *working consensus*. Kollock and O'Brien (1994) point out that though this public agreement may not reflect the private reality as to how communicators really feel about each other, it is the public reality that guides us in our interactions. Thus, though we may personally dislike a particular coworker, we allow our working consensus to guide our interactions.

Feeling Management

Previously, we examined how members of a society must learn a *hidden curriculum*, a concept introduced by Gerbner (1974) to designate the very broad body of information that humans must learn about behaving in their culture. Gerbner defines it as "a lesson plan that no one teaches, but everyone learns" (p. 476). The hidden curriculum includes both implicit and explicit communication rules. These suggest how we should behave in a variety of communication contexts, (e.g., how we should relate to others in our family; how we should behave during a classroom lecture). The curriculum is considered to be "hidden" because this immense and ever-changing body of knowledge is not contained within any one available format. Instead, the content is transmitted to the children and adults of our culture via verbal, non-verbal and paralinguistic communication, and emerges over their lifetimes.

Could it be that the hidden curriculum also includes lessons as to how we should *feel* about ourselves, others, events, and institutions? Research by Simon and colleagues (1994) suggests that societal communication also guides the development of feeling norms. These authors engaged in biweekly observations and conducted in-depth interviews of a total of ten peer groups in sixth, seventh, and eighth grade—primarily white females in a middle school cafeteria setting. The researchers discovered that heterosexual adolescent girls hold norms that dictate whether (or not) to love, whom to love, and the extent to which one should love. The norms that emerged are as follows:

Norm 1:   Romantic relationships should be important, but not everything in life.

Norm 2:   One should have romantic feelings only for someone of the opposite sex.

Norm 3:   One should not have romantic feelings for a boy who is already attached.

Norm 4:   One should have romantic feelings for only one boy at a time.

Norm 5:   One should always be in love.

Simon and colleagues also described a variety of discourse strategies used by adolescent girls to communicate the norms to their friends, and then, to reinforce the norms. Common discourse strategies included humor (i.e., joking and teasing), gossip and confrontation.

The process of emotional or affective socialization described by Simon and colleagues (1992) begins much before adolescence, even in infancy, as babies are encouraged to kiss the baby doll and to "make nice" to the family pet, whereas their older siblings are told that they must "love" the new intruder into their family unit.

Acting Techniques

A substantial part of our daily communication incorporates acting. Hochschild (1994) describes this as follows:

> "We all do a certain amount of acting. We may act in two ways. In the first way, we try to change how we outwardly appear. As it is for the people observed by Erving Goffman, the action is in the body language, the put-on sneer, the posed shrug, the controlled sigh. This is *surface acting*. The other way is *deep acting*. Here, display is a natural result of working on feeling; the actor does not try to seem happy or sad but rather expresses spontaneously, as the Russian director Constantin Stanislavski urged, a *real feeling* that has been self-induced."

> "In our daily lives, offstage as it were, we also develop feeling for the parts we play; and along with the workday props of the kitchen table, or office restroom mirror, we also use deep acting, emotion memory, and the sense of 'as if this were true' in the course of trying to feel what we sense we ought to feel or want."

Hochschild notes that acting also occurs in institutions:

> "something more operates when institutions are involved, for within institutions various elements of acting are taken away from the individual and replaced by institutional mechanisms. The locus of acting, of *emotion management*, moves up to the level of the institution."

He further explains:

> "Officials in institutions believe they have done things right when they have established illusions that foster the desired feelings in workers, when they have placed parameters around a worker's emotion memories."

Institutions use various means to accomplish what Hochschild suggests. They require adherence to a policies and procedures manual, and the company's mission statement. Quality assurance programs, and corporate-wide training promotes the treatment of customers and fellow employees alike as "valued customers." As examples, in the early 1990s, the Pontiac Division of General Motors, Inc. trained employees at every level of the organization to work together to satisfy the customer with enthusiasm (note the prescribed emotional state). Gap Inc.'s website (2007) states that "the work is fun," "we work hard," and "we thrive on a spirit of exploration, creativity, excellence, and teamwork in everything we do." Starbucks (2007) even extends the desired feeling management to its customers, striving to "develop enthusiastically satisfied customers all of the time."

Institutions that engage in military training, medical education, legal education and clinical psychological training may also be quite explicit in "directing" their employees' emotional management. Such training often exposes employees to the finer points of deep and surface acting as it applies to their future professional conduct.

Performance Disruptions

Try as we may to produce a communication performance that will project the desired impression to others, it is inevitable that disruptions will occur. Goffman (1995) describes various types of disruptions. These include "unmeant gestures, inopportune intrusions, and faux pas," that might result in anxiety or embarrassment.

Performance disruptions often occur in the presence of others and disrupt the situation, or "scene" within which one acts. Imagine a wedding where a jealous ex-lover walks into the chapel, witnesses the object of his affections in the process of marrying someone else, and brings the ceremony to a halt. This disruption would undoubtedly threaten the harmony of the situation and even go so far as to disrupt the "polite consensus" of a group. The wedding crasher could necessitate the creation a new "scene," in which the original team (i.e., the guests at the party) splits into two or more teams (i.e., the brides, the grooms, and the intruder's friends), each with a different interpretation of the disruption. We commonly hear reference to this in statements like, "what a scene!" or, "you really created quite a scene today!"

Performers and audiences alike protect the definition of the situation in the face of a potential or actual performance disruption. Goffman describes three key defensive attributes and practices:

Dramaturgical Loyalty

Dramaturgical loyalty operates when members of a team (e.g., a family) protect the secrets of the team between communication "performances." Goffman cites the examples of parents not discussing gossip in front of their children, lest the children betray the confidence to their friends.

In eighteenth century England, the "dumb-waiter," was introduced. This was a large, multi-tiered table upon which food was placed so that guests could serve themselves without the assistance of servants. The dumb-waiter functioned as a *dramaturgical device* in that its presence helped to keep team secrets from employees.

Dramaturgical loyalty can be compromised if performers form excessively close ties with the audience, as in the case of a department store clerk who tells key customers the dates of upcoming sales that have not yet been publicized. Some retail establishments avoid these problems by routinely altering the clerks' work schedule and locations so they do not become too well-acquainted with "the consumer audience." Another technique is to make a concerted effort to develop high-group team solidarity so that "performers" will not seek an overly-familiar relationship with the audience. This is frequently legislated within organizations, such that supervisors are not allowed to become romantically involved with the individuals they supervise.

Dramaturgical Discipline

The exercise of dramaturgical discipline requires that team members focus on their role in the team's performance, but that they do not become so engrossed with their own performance that they fail to recognize when they must counteract the effects of potential disruptions. Parents with young children in the car on a long trip, for example, must be able to continue giving directions and driving the car safely, while ensuring that the children maintain decorum in the back seat.

The "disciplined performer" also knows their part and performs without committing faux pas or mistakes. They will be able to carry on despite mistakes made by other members of the team, and to immediately compensate for the mistakes to make them seem as if they were just be "part of the act." The disciplined performer will accomplish all of this without the actor calling undue attention to the mistake or their assistance.

Dramaturgical Circumspection

Actors must engage in dramaturgical circumspection. This means that they need to consciously and analytically consider how best to "stage the show." This might involve strategic planning of their appearance as well as the timing, structure and content of a communication (e.g., "I'll ask Dad for the car keys after dinner when he's relaxed. I'll start off by telling him about my good grades this semester.").

Another result of dramaturgical circumspection may result in strategic selection of the audience, as in the case of jury selection.

Both audiences and performers employ protective practices so that the performance is not disrupted. The exercise of tact is an important protective mechanism, (e.g., clearing your throat to alert others to your presence). Sometimes staying away from a scene, (e.g., not attending a party where your presence would be awkward for others), or advising others to do so can also protect the performance.

When performance disruptions do occur, it is interesting to consider the nature of the disruption, and the responses of both the actor and the audience. Often, remedial strategies are employed to lessen the effect of an embarrassing incident. These might include: ignoring the disruption, taking action to "fix" the problem, use of humor, offering an apology, verbally justifying the disruption, expressing empathy to the embarrassed party or even fleeing the scene.

The Reality of Our Identity

Who am I? How do I view myself? Who are you? Neurologist Oliver Sacks (1994) approaches these questions through the eyes of a patient with severe Korsakov's amnesia. The patient is not only unable to remember others, but cannot recall his own identity and history. Sacks points out that it is particularly disabling since each of us possesses a life history, a series of narratives, and that:

> "If we wish to know about a man, we must ask, 'what is his life story—his real, inmost story?'—for each of us is a single narrative, which is constructed, continually, unconsciously, by, through and in us—through our perceptions, our feelings, our thoughts, our actions; and, not in the least, our discourse, our spoken narrations. Biologically, physiologically we are not so different from each other; historically, as narratives—we are each of us unique."

Imagine the confusion created by amnesia, or the disruption in personal identity caused by the need for an informant in the United States Witness Protection Program to shed a lifelong identity. Such scenarios would be devastating to one's sense of personal identity because the series of narratives that we tell ourselves, and others that are the keys to the reality of our identity, are either irretrievable or must be refabricated.

Gender Identity

Before the birth of a baby, it is not uncommon for the parents to learn the sex of the infant. Indeed, some engage in practices that ensure the offspring's sex will match their preference. In many cases, the selected name, color of the baby clothes, and the hue of the nursery's walls reflect this knowledge.

We now ask you to read Heritage's (1984) chapter (largely based upon the work of Garfinkel), which presents a case study that illuminates how gender is constructed via our communication with self and others. The case describes 'Agnes'—a pseudonym for a male born with typically appearing male genitals. Until age 17, Agnes presented himself as a boy. However, by age 19, Agnes appeared "convincingly female," (p. 180) to all but her parents, relatives, medical staff, and ultimately, her boyfriend. Agnes sought and underwent surgery to change her sex from male to female. The reading describes how Agnes attempted to construct a new gender identity, and how much of this was achieved via her verbal and non-verbal communication.

Summary

In this chapter, we have addressed the construction of "the self," and how our individual identities are influenced by larger physical environment, our biology, culture, family, and peers. Each of these elements, and "the self," interact across the life span, from birth to death.

It equally important in this final chapter to reflect upon the role of individual choice and intent. Do you believe that others, including the larger culture, dictate your roles and success (external locus of control) or, that you can proactively determine your own destiny (internal locus of control)? Do you fulfill others' prophecies as to how you will or will not succeed—or proactively create your own visions and maps to success? Does spirituality play a role in your communication with self and others?

Ultimately, it is communication within the self (intrapersonal communication) that most influences our being. We hope that this book will have had some small part in elucidating that process, and wish you, our reader, much joy and future success in that journey.

Maintaining Institutional Realities

John Heritage

For Kant the moral order 'within' was an awesome mystery; for sociologists the moral order 'without' is a technical mystery. A society's members encounter and know the moral order as perceivedly normal courses of action—familiar scenes of everyday affairs, the world of daily life known in common with others and with others taken for granted.

Garfinkel, *Studies in Ethnomethodology*

In the preceding chapters, we began to examine the consequences of viewing social action as fundamentally organized with respect to its reflexivity and accountability. A major finding of that examination was that the intersubjective intelligibility of actions ultimately rests on a symmetry between the production of actions on the one hand and their recognition on the other. This symmetry is one of *method* or *procedure* and Garfinkel forcefully recommends it when he proposes that

> the activities whereby members produce and manage settings of ordinary everyday affairs are identical with members' procedures for making those settings 'accountable.' (Garfinkel, 1967a: 1)

As we have seen, this symmetry of method is both assumed and achieved *by the actors* in settings of ordinary social activity. Its *assumption* permits actors to design their actions in relation to their circumstances so as to permit others, by methodically taking account of the circumstances, to recognize the action for what it is. The symmetry is also *achieved* and hence it is contingent. For the production and recognition of actions is dependent upon the parties supplying, and trusting one another to supply, an array of unstated assumptions so as to establish the recognizable sense of an action. A final conclusion to recall is that the production of an action will always reflexively redetermine (i.e. maintain, elaborate or alter) the circumstances in which it occurs.

We are now in a position to add a further 'layer' to the analysis of action—the layer of social institutions. For although we have deliberately ignored the fact until now, it will be obvious that, in maintaining, elaborating or transforming their circumstances by their actions, the actors are also simultaneously reproducing, developing or modifying the institutional realities which envelop those actions. In the present chapter, we shall be concerned with the phenomenon of institutional reality maintenance under a variety of circumstances ranging from overwhelming normative consensus to chronic structured conflict. The four case studies discussed in this chapter all focus on relatively diffuse institutional phenomena. The more recent 'studies of work' undertaken by Garfinkel and his students (Garfinkel, forthcoming) deal with a range of more concrete cases. We begin with Garfinkel's famous discussion of 'Agnes' (Garfinkel, 1967e).

Case 1: Agnes and the Institution of Gender

'Agnes' is the pseudonym of a patient who was referred to the Department of Psychiatry at the University of California at Los Angeles (UCLA) in 1958. She was born a boy with normal appearing male genitals, certified and named appropriately and, until the age of 17, was generally recognized to be a boy (ibid. 120). Nonetheless, by the time she presented herself at UCLA at the age of 19,

> Agnes's appearance was convincingly female. She was tall, slim, with a very female shape. Her measurements were 38–25–38. She had long, fine dark-blond hair, a young face with pretty features, a peaches-and-cream complexion, no facial hair, subtly plucked eyebrows, and no make-up except for lipstick . . . Her usual manner of dress did not distinguish her from a typical girl of her age or class. There was nothing garish or exhibitionistic in her attire, nor was there any hint of poor taste or that she was ill at ease in her clothing . . . Her manner was appropriately feminine with a slight awkwardness that is typical of middle adolescence. (ibid. 119)

Agnes's purpose in presenting herself at UCLA was to obtain a sex-change operation and, prior to this, she was examined by a number of specialists. The latter were interested in a range of her characteristics, including her unique endocrinological configuration (Schwabe et al., 1962), her psychological make-up, her gender identity, the causes of her desire to be made anatomically female and her psychiatric management (Stoller, Garfinkel and Rosen, 1960; 1962; Stoller, 1968; 1975). Garfinkel, however, used her case as an occasion to focus on the ways in which sexual identity is produced and managed as a 'seen but unnoticed,' but nonetheless institutionalized, feature of ordinary social interactions and institutional workings. He conducted the investigation with the use of tape-recorded conversations with Agnes in which the latter discussed her biography and prospects, triumphs and disasters and the hopes and fears associated with her self-imposed task of 'passing' for a woman. The result of this investigation was a profound analysis of gender considered as a produced institutional fact.

This last observation requires some additional comment. In studies of gender, it has been traditional to treat the conventional categories 'male' and 'female' as starting points from which to portray the different outlooks, life chances and activities of the sexes in relation to social structure. Despite their various differences, this analytic standpoint unites writings as divergent as Parsons's classic essays on sex roles and the family (Parsons, 1940; 1942; 1943; 1954), Engels's (1968) *The Origin of the Family, Private Property and the State* and more recent feminist writings (e.g. Kuhn and Wolpe, 1978). In these studies, sexual status is treated as a 'social fact' in a fully Durkheimian sense as an 'external and constraining' phenomenon. Garfinkel, by contrast, wanted to treat sexual status as a produced and reproduced fact. It is the constitution and reproduction of the ordinary facts of gender which is the object of inquiry. The reproduced differentiation of culturally specific 'males' and 'females' is thus the terminus of his investigation rather than its starting point. This differentiation is an overwhelming fact of social structure. Its reproduction, he proposes, is the outcome of a mass of indiscernible, yet familiar, socially organized practices. It was these latter which, in 1958, Garfinkel sought to disclose with the assistance of Agnes—a person whose determination to achieve 'femininity' and whose insight into its component features greatly helped Garfinkel to distance himself from the familiar phenomena of gender and to come to view them as 'anthropologically strange.'

In reading Garfinkel's account of Agnes, it is useful to bear in mind that she was, in effect, presented with two separate, but overlapping, problems in managing her claims to be female. First, she had the problem of dealing with those who took her at 'face value' and knew nothing of her potentially discrediting male genitalia and previously masculine biography. With these persons—the majority of her associates—Agnes was preoccupied with generating and living within a female identity which was above suspicion. Second, Agnes, was compelled to deal with a range of persons—her parents and relatives, the medical and psychiatric staff at UCLA and, ultimately, her boyfriend Bill—who knew about these incongruous aspects of her anatomy and biography. With this second group of persons, Agnes's task became one of insisting that, despite the incongruities, she was 'essentially' and 'all along and in the first place' a female. This task, as we shall see, was necessitated as part of her long-term campaign to secure the sex-change operation as a moral right.

Agnes: Sexual Status as a Methodic Production

As part of her task of maintaining herself as a bona fide female, Agnes—like other 'intersexed' persons—had become a sensitive ethnographer of gender. Continually anxious about the successful management of her self-presentation as a woman, she had indeed become acutely aware of the ways in which sexual status can have implications for the conduct of ordinary social activities. The range and scope of these implications are so great and so easily overlooked (ibid. 118) that it is worth beginning with an initial list of some of their aspects.

There are, first of all, the self-evident problems of achieving convincingly female dress, make-up, grooming and accoutrements as an initial precondition of being taken for female. To judge from Garfinkel's description, Agnes had largely overcome these problems before she presented herself at UCLA for the first time. Then there are the problems of managing appropriately feminine comportment—the behavioural manifestations of femininity: 'sitting like a woman,' 'walking like a woman,' 'talking like a woman' and so on. These behaviours are minutely accountable. For example, Agnes recollected that her brother had complained about her carrying her books to school like a girl and had 'demonstrated to her and insisted that she carry them like a boy' (ibid. 152). While, once again, Agnes had clearly mastered fundamental aspects of female behavioural comportment by the time she arrived at UCLA, the tasks of 'talking like a woman' continued to prove troublesome. For, it turned out, to talk like a woman required a reservoir of biographical experiences and 'knowhow'—all of which had to have been experienced and appreciated in detail from the point of view of a girl. This reservoir of detailed experiences was necessary, first, to produce appropriately feminine talk and, secondly and more generally, to serve as an accumulating series of precedents with which to manage current situations (ibid. 130–1). In this context, Agnes repeatedly complained of her lack of an appropriate biography. After the change to living as a female, but before her operation, Agnes began to exchange 'gossip, and analyses of men, parties, and dating postmortems' with roommates and wider circles of girlfriends (ibid. 147). Here, Garfinkel comments, 'two years of arduous female activities furnished for her a fascinating input of new experiences' which she used as resources to construct and reconstruct her own biography (ibid. 178). In what follows, we will briefly consider some aspects of Agnes's management of her sexual identity with those who did not know her secrets and with those who did.

Managing with Those Who Were Ignorant

In dealing with those who knew nothing of her 'male' anatomy and biography, Agnes's central preoccupation was to avoid the disclosure of her secrets.

> In instance after instance the situation to be managed can be described in general as one in which the attainment of commonplace goals and attendant satisfactions involved with it a risk of exposure . . . Her characteristic situation in passing was one in which she had to be prepared to choose, and frequently chose, between securing the feminine identity and accomplishing *ordinary* goals . . . Security was to be protected first. The common satisfactions were to be obtained only if the prior conditions of the secured identity could be satisfied. Risks in this direction entailed the sacrifice of the other satisfactions. (ibid. 139–40)

The nature and overriding extent of Agnes's sacrifices of ordinary satisfactions can be glossed by noting that, although she could drive, Agnes did not own a car because she feared the exposure of her secret while unconscious from an accident (ibid. 141).

In order to protect her identity, Agnes engaged in extensive pre-planning and rehearsal of ordinary activities so as to minimize the risk of enforced exposure. In 'open' or 'unplannable' situations she adopted a range of procedures, which Garfinkel refers to as acting as a 'secret apprentice' and 'anticipatory following,' through which she remained inconspicuous while acquiring important feminine 'knowhow.' In all situations, Agnes was concerned not only with managing to present herself as an accountable (i.e. 'observable-reportable') female, but also with the accountability of her management strategies themselves.

Thus, in pre-planning a medical examination for a job, Agnes determined in advance that under no circumstances would she permit the examination to proceed lower than her abdomen. At the same time, she formulated the reasonable grounds ('modesty') in terms of which her refusal, if necessary, would be made accountable. These same grounds provided the basis for a 'no nudity' rule which Agnes and a girlfriend adopted in their shared apartment. Or again, in visiting the beach,

> She would go along with the crowd, reciprocating their enthusiasm for bathing, if or until it was clear that a bathroom or the bedroom of a private home would be available in which to change to her bathing suit. Public baths and automobiles were to be avoided. If the necessary facilities were not available excuses were easy to make. As she pointed out, one is permitted not to be 'in the mood' to go bathing, though to like very much to sit on the beach. (ibid)

Here then, as in the other cases, there was a concern to make contingent on-the-spot decisions necessary for securing the female identity together with a concern for the secondary accountability of the management devices themselves.

A similar duality is evident in less structured contexts. In the context of gossip exchanges, post-mortems on social events or commentaries on the behaviour of other women, Agnes tended to play a passive role permitting the talk to instruct her as to proper conduct. Here, as Garfinkel comments, 'not only did she adopt the pose of passive acceptance of instructions, but she learned as well the value of passive acceptance as a desirable feminine character trait' (ibid, 147). Or again,

> Another common set of occasions arose when she engaged in friendly conversation without having biographical or group affiliation data to swap off with her conversational partner. As Agnes said, 'Can you imagine all the blank years I have to fill in? Sixteen or seventeen years of my life that I have to make up for. I have to be careful of the things that I say, just natural things that could slip out . . . I just never say anything at all about my past that in any way would make a person ask what my

past life was like. I say general things. I don't say anything that could be miscon-strued.' Agnes said that with men she was able to pass as an interesting conversa-tionalist by encouraging her male partners to talk about themselves. Women partners, she said, explained the general and indefinite character of her biographi-cal remarks, which she delivered with a friendly manner, by a combination of her niceness and modesty. 'They probably figure that I just don't like to talk about myself.' (ibid. 148)

In these remarks, once again, we find the 'dual accountability' constraints to which Agnes ori-ented. They surface too in other aspects of her 'secret apprenticeship.' For example, in permitting her boyfriend's mother to teach her to cook Dutch national dishes, Agnes simultaneously learned how to cook, *tout court*. This learning, secretly accomplished, was done under the accountable aus-pices of 'learning to cook Dutch-style.'

In reviewing Agnes's practices for passing with the ignorant, Garfinkel emphasizes the excep-tional precision and detail of her observation of the particulars of ordinary social arrangements. He points to the fact that she was compelled to protect her identity across ranges of contingencies which could not be known in advance and 'in situations known with the most faltering knowl-edge, having marked uncertainties about the rules of practice' (ibid. 136). In an eloquent descrip-tion of Agnes's predicament, Garfinkel summarizes it as follows:

In the conduct of her everyday affairs she had to choose among alternative courses of action even though the goal that she was trying to achieve was most frequently not clear to her prior to her having to take the actions whereby some goal might in the end have been realized. Nor had she any assurances of what the consequences of the choice might be prior to or apart from her having to deal with them. Nor were there clear rules that she could consult to decide the wisdom of the choice before the choice had to be exercised. For Agnes, stable routines of everyday life were 'disengageable' attainments assured by unremitting, momentary, situated courses of improvisation. Throughout these was the inhabiting presence of talk, so that however the action turned out, poorly or well, she would have been required to 'explain' herself, to have furnished 'good reasons' for having acted as she did. (ibid. 184)

The nature of Agnes's task in managing, constructing and reconstructing her social identity is thus perhaps well caught by the famous Neurath-Quine metaphor of being compelled to build the boat while already being out on the ocean. It was, unavoidably, a bootstrapping operation.

Above all, Garfinkel emphasizes, Agnes encountered scarcely any situations which could be treated as 'time out' from the work of passing. Always 'on parade,' Agnes was compelled at all times to secure her female identity 'by the acquisition and use of skills and capacities, the efficacious dis-play of female appearances and performances and the mobilization of appropriate feelings and pur-poses' (ibid. 134). In this context,

the work and socially structured occasions of sexual passing were obstinately unyielding to (her) attempts to routinize the grounds of daily activities. This obsti-nacy points to the omnirelevance of sexual statuses to affairs of daily life as an invariant but unnoticed background in the texture of relevances that comprise the changing actual scenes of everyday life. (ibid. 118)

These problems and relevancies extended to the tasks of passing with those who, in part at least (see ibid. 285–8), knew of her secrets and it is to these latter that we now turn.

Managing with Those Who Knew

As we have seen, Agnes's purpose in coming to UCLA was to secure a sex-change operation. This operation was the central preoccupation of her life and, as time progressed, it also became critical for the continuation of the relationship with her boyfriend which she treated as a major emblem of her femininity. In order to obtain this operation, Agnes had to undergo a wide variety of tests—anatomical, physiological, psychological and psychiatric—the results of which would form the basis on which the decision to operate or not would be made. In this context, Agnes's task became one of insisting that she had a right to the operation regardless of the results of the technical tests by doctors and others. She treated this right as a *moral* right and advanced it on the basis of what she urged as the *natural facts* of her femininity. Her task then, in a nutshell, was to insist that she was 'all along and in the first place' a *natural* female despite the incongruous anatomical, physiological, psychological and biological facts which might be amassed against the claim, and, on this basis, to urge the surgeons to remedy her condition in the direction 'intended by nature.'

It is clear, especially with the advantage of hindsight, that the task of presenting herself to those who knew her secrets as a 'natural-female-despite-the-incongruities' presented Agnes with management problems every bit as serious as those she encountered in presenting herself as a normal female to those who did not know them.

In her dealings with the specialists, Agnes systematically emphasized all aspects of her appearance, behaviour, motivation, biography and anatomy which could be held to be bona fide 'female' in character. Simultaneously, she down-graded every aspect which could be treated as evidence of her masculinity. Thus, in addition to her very feminine physical appearance described above, Agnes presented herself as 'ultra-female' both in her descriptions of her conduct and motivation in real world situations and in her actual conversations with the medical and psychiatric specialists who, indeed, 'came to refer to her presentation of the 120 percent female' (ibid. 129). Throughout

> Agnes was the coy, sexually innocent, fun-loving, passive, receptive, 'young thing'. . . . As a kind of dialectical counterpart to the 120 per cent female Agnes portrayed her boyfriend as a 120 per cent male who, she said, when we first started to talk, and repeated through eight stressful weeks following the operation when post-operative complications had subsided and the recalcitrant vagina was finally turning out to be the thing the physicians had promised, 'wouldn't have been interested in me at all if I was abnormal.' (ibid.)

Closely aligned with this self-presentation was Agnes's account of her biography in which all 'evidences of a male upbringing were rigorously suppressed':

> The child Agnes of Agnes's accounts did not like to play rough games like baseball; her *'biggest'* problem was having to play boys' games; Agnes was more or less considered a sissy; Agnes was always the littlest one; Agnes played with dolls and cooked mud patty cakes for her brother; Agnes helped her mother with the household duties; Agnes doesn't remember what kinds of gifts she received from her father when she was a child. (ibid. 128–9)

Similarly, evidences of male sexual feelings were never avowed:

> The penis of Agnes's accounts had never been erect; she was never curious about it; it was never scrutinized by her or by others; it never entered into games with other children; it never moved 'voluntarily'; it was never a source of pleasurable feelings. (ibid.)

Related to this suppression of Agnes's male biography and her non-acknowledgement of male sexual feelings was her attitude to her present anatomical state. Here Agnes downgraded her incongruous anatomical features within a *moral* idiom while upgrading those anatomical features which supported her claims to be female in a *naturalistic* way. Thus Agnes's penis 'had always been an accidental appendage stuck on by a cruel trick of fate' (ibid.). While,

> with genitals ruled out as essential signs of her femininity, and needing essential and natural signs of female sexuality, she counted instead the life-long desire to be female and her prominent breasts. . . . Before all she counted her breasts as essential insignia. On several occasions in our conversations she expressed the relief and joy she felt when she noticed at the age of twelve that her breasts were starying to develop. (ibid. 13.1–2)

In this way, Agnes presented both her physical development and her female psychological make-up as corresponding elements of a natural feminine development. This insistence on a naturalistic orientation to her female insignia would cost her dear after the operation was finally performed:

> Thus, after the operation she was a female with a 'man-made' vagina. In her anxious words, 'Nothing that is made by man can ever be as good as something that nature makes.' She and her boyfriend were agreed on this. In fact, her boyfriend who, in her accounts of him, prided himself as a harsh realist, insisted on this and taught it to her to her dismayed agreement. (ibid. 134)

It is significant, in this context, that Agnes made her final disclosures concerning the origins of her condition only after a further five years of successful life as a woman and after a leading urologist had told her 'unequivocally that her genitalia were quite beyond suspicion' (ibid. 286–7).

Agnes's successful 'feminization' of her biography was not without its lacunae. Reviewing the data obtained by all the researchers on her case, it was found that, despite their best efforts, no data were available about

> (1) the possibility of an exogenous source of hormones; (2) the nature and extent of collaboration that occurred between Agnes and her mother and other persons; (3) any usable evidence let alone any detailed findings dealing with her male feelings and her male biography; (4) what her penis had been used for besides urination; (5) how she sexually satisfied herself and others and most particularly her boyfriend both before and after the disclosure; (6) the nature of any homosexual feelings, fears, thoughts and activities; (7) her feelings about herself as a 'phony female.' (ibid. 163)

In presenting herself as a natural female, Agnes was concerned to avoid saying or doing anything which might permit others to include her within a category of persons—homosexuals or transvestites—who could be held to be essentially masculine. She had no interest in meeting 'other trans-sexuals' on the grounds of having nothing in common (ibid. 131). She insisted that she had always 'steered clear of boys that acted like sissies' (ibid.) and 'just as normals frequently will be at a loss to understand "why a person would do that," i.e. engage in homosexual activities or dress as a member of the opposite sex, so did Agnes display the same lack of "understanding" for such behaviour' (ibid.). Here, then, Agnes sought to avoid any contamination of her essential femininity which might arise from an interest in, or understanding of, or having something in common with persons whose essential identities could be held to be other than female. Her concern, once again, was to portray herself as an exclusively normal, natural female who was such 'without residue.' So scrupulous was this concern that she would not even permit verbal formulations of her desires and achievements in such terms as 'living or being treated *as a female.*' In these contexts she would insist 'not as a female, naturally' (ibid. 170).

Finally, it will be recalled that Agnes treated her own desire to live as a female as itself evidence of her natural sexual status. In this context, she portrayed these desires as fundamental, axiomatic and inexplicable and avoided any psychological or other form of explanation or them that would relativize their status. Instead, she appealed to their life-long biographical continuity as evidence for their naturalness. Thus,

> In common with normals, she treated her femininity as independent of the conditions of its occurrence and invariant to the vicissitudes of desires, agreements, random or wilful election, accident, considerations of advantage, available resources and opportunities . . . It remained the self-same thing in essence under all imaginable transformations of actual appearances, time, and circumstances. It withstood all exigencies. (ibid. 133–4)

This achievement of the objectivity, transcendence and naturalness of her femininity was critical for the advancement of Agnes's moral claim to the body which she felt she should have had all along. The nature of her claim, in turn, was sensitive to the character of sexual status as a 'natural-moral' institution, which we will now discuss.

Sexuality: A 'Natural-Moral' Institution

As indicated in the preceding chapters, one of Garfinkel's theoretical preoccupations is with the 'double-edged' character of the accountable objects, events and activities which are treated as existent within a society or collectivity. When he proposes that 'a society's members encounter and know the moral order as perceivedly normal courses of action' or, reversing the formulation, that the real-world features of a society are treated by its members as 'objective, institutionalized facts, i.e. moral facts,' he announces an interest in the fact that the ordinary members of a society treat its undoubted, objective features as both 'normal' and 'moral.' Social facts are treated both as 'factual,' 'natural' and 'regular' and as phenomena which the member is morally required to attend to, take into account and respect.

This interpenetration of the 'factual' and 'moral' aspects of social activities, Garfinkel proposes, is a core feature of the ways in which society members orient towards the world of everyday life:

> They refer to this world as the 'natural facts of life' which, for members, are through and through moral facts of life. For members not only are matters so about familiar scenes, but they are so because it is morally right or wrong that they are so. (ibid. 35)

In sum, the everyday world as an institutionalized and institutionally provided-for domain of accountably real objects, events and activities is, from the society member's point of view, a 'natural-moral' world.

Sexual status is not excluded from this characterization. On the contrary, it vividly illustrates Garfinkel's analysis of the mutual interpenetration of the 'natural' with the 'moral.' As Garfinkel pointedly puts it, if one examines sexual status from the point of view of those who can take their own normally sexed status for granted, then 'perceived environments of sexed persons are populated with natural males, natural females, and persons who stand in moral contrast with them, i.e. incompetent, criminal, sick and sinful' (ibid. 122). The evidence from Garfinkel's study of Agnes profoundly illustrates this phenomenon. It indicates that everyone—the 'man on the street,' Agnes's relatives, the physicians on the case and Agnes herself—treated sexual status as a matter of 'objective, institutionalized facts, i.e. moral facts' (ibid.). Let us briefly review each of their attitudes in turn.

Garfinkel begins by noting that the ordinary member of society finds it odd to claim that decisions about sexuality can be problematic.

> The normal finds it strange and difficult to lend credence to 'scientific' distributions of *both* male and female characteristics among persons, or a procedure for deciding sexuality which adds up lists of male and female characteristics and takes the excess as the criterion of the member's sex. (ibid. 123–4)

The normal, Garfinkel continues, finds these assertions strange because he (or she) cannot treat normal sexuality as a matter of technical niceties or of purely theoretical interest. Ordinary people are interested in normal sexual status as the legitimate grounds for initiating morally sanctionable and morally appropriate (i.e. accountable) courses of action. In this context, normal sexual status is treated as decided by reference to the 'sexual insignia' witnessed from birth onwards and 'decided by *nature*' (ibid.). These insignia subsequently form the accountable grounds for differentiated courses of treatment to their bearers. Decisions about sexual status cannot, if social life is to proceed smoothly, and need not await authoritative zoological or psychiatric determination.

The fact that this 'natural' distribution of sexual status is, simultaneously, a 'moral' distribution is revealed by ordinary reactions to persons who perceivedly deviate from the distribution. These reactions commonly take the form of moral retribution. The reactions of Agnes's family to her various changes illustrate this phenomenon and its vicissitudes. After her initial assumption of female status, Agnes reported, her cousin's attitude changed from one which was favourable to Agnes to one of strong disapproval. Other family members displayed 'open hostility' and 'consternation and severe disapproval' (ibid. 128). Thus, although philosophers have extensively criticized the 'naturalistic fallacy' (that is, reasoning from what is the case to what ought to be the case), Agnes's family members repeatedly employed this device to assert the grounds (Agnes's upbringing as a boy) on which she should mend her ways.

However, if the employment of the 'naturalistic fallacy' worked against Agnes before the operation, it worked in her favour afterwards when family members exhibited 'relieved acceptance and treatment of her as a "real female after all"' (ibid.). In this context, Garfinkel comments:

> . . . although the vagina was man-made it *was* a case of the real thing since it was what she was now seen to have been entitled to all along. Both the aunt and the mother were strongly impressed by the fact that the operation had been done at all

'in this country.' That the physicians at the UCLA Medical Centre by their actions reconstructed and validated Agnes's claim to her status as a natural female needs, of course, to be stressed. (ibid. 128)

Turning now to the physicians, it is again clear that, in making the decision to operate or not, they also sought a determination of Agnes's sexual status and thus similarly employed an 'is-to-ought' line of reasoning to support their decision. This use of what Agnes 'naturally was' as grounds to support the line of treatment decided upon is vividly displayed in Stoller's account of Agnes's case (1968: 133–9). In that part of his account reproduced by Garfinkel (1967: 286–7), Stoller goes to considerable lengths to show the grounds on which he had determined that Agnes did not desire the operation as a matter of wilful election and, in particular, that her condition was not the product of ingesting female hormones (estrogens). He concludes the discussion by accounting for the decision to operate as follows: 'Not being considered a transsexual, her genitalia were surgically transformed so that she now had the penis and testes removed and an artificial vagina constructed from the skin of the penis' (ibid. 286). The critical phrase in this passage is the first: 'not being considered a transsexual.' It expresses the belief of Stoller and his colleagues that Agnes was 'fundamentally' female and did not simply desire to be female as a matter of deliberate choice. The phrase indicates that, despite the technical expertise of Stoller and his colleagues, the fundamental grounds in terms of which he presented their decision to an audience of medical professionals—were the same 'natural-moral' grounds which were invoked as the basis of their treatments of Agnes by all of her 'significant others.'

Thus in her dealings with her entire world of associates—family, friends, boyfriend, medical specialists, psychiatrists and Garfinkel himself—Agnes was presented with one consuming and overriding problem: the presentation of herself as someone who was naturally, all along and in the first place a bona fide female. The task had to be carried forward across every possible exigency, across every possible or actual state of knowledge possessed individually or severally by these others. And it had to be managed as a condition, not only of acquiring the 'sexual insignia' which would place her beyond suspicion with those who would meet her in the future, but also as a condition of convincing those who, fully knowing her past, could nonetheless be persuaded that she was, finally, what she had claimed to be all along. To meet these tasks, Agnes had only one asset: her skills as a 'practical methodologist' acquired as a student of normal sexuality:

> Her studies armed her with knowledge of how the organized features of ordinary settings are used by members as procedures for making appearances-of-sexuality-as-usual decidable as a matter of course. The scrutiny that she paid to appearances; her concerns for adequate motivation, relevance, evidence and demonstration; her sensitivity to devices of talk; her skill in detecting and managing 'tests' were attained as part of her mastery of trivial but necessary social tasks, to secure ordinary rights to live. Agnes was self-consciously equipped to teach normals how normals make sexuality happen in commonplace settings as an obvious, familiar, recognizable, natural, and serious matter of fact. Her specialty consisted of treating the 'natural facts of life' of socially recognized, socially managed sexuality as a managed production so as to be making these facts of life true, relevant, demonstrable, testable, countable, and available to inventory, cursory representation, anecdote, enumeration, or professional psychological assessment; in short, so as unavoidably in concert with others to be making these facts of life visible andreportable—accountable—for all practical purposes. (ibid. 180)

To summarize: Agnes subscribed to the 'natural-moral' order of sexual status within which normal sexual status is treated as a 'natural fact' while aberrations from the norm are treated as morally accountable. She subscribed to the objective reality of normal sexual status, despite her knowledge of its intricate management in daily life, both as a condition or maintaining her own identity and as a condition or achieving her desired objective—the operation. In this regard, as Garfinkel remarks, Agnes was no revolutionary (ibid. 177–8). Rather, in deploying her considerable methodological talents, Agnes sought in every way to conform with (and thus reproduce) the 'natural-moral' institutional order in which she so dearly wished to participate—as a normal, natural female.

The Objective Reality of Sexual Status and Its Maintenance

The variety or Agnes's management strategies and procedures, the resistance of ordinary social occasions to her attempts to routinize her daily life as a female and the fact that almost every occasion could somehow take on the features of a '"character and fitness" test' (ibid. 136) suggest that, in almost any occasion of social life, institutionalized features of sexual status are being produced and reproduced by 'normally sexed' males and females. Agnes's case further suggests that, while institutionalized sexuality is being produced and reproduced in this way as a supremely natural 'matter of fact,' its reproduction is simultaneously supported by a massive 'repair machinery' of moral accountability which is brought to bear in cases of discrepancy or deviance. To make these—potentially relativizing—observations on the socially organized character of accountable sexuality is not to deny its objectivity or facticity. On the contrary, it is to begin to gain some appreciation of what its objectivity and facticity consist of. As Garfinkel summarizes it:

> Agnes's methodological practices are our sources of authority for the finding, and recommended study policy, that normally sexed persons are cultural events in societies whose character as visible orders of practical activities consist of members' recognition and production practices. We learned from Agnes, who treated sexed persons as cultural events that members make happen, that members' practices alone produce the observable-tellable normal sexuality of persons, and do so only, entirely, exclusively in actual, singular, particular occasions through actual witnessed displays of common talk and conduct. . . . The inordinate stresses in Agnes's life were part and parcel of the concerted practices with normals, whereby the 'normal, natural female' as a moral thing to be and a moral way to feel and act was made to be happening, in demonstrable evidence, for all practical purposes. (ibid. 181)

This reference to the stresses which Agnes experienced, however, raises a core problem in Agnes's management of 'normality.' While normals can routinize their management and detection of displays of 'normally sexed' conduct so that the latter become a 'seen but unnoticed' background to the texture of commonplace events, Agnes's secrets were such that she could not lose sight of what, for normals, is so massively invisible:

> For Agnes, in contrast to normals, the commonplace recognition of normal sexuality as a 'case of the real thing' consisted of a serious, situated, and prevailing accomplishment . . . Her anguish and triumphs resided in the observability, which was particular to her and uncommunicable, of the steps whereby the society hides from its members its activities of organization and thus leads them to see its features as

determinate and independent objects. For Agnes the observably normally sexed person *consisted* of inexorable, organizationally located work that provided the way that such objects arise. (ibid. 182)

In this context, Garfinkel remarks that Agnes found psychological and sociological theories of the 'judgmental dope' variety flattering (ibid. 183–4). For these approaches 'theorized out of recognition' her excruciating perception of the work of managing sexual status. They thus 'naturalized' (in the way that ordinary society members 'naturalize') the sexual status which she longed to treat as just that—*natural*. Within these theories, sexual status is unproblematically treated as ascribed and internalized. Whereas what Agnes knew without doubt was that this 'ascribed' status is through and through *achieved* as the product of unnoticed, yet unremitting, work.

Reflecting for a moment on the Agnes study, it is surprising to realize the extent to which gender differentiation consists of a filigree of small-scale, socially organized behaviours which are unceasingly iterated. Together these—individually insignificant—behaviours interlock to constitute the great public institution of gender as a morally-organized-as-natural fact of life. This institution is comparatively resistant to change. To adapt Wittgenstein's famous analogy, the social construction of gender from a mass of individual social practices resembles the spinning of a thread in which fibre is spun on fibre. And, as Wittgenstein points out, 'the strength of the thread does not reside in the fact that some one fibre runs through its whole length, but in the overlapping of many fibres' (Wittgenstein, 1958: para. 67e). But if gender manifests itself as a density of minutiae, the latter are nonetheless stabilized both individually and collectively by the apparatus of moral accountability which we have repeatedly seen in action. In this context it is perhaps ironic that Freud could not trust the facts of culture sufficiently to base his account of the differentiation between the sexes on cultural mechanisms. For Freud, gender differentiation is ultimately based on a single slender thread: the psychological responses of males and females to the facts of anatomy. For Garfinkel, by contrast, the institution of gender appears as a densely woven fabric of morally accountable cultural practices which are throughout both accountable, and accountably treated, as natural.

Sources Cited

Alderfer, C. P. (1969). An empirical test of a new theory of human needs, *Organizational Behavior and Human Performance*, 4, 142–175.

American Heritage® Dictionary of the English Language, Fourth Edition. (2000). Boston, MA: Houghton Mifflin Company.

Arden, H. (1975). The pious ones. *National Geographic*, 276–298.

Aspy, D. N. (1975). "Empathy: Let's Get the Hell on with It," *The Counseling Psychologist*, 5, 10–14.

Baron R. A. (1986). *Behaviour in Organisations: Understanding and Managing the Human Side of Work.* Boston, MA: Allyn and Bacon.

Barker, L., Wahkler, K., Watson, K., & Kibler, R. (1991). *Groups in Process: An Introduction to Small Group Communication.* Englewood Cliffs, NJ: Prentice-Hall.

Bateson, G. (1972). *Steps to an Ecology of Mind.* New York: Chandler.

Bateson, G. (1978). The pattern that connects. *The Coevolution Quarterly*, 4–15.

Benne, K. D., & Sheats, P. H. (1948). Functional roles of group members. *Journal of Social Issues*, 4, 41–49.

Birdwhistell, R. (1970). *Kinesics in Context.* University of Pennsylvania Press, Philadelphia.

Bormann, E. G. (1990). Small Group Communication: Theory and Practice. New York: Holt, Rinehart and Winston.

Buber, M. (1965). *Between Man and Man.* New York: Macmillan Publishing Co.

Burgoon, M., & Ruffner, M. (1978). *Human Communication.* New York: Holt, Rinehart and Winston.

Burke, K. (1968). *Language as Symbolic Action.* Berkeley, CA: University of California Press.

Carroll, J. B. (ed.) [1956] (1997). *Language, Thought, and Reality: Selected Writings of Benjamin Lee Whorf.* Cambridge, MA: Technology Press of Massachusetts Institute of Technology.

Cato, J. (2005). Pay phones losing connection. *Pittsburgh Tribune-Review.* Retrieved June 12, 2007, from http://www.pittsburghlive.com/x/pittsburghtrib/s_386852.html

Cohn, E. R. (1996). *The Communication Process*, 6th ed. University of Pittsburgh External Studies Program, Center for Instructional Development and Distance Education.

Cooley, C. H. (1994). Looking-glass self. In Kollock, P., & O'Brien, J. (eds.) *The production of reality-essays and readings in social psychology* (pp. 266–268). Thousand Oaks, CA: Pine Forge Press.

Cullen, L. (11/16/06). WPTT 1360, Pittsburgh, PA.

Dance, F. (1970). "The 'concept' of communication. *Journal of Communication*, 20, 201–210.

Davis, F. (1989). Of maids' uniforms and blue jeans: The drama of status ambivalences in clothing and fashion. *Qualitative Sociology*, 12(4), 337–355.

DeVito, J. (1991). *Human Communication.* New York: Harper Collins.

Eakins, B. W., & Eakins, R. G. (1981). Power, sec and talk. In Civikly, J. M. (ed.) *Contexts of Communication.* New York: Holt, Rinehart and Winston.

Ford, F. (1983). Rules: The invisible family. *Family Process*, 22 (2), 135–145.

Foxman, C. (1988). *Speak with Sense: Asha.* Washington, DC: American Speech-Language and Hearing Association, pp. 46–47.

Gareis, J. W. (1991). *Characteristics of Empathic Exchanges in Human Interaction*, Unpublished dissertation, University of Pittsburgh.

Garfinkel, H. (1967). *Ethnomethodology.* Englewood Cliffs, NJ: Prentice-Hall.

Geertz, C. (1973). *The Interpretation of Cultures*. New York: Basic Books.

Gerbner, G. (1974). Teacher image in mass culture: Symbolic functions of the "hidden curriculum." In: Olson, D. R. (ed.) *Media and Symbols: The Forms of Expression, Communication, and Education: The Seventy-third Yearbook of the National Society for the Study of Education*, part I. Chicago: University of Chicago Press.

Gladstein, G. A. (1987). *Empathy and Counseling: Explorations in Theory and Research*, New York: Springer-Verlag.

Goffman, E. (1994). The art of impression management. In: Kollock, P. & O'Brien, J. (eds.). *The Production of Reality: Essays and Readings in Social Psychology* (pp. 212–246). Thousand Oaks, CA: Pine Forge Press.

Goffman, E. (1959). *The Presentation of Self in Everyday Life*. New York: Doubleday Anchor.

Goffman, E. (1974). *Frame Analysis*. New York: Harper Company.

Hamilton, C., & Parker, C. (1990). *Communicating for Results: A Guide for Business and the Professions*. Belmont, CA: Wadsworth.

Handwerk, B. (2003). *Uniting Iraq's Disparate Cultures a Challenge, Experts Say*. National Geographic News.

Hayalawa, S. I. (1962). *Language in Thought and Action*, (2nd ed). New York: Harcourt, Brace & World.

Heritage, J. (1984). *Garfinkel and Ethnomethodology*. Cambridge: Polity Press, pp. 179–232.

Hickson, M., & Stacks, D. (1985). Communication studies and applications. *Nonverbal Communication*. Dubuque, IA: Wm. C. Brown Publishers.

Highwater, J. (1981). *The primal mind, vision and reality in Indian America: The Intellectual Savage*. New York: Harper and Row.

Hochschild, A. (1994). Managing feeling. In Kollock, P., & O'Brien, J. (Eds.), *The Production of Reality-Essays and Readings in Social Psychology* (pp. 159–171). Thousand Oaks, CA: Pine Forge Press.

Janis, I.L. (1982). *Victims of groupthink*. Boston: Houghton-Mifflin.

Kollock, P., & O'Brien, J. (Eds.). (1994). *The Production of Reality-Essays and Readings in Social Psychology*. Thousand Oaks, CA: Pine California, Pine Forge Press.

Laing R. D., Phillipson, H., & Lee, A. R. (1966). *Interpersonal Perception: A Theory and a Method of Research*. New York: Springer.

Lakoff, G., & Johnson, M. (1980). *Metaphors We Live By*. Chicago: University of Chicago Press.

Leeds-Hurwitz, W. (1992). *Communication in Everyday Life—A Social Interpretation*. Norwood, NJ: Ablex Publishing Co.

Lindahl, K. (2003). Practicing the sacred art of listening: a guide to enrich your relationships and kindle your spiritual life. Woodstock, VT: SkyLight Paths Pub. In: Stewart, J. (2006). *Bridges Not Walls*. New York: McGraw Hill.

Linton, W. J. (ed). (1878). *Poetry of America: Selections from One Hundred American Poets from 1776 to 1876*. London: G. Bell, pp. 150–152.

Luft, J. (1969). *Of Human Interaction*. Palo Alto, CA: National Books Press.

Maslow, A. (1970). *Motivation and Personality*. New York: Harper and Row.

Mehl, M. R., Vazire, S., Ramírez-Esparza, N. R. B. Slatcher, & J. W. Pennebaker. (2007). Are women really more talkative than men? *Science* 317(5834), 82.

Mehrabian, A. (1981). Silent messages: Implicit communication of emotions and attitudes. In Olson, X (ed.) *Media and Symbols: The Frames of Expression, Communication and Education* (pp. 470–497). Chicago, IL: University of Chicago Press.

Miller, G. (1972). *An Introduction to Speech Communication*, Indianapolis: Bobbs-Merrill, Inc.

Miller, K. (2002). *Communication Theories*. New York: McGraw-Hill.

Osgood, C., Suci, G., & Tannenbaum, P. *The Measurement of Meaning*. Urbana: University of Illinois Press.

Pearce, W. B. (1994). *Interpersonal Communication: Making Social Worlds*. New York: Harper Collins College Division.

Piaget, J. (1962). *Language and Thought of the Child*. Atlantic Highlands, NJ: Humanities Press.

Poulakos, J. (1995). *Sophistical Rhetoric in Classical Greece*. Columbia, SC: University of South Carolina Press.

Reiss, D. (1981). *The Family's Construction of Reality.* Cambridge, MA: Harvard University Press.

Rogers, C. (1975). *Empathic: An Unappreciated Way of Being.* The Counseling Psychologist, Vol 5, No 2; 2–10 (1975).

Rogers, E. M. (1994). *A History of Communication Study: A Biographical Approach.* New York: The Free Press.

Rogers, E. M., & Argarwala-Rogers, R. (1975). Organizational communication. In. G. J. Hannenman & W. J. McEwan (Eds.), *Communication and behavior* (pp. 218–236). Wesley, MA: Addison.

Ruben, B. (1988). *Communication and Human Behavior.* New York: Macmillan Co.

Sachs, O. (1994). A matter of identity. In Kollock, P., & O'Brien, J. (eds.), *The Production of Reality-Essays and Readings in Social Psychology* (pp. 85–89). Thousand Oaks, CA: Pine Forge Press.

Shannon, C. E., & Weaver, W. (1949). *The Mathematical Theory of Communication.* Urbana: University of Illinois Press.

Shimanoff, S. B. (1980). *Communication Rules: Theory and Research.* Beverly Hills, CA: Sage.

Simon, R. W., Eder, D., & Evans, C. (1992). "The development of feeling norms underlying romantic love among adolescent females." *Social Psychology Quarterly,* 55:1, 29–46.

Smith, M. J. (1988). *Contemporary Communication Research Methods.* New York: Wadsworth.

Stein, E. (1970). *On the Problem of Empathy,* Waltraut Stein, trans., The Hague: Martinus Nijhoff.

Tannen, D. (1993). *Gender and Conversational Interaction.* Oxford: Oxford University Press.

Triplett, N. (1897). The dynamogenic factors in pace-making and competition. *American Journal of Psychology,* 507–533.

Tubbs, S. L., & Moss, S. (1994). *Human Communication.* New York: McGraw-Hill.

Watzlawick, P., Beavin, J., & Jackson, D. (1967). *Pragmatics of Communication.* New York: W.W. Norton.

Watzlawick, P. (1977). *How Real Is Real: Confusion, Disinformation, and Communication.* New York: Vintage Books.

Webster's Encyclopedia Unabridged Dictionary of the English Language. (1989). New York: Portland Hall.

West, R., & Turner, L. (2000). *Introducing Communication Theory.* Mountain View, CA: Mayfield Publishing Company.

Wood, J. (2006). *Communication Mosaics: An Introduction to the Field of Communication.* Belmont, CA: Wadsworth/Thomson Learning.

Websites Cited

http://www.boston.com/news/globe/editorial_opinion/oped/articles/2004/07/11/new_look_at_bushs_16_words/

http://www.facebook.com/

http://www.gapinc.com/public/Careers/car_culture.shtml

http://www.natcom.org/nca/Template2.asp?bid=1143

http://www.pittsburghlive.com/x/pittsburghtrib/s_386852.html

http://www.starbucks.com/aboutus/environment.asp

Chapter Exercises

CHAPTER 1

Introduction to Communication as Culture

EXERCISES

Exercise 1: Garfinkeling Assignment

- You and a partner are to identify a rule or "norm" of social interaction (or what you think is a rule of social interaction).
- With your partner observing, go into a public setting and act in a way that violates your rule of social interaction. Both you and your partner should violate the rule at least three times (total of six) *each* while the other acts as observer.
- The observer will record responses from your "victims" on the *Garfinkeling Assignment Report Form*.
- Have fun, but DO NOT ACT IN A WAY THAT PUTS YOU OR ANOTHER IN ANY IMMEDIATE OR PERCEIVED DANGER.

GARFINKELING ASSIGNMENT REPORT FORM

1. Write your rule of social interaction in the If/then format (i.e.: If you answer a telephone, then you use a greeting like "Hello" or "Boyer residence.")

2. Describe your procedure for breaking the rule. (Remember to do nothing that puts you or others in immediate or perceived danger). Include a description of the setting.

3. Record reactions of the "victims" noting gender, age, or any information related to your experience.

   PERSON 1:

   PERSON 2:

   PERSON 3:

   PERSON 4:

   PERSON 5:

   PERSON 6:

4. Write a paragraph in which you discuss two to four conclusions regarding the importance and function of your rule.

Exercise 2: Identifying Rules

Write five *explicit rules* and *five implicit* rules that you see operating in your communication class.

EXPLICIT RULES

     1.

     2.

     3.

     4.

     5.

IMPLICIT RULES

     1.

     2.

     3.

     4.

     5.

KEY TERMS

Culture is:

Learned _____

Created _____

Rule-governed _____

Contains symbol systems _____

Dynamic (changes) _____

Distinctive _____

Constraining _____

Phonological system _____

Semantic system _____

Syntactic system _____

Morphophonemic system _____

Pragmatic system _____

Egocentric speech _____

Sociocentric speech _____

Segmented worldview _____

Communication _____

Perception _____

Self _____

Inverted Triangle Approach (to study communication) _____

Cross-cultural studies _____

Hidden curriculum _____

Leave-taking behavior _____

Semiotic _____

Rules

    Prescriptive _____

    Explicit _____

    Implicit _____

    Behavior-specific _____

    Contextual _____

Symbols _____

Symbol systems _____

Verbal codes _____

Non-verbal codes _____

Horizons _____

Boundaries _____

Ethnography _____

Participant observer _____

Anthropologically strange _____

Ethnomethodology _____

Breaching experiments _____

TEST YOUR KNOWLEDGE

1. In their breaching experiments, Garfinkel and his students challenged people's beliefs in the stability of reality by breaking taken-for-granted rules of conduct.
   a. True
   b. False

2. Context includes:
   a. the physical setting.
   b. the people in the setting.
   c. when behavior occurs.
   d. all of the above.

3. Which of the following is *most likely* to be an explicit rule in the workplace?
   a. "Report to work by 8:00 AM."
   b. "Don't sit in the supervisor's seat in the lunchroom."
   c. "Don't tell jokes in the elevator when customers are present."
   d. "Don't work harder than your office mates."
   e. "If you have a problem at home, don't discuss it at work."

4. Ethnography is:
   a. limited to study of one ethnic group.
   b. employed to provide a detailed description of a culture or group.
   c. a quantitative and technical process.
   d. a and b
   e. all of the above.

5. Culture is:
   a. a universally similar phenomenon.
   b. learned.
   c. historically transmitted.
   d. biologically transmitted.
   e. b and c only

6. A parent tells their child, "Never talk to a stranger. But if you get lost, find a police officer. The last piece of advice is an example of:
   a. the rule.
   b. the counter rule.
   c. the rule about qualifications and exceptions.
   d. the rule about consequences of breaking the rule.
   e. the rule that tells how the rule is to be implemented.

CHAPTER 2

Definition of Communication

EXERCISE

Exercise 1: Scholarly Article Assignment

Select a scholarly article from an academic communication research journal,[1] published within the last five years. Record the following information:

1. The full citation of the article using the MLA Style.[2]

---

[1]**Sample Communication Journals**
Argumentation and Advocacy
Central States Speech Journal
Communication and Critical/Cultural Studies
Communication Monographs (formerly Speech Monographs)
Communication Quarterly
Communication Research
Communication Theory
Critical Studies in Mass Communication
Critical Studies in Media Communication
Cultural Studies
Differences
Discourse & Society
Feminist Studies
Human Communication Research
Media, Culture and Society
Philosophy & Rhetoric
Qualitative Research Reports in Communication
Quarterly Journal of Speech
Southern Speech Communication Journal
Western Journal of Communication (formerly Western Speech; Western Journal of Speech Communication)

[2] MLA citation style is summarized on The OWL at Purdue website, http://owl.english.purdue.edu/owl/resource/557/01/

2. The author(s) name(s).

3. The thesis of the article [What is/are the main argument(s) that the article is trying to make? What point is "proved" by this article?]

4. An explanation of the research questions that drive the article [What does the author want to learn? What communication aspects does the author deal with?]

5. A brief description of how the scholar conducted their research [Is it a qualitative or quantitative? Explain your decision.]

6. A summary of the article's results or findings. [What research questions were answered?]

KEY TERMS

Communication _____

    Transactional _____

    Process _____

    Irreversible _____

    Unrepeatable _____

    Creates and sustains social order _____

    Involves meaning _____

    Context shaped _____

    Context shaping _____

Humans: symbolic using animal _____

Metacommunication _____

Theory _____

Inductive _____

Deductive _____

Quantitative research methods _____

Scientific Method _____

Hypothesis _____

Variables _____

Methodology _____

Data _____

Qualitative research methods _____

Metatheoretical positions _____

Ontology _____

Epistemology _____

Axiology _____

Pragmatics _____

Communication axioms _____

TEST YOUR KNOWLEDGE

1. Your instructor tells a joke in class that simultaneously imparts information, discusses the expectations of class performance and serves an entertainment function. This is an example of communication as:
   a. a behavior with pattern.
   b. a behavior we learn.
   c. a behavior in context.
   d. multichannel behavior.
   e. multifunctional behavior.

2. Sue tells her roommate, "You really have some nerve embarrassing me like that." Sue is engaging in:
   a. double-bind communication
   b. metacommunication
   c. phatic communication
   d. self-prophesizing communication
   e. empathic communication

3. Meanings in a conversation are usually absolute, and are not topics for negotiations. The meanings are assigned.
   a. True
   b. False

4. Communication scholars have arrived one agreed-upon definition of communication.
   a. True
   b. False

5. Communication is irreversible.
   a. True
   b. False

6. We cannot, not communicate.
   a. True
   b. False

CHAPTER 3

A Short History of the Study of Communication

EXERCISES

Exercise 1: Create a Communication Model

Because models are "arbitrary," some classification systems are likely to be more representative of the communication process, as you perceive it, than others. You are therefore urged to create a model of communication that is most representative of your understanding of and experience with the process. Ask yourself what is the starting point for communication, and whether communication is seen as a linear or a cyclical process. You should also determine whether your model is best represented in pictures or words. Be thoughtful and creative with your work.

Exercise 2: Personal Small Group Inventory

Take a moment to guess how many small groups you currently belong to. Now, make note of groups that you belong to in each category:

Primary:

Social:

Educational:

Empathic/Therapy:

Problem solving/Task:

Exercise 3: Personal Small Group Role Reflection

Reflect upon the following, as they relate to your participation in small groups.

a. Group task roles
b. Group building and maintenance roles
c. Self-centered roles

What of these roles do you want to see maintained? increased? decreased?

Exercise 4: Groupthink Analysis

Identify an historical, or work-related event in which groupthink may have operated to produce an undesired result. Which of the following symptoms of unhealthy group conformity existed? Provide examples.

Illusion of invulnerability:

Collective rationalization of shortcomings or failures:

Accept group's morality; ignore ethical or moral implications of decision:

Pressure a dissident group member to conform:

Illusion of unanimity:

Stereotype the "enemy" negatively and inaccurately:

Contains self-appointed "mind guards":

Exercise: Organizational Chart

Without using references, draw an organizational chart of your university that shows where the Department of Communication, and this class reside. Then refer to the university website to determine your accuracy.

KEY TERMS

Rhetoric _____

Sophists _____

Plato; *Dialogue* _____

Aristotle; *On Rhetoric* _____

Ethos _____

Pathos _____

Logos _____

Unidirectional communication _____

Chicago School _____

Symbolic interactionism _____

Mathematical model of communication _____

Information source _____

Message _____

Transmitter _____

Signal _____

Noise

   Physical _____

   Psychological _____

   Semantic _____

   Intra-listener discomfort _____

Receiver _____

Message destination _____

Models of communication _____

Organization (definition) _____

Organization types

    Business organization _____

    Service organization _____

    Mutual benefit organization _____

    Commercial or commonwealth organization _____

    Coercive organization _____

    Utilitarian organization _____

    Normative organization _____

Division of labor _____

Span of control _____

Hierarchy _____

Chain of command _____

Formal communication _____

Informal communication _____

Upward communication _____

Downward communication _____

Information loss _____

Horizontal communication _____

Organizational/institutional objective reality _____

Institutional knowledge transmission _____

Institutional time _____

Small group communication _____

Small groups: types

Primary _____

Social _____

Educational _____

Therapy _____

Problem solving/task _____

Small groups: characteristics

Assembly effect bonus _____

Dynamogenic effect _____

Group personality _____

Group norms _____

Group cohesiveness _____

Commitment to task _____

Group size _____

Groupthink _____

Risky shift phenomenon _____

Small groups: development

Orientation stage _____

Conflict stage _____

Emergence stage _____

Reinforcement stage _____

Small groups: roles

Task _____

Group building and maintenance _____

Self-centered _____

Task roles

Coordinator _____

Elaborator _____

Evaluator-critic _____

Energizer _____

Information-giver _____

Information-seeker _____

Procedural technician _____

Recorder _____

Group building and maintenance roles

Compromiser _____

Encourager _____

Follower _____

Gatekeeper _____

Group observer _____

Harmonizer _____

Self-centered roles

Aggressor _____

Blocker _____

Dominator _____

Help-seeker _____

Social-loafer _____

Self-confessor _____

Special-interest pleader _____

Group leadership

Task leader _____

Social-emotional leader _____

Interpersonal communication _____

Relationship types _____

Relationship development (reasons for)

Proximity _____

Reinforcement _____

Similarity _____

Complementarity _____

Stages of relationship development _____

Relationship ending strategies

Behavioral de-escalation _____

Negative management identity _____

Justification _____

De-escalation _____

Positive tone _____

Intrapersonal communication _____

Cognitive strategies _____

Personal orientation

Values _____

Attitudes _____

Beliefs _____

Prejudices/stereotypes _____

Personality traits

Locus of control _____

Manipulation _____

Dogmatism _____

Tolerance of ambiguous information _____

Self-esteem _____

Maturity _____

Defense mechanisms

Repression _____

Rationalization _____

Projection _____

Identification _____

National Communication Association _____

TEST YOUR KNOWLEDGE

1. Models of communication:
   a. are arbitrary representations of reality.
   b. are all equally valid.
   c. reflect the theoretical orientation of their author.
   d. are symbolic of communication.
   e. all of the above.

2. The fraternity's finance committee cannot seem to agree on a budget. They argue back and forth. Finally, the newest member of the group says, "I have an idea." The members stop arguing, listen, and say things like, "that might work," but they do not quite commit to a decision. What stage of group decision-making is the group entering?
   a. orientation
   b. conflict
   c. emergence
   d. reinforcement
   e. risky shift

3. The high school debate team is scheduled to defend their state title against a team that they consider far less experienced and worthy. The captain and teammates ignore their coach's advice to prepare rigorously. Instead, they tell each other: "we're the best;" "we all agree we should party tonight," "they're a joke," and "don't worry if we need to make up the statistics." The team loses their title. Their pre-debate behavior is characteristic of what problem that may surface in small group communication?
   a. Hidden agenda
   b. Risky shift phenomenon
   c. Groupthink
   d. Group building
   e. Critical thinking

4. A study group of first year law students has been working most of the day to prepare for final exams. They are tense, hungry, and irritable. John, a student in the group, gets his classmates to laugh, implores them to take a one-hour dinner break, and consoles a panicked fellow student. John has demonstrated:
   a. Gatekeeper functions
   b. Task leadership
   c. Social-emotional maintenance leadership
   d. Self-centered leadership
   e. Social-loafing

5. The managing partner of an accounting firm sends an e-mail to all employees imploring them to donate to United Way, so the firm can meet its participation goal. This is an example of:
   a. illusion of unanimity
   b. horizontal communication
   c. downward communication
   d. upward communication
   e. chain of command

CHAPTER 4

Perception and Reality

EXERCISES

What were they thinking?

Look at the front cover of this textbook and do the following:

1. Given what you have learned about the authors, write a paragraph explaining why they choose this picture.

2. Write a short (ten-line minimum) dialogue that might be occurring between these two people.

3. Write a caption for this picture.

Cultural Perspective/Understanding

1. Sometime this week you are to read a periodical, watch a television show, or attend a cultural event that reflects a cultural experience quite different from your own (i.e., a political liberal might listen to Rush Limbaugh or a Christian might attend a Jewish or Islamic service).

2. Write a short reflection paper in which you:
   - Describe the article, show, or event
   - Offer your perceptions of the kind(s) of people who comprise the normal audience.
   - Offer two or three things you learned about yourself as you read, watched, or attended.

KEY TERMS

Ambiguous or optical illusion _____

Perception _____

Sophistry (Gorgias') threefold summary of reality _____

Reality (and relationship to communication) _____

Multiple internal realities _____

Perceptual process

    Selection _____

    Organization _____

        Figure-ground _____

        Patterning (pattern) _____

Sensory overload _____

Interpretation _____

First-order reality _____

Second-order reality _____

Spiral of interpersonal perceptions _____

TEST YOUR KNOWLEDGE

1. According to symbolic interactionists, all meaning is relative.
   a. True
   b. False

2. Which of the following is true of a second order reality?
   a. It is a purely physical reality.
   b. It is objective.
   c. It is repeatable.
   d. It is based upon actuality.
   e. It is based upon communication and how this is perceived.

3. Human pattern recognition helps us to avoid sensory overload in a world filled with constant stimulation.
   a. True
   b. False

4. Humans are cognitively predisposed to seek evidence of old patterns when faced with new information.
   a. True
   b. False

5. Communication helps humans to achieve continuity between the past and the present.
   a. True
   b. False

6. John believes that the United States' presence in Somalia represents a humanitarian effort, whereas Jack believes our presence there is for the purpose of imperialistic nation building. John and Jack differ in:
   a. their waking conscious reality.
   b. their interpretation of cosmic time.
   c. their metacommunication.
   d. their construction of second order reality.
   e. their construction of first order reality.

CHAPTER 5

Verbal Communication

EXERCISES

Exercise 1: The Motorcycle Accident Exercise

1. **Read** the accompanying *Transcript of the Motor Cycle Accident Report* and determine the gender of each of the speakers. (Which, if any, is female? Which, if any, is male? Are they both the same gender?).

   one page minimum

2. **Write** a two page explanation of the reasons you identified the speakers gender(s), as you did, using communication concepts to support your hypotheses.

3. **Ask** five other people (not in your class) to read the dialogue and identify the gender(s) of the speakers, giving reasons for their answers. Make sure you ask both females and males to respond. Record your findings on the *Motor Cycle Accident Project* page that follows. Be sure to note the gender of your respondents.

   pg. 71 & 72 for difference between gender communication

Transcript of the Motor Cycle Accident Report

Transcript symbols:

A	Person A
B	Person B
(.)	Short pause
(h)	Exhaled laughter in words
(3.0)	Timed pause
=	Latching symbol, indicates no break between words or phrases

The following transcript began as the 46th utterance in a conversation that transpired between two friends.

1.   A: I hope them Pirates get somethin' goin'

2.   B: Hmmm?

3.   A: I—I'd like to see the Pirates do somethin' (3.0)

4.   B: Yeah

5.   A: They suck.

6.   B: Hmm, the t-shirts wo(h)uld g(h)o al(h)ot fa(h)ster

7.   ((both laugh together))

8.   A: hey, can I use your bathroom?

(bathroom break—30 sec.)

9.   B: You know, ever since (.) you noticed these (.) I've been looking in the m(h)irror.

10.   (.) trying to see if they're really obvious or not remember Saturday night?

11.   A: Noticed what

12.   B: These?

13.   A: What is that a scar?

14.   B: I have'em all on my neck and stuff

15.   A: From what

16.   B: Do you remember that? When we were in the lobby?

17.   A: Fer-How 'dja get 'em

18.   B: you're like, what's that on your neck What is it!

19.   What is it! What is it!

20.   A: How 'dja get it?

21.   B: Just from an accident (.) When I was in the eighth grade

22.   A: Car accident?

23.   B: Quad motorcycle (.) Head on

24.   A: ((sniffs))

25.   B: I was on the motorcycle

26.   A: 'dja have a helmet?

27.   B: Yeah, but it went (.) Se:e y:a!!

28.   A: Oh really

29.   B: I didn't have it strapped

       A: I wrecked (.) One time I wrecked so bad I wasn't (.) I-I was jumpin' and

31.   I-I was gonna take off my ah, helmet (.) and I said after I make this jump

32.   I'm gonna take my helmet off, I went up (.) and my (.) bike I got stick in

33.   a-a second gutch pow-sec-er for (.) second or first gear power band (.) I

34.   hit the thing, and I just went sjroooom! =

35.   B: Tssssss ((laugh))

36.   A: = Me and the bike were standin' in the air like 'is and then I fell off,

37.   bounced on my head (.) If I didn't have a helmet on I would be f—ed

38.   up (3.0)

39   B: I cam around a blind turn (.) I was on a little (.) KX80 and (.) she was on

40   a um (.) Honda 300 quad (.c) Guess who l(h)ost

41.   A: Hmmm

42.   B: She was fine (.) The quad was fine (.) I was a mess

43.   A. Hmmm

44.   B: Broke my leg, sprained my ankle, broke my thumb

45.   sprained my wrist, got seven stitches ( )

46.   A: Oooh okay that's enough that's enough that's enough I'm ah, oh, yeah

45.   B: Yeah (.) and the bike is a little bit shorter now hhh

47.   A: Really

48.   B: Ye(h) ah (.) l(h)t still ru(h)ns i(h)ts j(h)ust a li(h)ttle bi(h)t sho(h)rter

Motorcycle Accident Project

Circle the answer of your respondents and write their reasons for their choices.

Respondent 1 (M F)

    Gender of "A": M F   Reasons:

    Gender of "B": M F   Reasons:

Respondent 2 (M F)

    Gender of "A": M F   Reasons:

    Gender of "B": M F   Reasons:

Respondent 3 (M F)

    Gender of "A": M F   Reasons:

    Gender of "B": M F   Reasons:

Respondent 4 (M F)

    Gender of "A": M F   Reasons:

    Gender of "B": M F   Reasons:

Respondent 5 (M F)

    Gender of "A": M F   Reasons:

    Gender of "B": M F   Reasons:

Exercise 2: Create a New Word

Coin a new word to describe a common object or phenomenon. To accomplish this you will: write the word; identify it as a noun, verb, adjective or adverb; and use the word in three different sentences. You will be judged on your word's usefulness and your creativity.

KEY TERMS

Language _____

Sapir-Whorf hypothesis _____

Linguistic meaning _____

Semantic differential

    Evaluation _____

    Potency _____

    Activity _____

Dialectal differences (vs. deviations) _____

Private, idiosyncratic language _____

Gender difference in communication _____

Tag questions _____

Filler _____

Qualifiers _____

Disclaimers

    Suspension of judgment _____

    Cognitive disclaimers _____

    Sin license _____

    Credentialing _____

    Hedging _____

Translation problems _____

Back-translation _____

TEST YOUR KNOWLEDGE

1. "Back-translation" is a useful technique to be certain that linguistic translation has accurately proceeded.
   a. True
   b. False

2. Which of the following descriptions of social life best represents the use of a metaphor?
   a. Humans learn to participate in social life through their interactions with other human beings.
   b. Humans are both rational and emotional creators.
   c. Humans often overstate the importance of individual effort and personal experience.
   d. Humans are like actors on a stage playing parts and having an important role in social life.

3. Which of the following best illustrates Whorf's finding that people act based on the linguistic meaning a situation has for them?
   a. A person who puts out their cigarette around full gas drums since gas is dangerous around fire.
   b. A woman who does not drink alcohol during her pregnancy so as not to harm her baby.
   c. A man who does not put on his seat-belt because he thinks that they are more dangerous than driving without one.
   d. All illustrate Whorf's finding.
   e. Only a and c

4. Meanings in a conversation are not usually absolute, and are not topics for negotiations.
   a. True
   b. False

5. Examples of paralanguage include all *except:*
   a. coughing
   b. vocal quality
   c. vocal pitch
   d. laughing
   e. American Sign Language

6. According to Highwater, the word "duck" accurately represents his second order reality for the word "méksikaatsi."
   a. True
   b. False

CHAPTER 6

Non-Verbal Communication

EXERCISES

Exercise 1: One Cannot *Not* Communicate

Provide a college classroom based example of non-verbal communication that demonstrates that "one cannot *not* communicate."

Exercise 2: Non-Verbal Communication "Rules!"

Provide an example of how non-verbal communication might be used to contradict verbal communication between a couple that is not having a good time on a "first date."

Exercise 3: Power and NVC

Provide an example of how non-verbal communication is used to demonstrate status/power in the United States of America's White House. Contrast and compare this to non-verbal communication of status/power in England's Buckingham Palace.

Exercise 4: Comprehensive NVC Analysis

Provide an example of how each of the following is used to communicate in the Hasidic Jewish community described in Arden's article, *"The Pious Ones."*

a. Chronemics (the use of time)

b. Cosmetics (applicative or reconstructive)

c. Costuming (the use of dress)

d. Haptics (the use of touch)

e. Objectics (the use of objects)

f. Oculesics (the use of the eyes)

g. Olfactics (the use of smell)

h. Organismics (unalterable body characteristics)

i. Kinesics (body movement)

j. Proxemics (use of space)

k. Vocalics (voice and silence)

KEY TERMS

One cannot, not communicate _____

Channel

    Visual _____

    Auditory _____

    Olfactory _____

    Gustatory _____

    Tactile _____

Sensory-based communication styles _____

Verbal codes _____

Paralanguage codes _____

Non-verbal codes _____

Co-occurrence of codes _____

Context _____

Temporal reality _____

Culture _____

Categories of non-verbal communication

    Chronemics _____

    Cosmetics _____

    Costuming _____

    Haptics _____

Objectics

    Oculesics _____

Olfactics _____

Organismics _____

Kinesics

    Proxemics _____

        Intimate distance _____

        Personal distance _____

        Social distance _____

        Public distance _____

    Vocalics _____

Significance of non-verbal communication _____

Relationship between verbal and non-verbal communication (seven scenarios) _____

Communication redundancy _____

Turn yielding _____

Turn maintaining _____

Turn requesting _____

Turn denying _____

Communication metaphors

    Telegraph _____

    Orchestra _____

    Dance _____

Self-synchrony

    Interactional synchrony _____

    Asynchrony _____

TEST YOUR KNOWLEDGE

1. While Ed rambles on, Bill suddenly sits up, raises his finger, and audibly inspires air. Bill is exhibiting typical
   a. turn-yielding behavior.
   b. turn-requesting behavior.
   c. turn-denying behavior.
   d. turn-maintaining behavior.

2. The orchestra metaphor is a better metaphor for communication than the telegraph metaphor, because the orchestra, unlike the telegraph, transmits information via several channels.
   a. True
   b. False

3. Non-verbal behavior may substitute for verbal behavior.
   a. True
   b. False

4. Mehrabian estimated that in communication between two people, the majority of the message is conveyed:
   a. Vocally
   b. Facially
   c. Verbally
   d. Haptically

5. Which of the following is true about the use of silence to communicate?
   a. The use of silence differs in different cultures.
   b. Silence can be used in a manner that is intentionally hurtful to others.
   c. Silence can convey empathy, allowing the other person time to think.
   d. Silence can communicate an emotional response.
   e. All of the above.

6. Your employer seems to be a visual learner. It is best, therefore, to do all but the following:
   a. Supplement a work-related conversation with a typed outline of your plan.
   b. Dress well to make a good impression.
   c. Convey important information in person vs. on the phone.
   d. Use wording like: "I can picture that."
   e. Use vocabulary words such as: "feel," "firm," and "soft."

7. Which of the following descriptions of social life best represents the use of a metaphor?
   a. Humans learn to participate in social life through their interactions with other human beings.
   b. Humans are both rational and emotional creators.
   c. Humans often overstate the importance of individual effort and personal experience.
   d. Humans are like actors on a stage playing parts and having an important role in social life.

CHAPTER 7

Listening and Empathy

EXERCISES

Exercise 1. Listening Journal

Keep a listening journal for two weeks. Make one entry daily, five days per week. The journal should include:

a. Date
b. Type of listening: pleasurable, discriminative, critical, or empathic
c. Brief description of the situation
d. How you responded as the listener
e. What you learned from the experience

Exercise 2. Listening Improvement Module

a. On the basis of your Listening Journal, identify three of your listening:

   i.   Strengths

   ii. Weaknesses

b. Select one listening behavior you wish to improve, and plan to practice this behavior on at least one occasion.

   Example: I tend interrupt my employer when she talks to me. I will instead, allow her all the time she needs to talk. I will demonstrate good attending behaviors, including appropriate eye contact, relaxed and open posture, head nods, and verbal fillers (uh huh) to show I am engaged. I will not be quick to disagree with her; instead, I will respond briefly, using language that indicates I understand what she said.

c. Describe what you did, the outcome, and how you felt during this effort.

   Example: My efforts to pay attention to the lecture improved my retention. I took accurate notes, and sat in the front of the class. I turned off my cell phone, and didn't talk to my friends sitting nearby. It was tiring to concentrate, but I feel good that I grasped the instructor's comments. I didn't "feel lost" in the lecture.

KEY TERMS

Listening _____

Hearing _____

Intention _____

Attention _____

Selective attention _____

Retention _____

Redundancy _____

Obstacles to effective listening

    Situational obstacles _____

    Internal obstacles _____

Listening types

    Pleasurable _____

    Discriminative _____

    Critical _____

    Empathic _____

Empathy

    (is not) projection _____

    (is not) sympathy _____

    (is not) agreement _____

Empathic behaviors

    Elicit information _____

    Affirm content _____

Affirm the person _____

Vocal variance _____

Curvilinear effect _____

TEST YOUR KNOWLEDGE

1. Which of the following communication behaviors do humans use most often?
   a. Writing
   b. Reading
   c. Speaking
   d. Listening

2. Select the verbal response that *best* represents a display of empathy:
   a. My sympathies on your loss.
   b. You shouldn't feel sad. Be strong!
   c. Cheer up.
   d. I agree, entirely.
   e. You seem especially sad today.

3. Too much eye contact may have a curvilinear effect, and convey a lack of empathy.
   a. True
   b. False

4. Hearing is the same as listening.
   a. True
   b. False

5. Listening is automatically accomplished, and requires little or no intent.
   a. True
   b. False

6. The average person speaks 300 to 600 words per minute. The human mind can only process 100 to 160 words per minute. These facts explain why humans are such poor listeners.
   a. True
   b. False

CHAPTER 8

Communication and the Self

EXERCISES

Exercise 1: Your Johari Window: Current and Future

- Construct your own Johari Window, altering the sizes of each of the respective windows to reflect how you typically relate to your friends. Draw a second Johari Window, indicating how you would like the panes to be sized in your post-college employment site.

Exercise 2: Organizational "Feeling Management"

- Review five corporate websites (other than those discussed in this chapter), and locate evidence of the desired emotions relating to "feeling management" of its employees and/ customers.
- Review one U.S. military website and locate evidence of the desired emotions relating to "feeling management."

KEY TERMS

The Self _____

Communication: a basic life process _____

Systems Theory of Communication _____

Maslow's Hierarchy of Human Needs

    Self-actualization needs _____

    Physiological needs _____

    Esteem needs _____

    Social needs _____

    Safety needs _____

    Physiological needs _____

Alderfer's ERG Theory

    Existence Needs _____

    Relatedness Needs _____

    Growth Needs _____

Johari Window

    Open _____

    Blind _____

    Hidden _____

    Unknown _____

Self-disclosure (rules for) _____

Impression management/formation _____

Dramaturgy _____

Performances _____

Identity negotiation _____

Working consensus _____

Feeling management _____

Hidden curriculum _____

Norms _____

Acting techniques

    Surface acting _____

    Deep acting _____

Institutional emotion management _____

Emotion memories _____

Scenes _____

Performance disruptions

    Dramaturgical loyalty _____

    Dramaturgical discipline _____

    Disciplined performer _____

    Dramaturgical circumspection _____

Reality of our identity _____

Gender identity _____

Self-fulfilling prophecies _____

TEST YOUR KNOWLEDGE

1. According to Goffman's perspective on human interaction, dramaturgy is
   a. a false mask we wear to hide our "real selves" from others.
   b. the managed presentation of ourselves to others.
   c. a theatrical performance.
   d. the reactions of others to our claims of competence.

2. We typically behave in a way that will highlight facts that otherwise would go unnoticed (e.g., describing a position of responsibility one held in the past during a job interview). Goffman calls this:
   a. inflation.
   b. theatrical license.
   c. interactional ambiguity.
   d. dramatic circumspection.

3. Select the lowest (most basic) human need on Maslow's hierarchy:
   a. self-actualization need
   b. safety need
   c. physiological need
   d. social need
   e. esteem need

4. Abraham Maslow and Clayton Alderfer's theories of human need differ as follows:
   a. Alderfer omits reference to esteem needs.
   b. Unlike Maslow, Alderfer does not insist that the needs are activated in a specific, hierarchical order.
   c. Communication is only primary to Maslow's schema.
   d. All of the above.
   e. None of the above.

5. Beth told a stranger on a bus the details of her divorce, her health problems, and how much she dislikes her boss. Beth is over-disclosing, and, as per the Johari Window schema, should consider reducing the size of her:
   a. Open window
   b. Closed window
   c. Blind window
   d. Hidden window

TEST YOUR KNOWLEDGE: ANSWERS

Chapter 1
1. a
2. d
3. a
4. b
5. e
6. c

Chapter 2
1. e
2. b
3. b
4. b
5. a
6 a

Chapter 3
1. e
2. c
3. c
4. c
5. c

Chapter 4
1. a
2. e
3. a
4. a
5. a
6. d

Chapter 5
1. a
2. d
3. a
4. b
5. e
6. b

Chapter 6
1. b
2. a
3. a
4. b
5. e
6. e
7. d

Chapter 7
1. d
2. e
3. a
4. b
5. b
6. b

Chapter 8
1. b
2. d
3. c
4. b
5. a

Index